SOCIAL PSYCHOLOGY

THE BASICS

Social psychology explores some of the most important questions we face as people: how do we create and understand the social self? How does our 'social mind' influence our thoughts and behaviour? How do we relate to other individuals and groups?

In a jargon-free and accessible manner, *Social Psychology: The Basics* critically examines these fundamental principles of social psychology, and provides a thorough overview of this fascinating area. Discussing the theory and science behind our understanding of how people relate to others, this book explores how we understand ourselves, how we relate at an individual and group level, the key processes underpinning social influence, and the ways the discipline has evolved (and continues to evolve). It also looks at how the application of social psychology makes important differences in the real world.

Highlighting key issues, controversies and applications, including case studies, questions and biographies of important figures in the discipline, this is the essential introduction for students at undergraduate level and A-level who are approaching social psychology for the first time.

Daniel Frings is an Associate Professor at London South Bank University. He has taught social psychology at undergraduate and MSc levels and supervised numerous PhDs. His research interests include social identity, bio-psychosocial approaches to behaviour and addiction psychology. He has received research funding from prestigious funders such as the Economic Social Research Council, the British Academy and Cancer Research UK. Daniel is also an Associate Editor of the *Journal of Applied Social Psychology* and has guest edited special issues of the journal *Addictive Behavior Reports*.

THE BASICS SERIES

For a full list of titles in this series, please visit www.routledge.com/The-Basics/book-series/B

SOCIAL PSYCHOLOGY
THE BASICS

Daniel Frings

Routledge
Taylor & Francis Group

LONDON AND NEW YORK

First published, 2019
by Routledge
2 Park Square, Milton Park, Abingdon, Oxon OX14 4RN

and by Routledge
711 Third Avenue, New York, NY, 10017

Routledge is an imprint of the Taylor & Francis Group, an informa business

British Library Cataloguing-in-Publication Data
A catalogue record for this book is available from the British Library

Library of Congress Cataloging-in-Publication Data
A catalog record for this title has been requested

ISBN: 978-1-138-55198-5 (hbk)
ISBN: 978-1-138-55200-5 (pbk)
ISBN: 978-1-315-14788-8 (ebk)

Typeset in Bembo
by Out of House Publishing

This book is dedicated to

Louise, Katherine and Annabelle, for all the joy
they bring into my life

and to

Dominic and Ian, for giving me both the
confidence and the tools to (attempt to!)
tackle a book.

CONTENTS

PREFACE

All over the world, people are thinking about other people. In an office in Delhi, a manager frets about how to get more productivity from his team. At an ice rink in Canada, two ice hockey teams square up for a long-awaited rematch. In a flat in London, a young woman hopes to make a good impression at her job interview the next day. Not so far away, in a bedsit in Northern Ireland, a father worries his baby daughter will grow up in a renewed sectarian conflict. Meanwhile, in East Africa, an advertising account manager crosses her fingers that her latest campaign will go viral. These individuals are joined by countless others whose thoughts and action are directly linked to other people in some form or other.

As the above suggests, many, if not most, of our day-to-day activities and concerns involve other people. Social psychology is a body of ideas and research which attempts to understand how people think and behave in these social contexts. Drawing on a variety of experimental and non-experimental techniques, it attempts to uncover and understand all aspects of social behaviour. The levels of analysis are equally diverse, ranging from biological accounts of how the 'social brain' functions to models of intergroup conflict on an international scale. This volume will encapsulate this broad field in a critical yet accessible way, exploring the major areas of the discipline across nine topic-based chapters. Those covering the bulk of the theory and research which make up the field are split into three major themes: *self and motivation, social relationships* and *social influence*.

Before we reach these themes, the first chapter, 'A (very) brief history of social psychology', will outline how social psychology as a discipline defines itself, and contextualise how it has developed historically. In doing so, we will see it is a rich, varied and vibrant field which impacts on society in many important ways. However, we'll also see that social psychology is a 'young' science that is still finding its feet.

The next two chapters constitute the *self and motivation* theme. Here we will begin our tour of the theories and evidence that make up the body of social psychology by examining how we understand our own social selves and also the motivational processes which drive our thoughts and behaviour. The 'Understanding the self' chapter will begin by investigating theories of self, including group- and individual-level accounts. It will also consider the formation and function of self-esteem and the extent to which our social action and behaviours are controlled or automatic, and how our online and offline personas differ. Following on from this, the chapter on 'The ways we think' will examine how our cognition and motivation are affected by other factors such as cognitive dissonance, language and embodied social cognition. It will also discuss the importance of understanding the role of culture in social psychological phenomena.

We then move to our next theme: *social relationships*. In this theme we will examine relationships between the self and other individuals and groups. The 'Self and other people' chapter discusses classic concepts such as person perception (including impression formation), interpersonal attraction, attribution theory and bias, and non-verbal communication. In the 'Self and groups' chapter we will examine the definitions of groups; how groups form, evolve and dissolve; how social identities influence self-perception; and the psychology of intergroup relations – including stereotypes, stigmatisation and prejudice, and the psychology of intercultural adaptation (acculturation).

The following theme takes an in-depth look at *social influence* – exploring how we are both recipients of attempted social influences from others and sources of influence directed at the social world. The 'Conformity and obedience' chapter will cover the main topics in this area, including conformity and obedience from both classic and more contemporary perspectives. We will also examine how and when people and groups resist or overturn social influence by examining minority influence. The 'Persuasion' chapter will then overview the persuasion psychology literature, discussing models such as the Yale model, the elaboration likelihood model, fear arousal and 'rebound effects'. Cialdini's six principles of persuasion and behavioural science's 'nudge' approaches will also be explored.

Social psychology is often very applied in nature, and no overview of the field would be complete without a review of how it has been used to change things in the real world. The book's penultimate chapter ('Social psychology in applied context') will look at applications of psychology in everyday situations. Here we will begin by examining 'aggression' from biological and social perspectives, examining causes, process and interventions. The discussion will then move to the opposite behaviour by examining helping behaviour and bystander apathy. We will then look at the psychology of jury decision-making – exploring how many of the processes outlined in this book can be applied to reveal systematic biases in the judicial system, and how the discipline can help address these.

Finally, we will focus on an emerging area of literature – the social psychology of physical and mental health and well-being – exploring the practical application of a concept known as the '*social cure*'. For each topic, clear links will be drawn between the theories and concepts outlined previously and the topic at hand.

The final chapter, 'Future directions and common themes', will take a risk by speculating what social, technological and political drivers will shape the future of the discipline, and will suggest areas of study which are likely to be the focus for future work. Finally, we will round off our tour of social psychology by reviewing the main themes which emerge from the preceding chapters and make an attempt to find common factors which run across the discipline.

By the end of this book you will have a good grounding in the key theories and issues in the discipline. Along the way, we'll meet some fascinating characters that make up the leaders in the field, past and present, some counterintuitive findings which will make you 'think about how people think', and some theories and ideas which have literally changed society. We will learn about what brings us together, what pushes us apart and how we can start to make change happen ourselves.

But, for now, let us start with what social psychology actually is and where (and how) it all began.

A (VERY) BRIEF HISTORY
OF SOCIAL PSYCHOLOGY

WHAT IS SOCIAL PSYCHOLOGY?

Broadly speaking, social psychology is the study of human thought and behaviour which involves other people in any form. Gordon Allport (who, as we will see, is one of the 'heroes' of social psychology) classically defined the discipline more precisely as 'the scientific investigation of how the thoughts, feelings and behaviours of individuals are influenced by the actual, imagined or implied presence of others' (see Allport, 1954a, p. 5). Although over 60 years old, this summary captures the depth and nuance of the field pretty well.

UNPACKING ALLPORT'S DEFINITION

Let us pick apart this definition a little – looking at what implications this seemingly simple sentence has to offer, and what limitations it may have. Allport argues that social psychology is a 'scientific investigation'. In doing so, he suggests that the subject of study can be observed and measured and, importantly, that generalisations between a given study population and the wider world can be made. While the majority of psychological thinking and research takes such an *empiricist* approach (see below), this aspect of the definition is also somewhat limiting. One of the most significant historical events in the field (the 'first crisis'; see below) highlights how other non-scientific approaches are needed to fully understand an individual's experience and supports the argument that such research cannot really be generalised to a common human condition.

Allport also sets the scope of study to 'thoughts, feelings and behaviours'. This is important because it makes clear that it is not only actual behaviours which are of interest, but also the cognitive (thoughts) and affective (feelings) processes associated with them. It also highlights some methodological challenges faced by the discipline. For instance, we can directly measure someone's behaviour – I can measure if someone gives to charity, gives someone else a loud burst of static noise or chooses to go on a date with them. However, we can only ever infer someone's thoughts or feelings via a behaviour. For example, I can see what someone thinks about ice cream by their behavioural response to an attitude questionnaire, or their feelings towards another person via facial expressions. So, the study of social psychology often relies on indirect measures (although some approaches – such as *social neuroscience*, which we discuss below – are beginning to challenge this limitation).

Allport's definition also highlights the importance of *influence* – humans are not seen as isolated systems. Rather, they are social beings who both receive and respond to social information, while simultaneously being sources of information themselves. The definition also suggests that social information can be generated by people physically present (*actual*), *imagined* ('what would X say if they heard about this behaviour?') or *implied* (i.e. when the source of social influence is signified by cues in the environment, such as a Christian cross, or the behavioural norms we are socialised to adhere to).

By bringing all of these elements together, Allport neatly sums up his vision of (i) how we should approach the study of social psychology, (ii) the scope of this investigation and (iii) the processes which cause social behaviour. It is this triple whammy combination which makes it so popular – but the definition's prescriptive nature also means many areas of the discipline arguably fall outside its scope.

CRITICAL SPOTLIGHT: DEFINITIONS OF
PSYCHOLOGY

How well does Allport's definition actually describe social psychology? Once you have read through this (or another) chapter, why not
revisit this section, and test Allport's assumptions against what you
have learnt? How would you improve the definition yourself? What
are the benefits and disadvantages of a very narrow (or a very broad)
view of social psychology?

BC–1890s: EARLY APPROACHES TO SOCIAL
PSYCHOLOGY

PRE-SOCIAL PSYCHOLOGY

We have seen what social psychology is, but where did it come from?
Trying to understand why people behave the way they do is nothing
new. In *Politics*, Aristotle argued slightly cryptically that 'Anyone who
either cannot lead the common life or is so self-sufficient as not to
need to, and therefore does not partake of society, is either a beast or a
god' (Aristotle, trans. Jowett, 2000). This suggests that even in ancient
Greece people were thinking about the importance and ubiquity
of interpersonal and intergroup interactions. More directly, Plato
argued in many of his own dialogues that part of the state's role was
to shape social behaviour in acceptable ways. In making these claims,
both of these philosophers laid the groundwork for the idea that
individuals are shaped by social interactions, and that no-one is truly
separate from the social context they reside in. The ways in which
people could influence others was (perhaps inevitably) a source of
interest for a variety of other early political intellectuals as well. For
example, in his book *The Prince*, Venetian political adviser Machiavelli
advises rulers of 16th-century city states how to use both interpersonal relationships and also social emotions (such as love and fear) to
rule effectively on a national scale. Similarly, war strategist Sun Tze
argued that commanders should consider the psychological tempera-
ment of their opponents and leverage it to their own advantage in

his 5th-century book *The Art of War*. But when did this field of study become a 'discipline' in its own right?

SOCIAL PSYCHOLOGY AS A DISCIPLINE

While numerous other writers and thinkers wrote about similar themes, the formal recognition of 'social psychology' could arguably be attributed to Leipzig-based Wilhelm Wundt (and colleagues including Lazarus and Steinhal), who argued that psychology as a science should be separated into two sub-fields – individual psychology (focusing on individual-level cognition and behaviour) and '*Völkerpsychologie*' (roughly translated as 'ethnic' or 'folk' psychology). This later new branch of the discipline (Wundt's explanation of which was published in 1859 and ran to ten volumes!) aimed to focus on the *social aspects of experience* – with an emphasis on understanding people through the effects of language, mythology and moral systems (including jurisprudence and socialisation). It also argued strongly for a move away from the increasingly exclusive use of experimental methods (a theme we will see picked up later in the development of the discipline). In the years after its inception, the Völkerpsychologie movement faced criticism for being methodologically unsound and, perhaps more significantly, potentially racist in its aims to understand whole groups of people in stereotypical ways. Rebutting this latter criticism was made almost impossible by far-right advocates of its use – for instance, in the role it played in the German Nazi party's racial narratives. By the 1960s, the approach itself had virtually disappeared from mainstream study. Although we may look back at Völkerpsychologie with reservations, it is historically important for two reasons: it made a strong argument for treating social psychology as a discipline in its own right and it also highlighted the importance of diverse research methods. Perhaps fortunately, Wundt and his colleagues were not the only people shaping the field, and others had their own, often differing views …

1890s–1950s: THE BIRTH OF SOCIAL PSYCHOLOGICAL SCIENCE

SOCIAL PSYCHOLOGY AS AN EXPERIMENTAL SCIENCE

While Wundt was developing his ideas around non-experimental Völkerpsychologie in Leipzig, competing work on the other side of the Atlantic was taking a different tack – aiming to develop an *empirical science* approach to social behaviour. In particular, an Indiana-based psychologist and bicycle racing enthusiast named Norman Triplett was working out how to improve his bicycle racing times. In doing so, he also ended up undertaking what many psychologists argue was social psychology's first true empirical 'experiment'. Triplett's work during this period was focused on the effects of *social facilitation* (the effects of the presence of others on performance, which we examine in depth in Chapter 6). Triplett (1898) details an observation that cyclists achieved greater speeds when competing against each other than when competing against a clock. Triplett hypothesised that this was because the presence of others *energised* performance. The important step soon followed – Triplett took this hypothesis and tested in it a laboratory setting, by asking 40 children to wind fishing reels as quickly as they could while either alone or in pairs. He observed that many of the pairs wound quicker than children competing solely against a clock and concluded this indicated the presence of social facilitation. Interestingly, contemporary commentators argue that Triplett didn't actually find any strong evidence of social facilitation at all – the sample of people tested was too small to demonstrate reliable findings using modern statistical methods, and the design of the experiment was (perhaps understandably) not entirely adequate. Nonetheless – the idea of taking an *observable phenomenon* (cyclists increasing speed in the presence of others), developing a *hypothesis* (others energise us) and *testing* it in a lab in a controlled fashion (having children wind reels) put the study of social psychology on an experimental, scientific course. As we'll see, in the post-World War II period this proved a major boon, but in the 1960s and 1970s it was also almost the discipline's undoing.

CRITICAL SPOTLIGHT: WHO WAS NORMAN TRIPLETT?

Born in 1861, Norman Triplett was a psychologist who worked at Indiana University. His is most famous for his experiment detailing performance of people alone or in company. Although the scientific validity of the specific findings has come under question in recent years, his work was instrumental in putting social psychology on an empirical footing. Alongside his research on social facilitation,

Triplett also published some of the earliest psychological science on the topic of magic – detailing the 'Psychology of conjuring deceptions' in the *American Journal of Psychology* in 1900 (Triplett, 1900).

CROWD BEHAVIOUR AND SITUATIONISM

The study of social psychology did not remain limited to children and fishing reels for long. In 1895, Le Bon published an influential book outlining his '*group mind*' account of crowd behaviour (Le Bon, 1896). Working against a backdrop of widespread collective expressions of social discontent, Le Bon argued that when an individual becomes 'submerged' in a group, they lose their sense of personal responsibility and develop a group-based sense of invincibility and unrest. Le Bon also argued that crowds were subject to 'suggestibility' and 'contagion' – people within the crowd are influenced by base, primal emotions and thoughts which then spread and amplify unchallenged through the crowd. Le Bon also detailed how crowds' responses to situations could be manipulated to serve the state rather than advance the cause of social agitators. Le Bon's theories strongly influenced those who wished to harness the power of groups to their own ends (including figures such as Hitler and Mussolini). This cast a long shadow over the study of crowds – indeed, it was only with the advent of work by researchers such as John Drury and Steven Reicher that the idea of a 'mindless mob' was strongly challenged, and the complexity of the phenomena unpacked (see Drury & Reichher, 2009).

Le Bon's work also influenced the discipline in other ways. Although largely separated from the social context they were conceived in, Le Bon's writings also paved the way to the idea that individuals in society were subject to social stimuli – outside influences and cues which interacted to affect people's behaviour. This in turn set the scene for ideas around *situationism* and *field theory* – principally developed by a German psychologist named Kurt Lewis. Lewis was influenced by the *Gestalt movement*, which argued that often a given phenomenon was more complex and greater than an understanding of each individual part in isolation would suggest. Applying this to social psychology, Lewin (1936) argued that one cannot understand behaviour in isolation from the situations individuals find themselves in, and all the motives, experience and social history that accompany such experiences. He also argued that human behaviour could be studied in a similar way to maths and physics (see Lewin's equation) by using quantitative models. In some ways, this work foreshadowed the *cognitive revolution* in social psychology (see below).

CRITICAL SPOTLIGHT: LEWIN'S EQUATION

Lewin (1936) argued behaviour could be understood in a similar way to physics or maths, and even quantified *all* human behaviour in an equation:

$$B = f(P,E)$$

where *B* is behaviour, *P* is person and *E* represents the environment. Quite what one is supposed to do with this equation is unclear, but the idea that you can understand behaviour without necessarily referring to both an individual's unique characteristics and the social context they are in became (for a while!) a cornerstone of social psychology.

1950S–1980S: RAPID PROGRESS AND FUNDAMENTAL QUESTIONS

THE SOCIAL-COGNITIVE REVOLUTION AND US DOMINATION

The next major shift in the field was a move away from *behaviourist* accounts of behaviour (which view behaviour as a set of responses conditioned to occur by previous rewards or punishments), and relatively isolated theories such as crowd theory, towards a more unifying meta-theory (a general theoretical framework which can be applied to multiple domains within a discipline). During the late 1950s, theorists began thinking of psychology (in general) as a form of *information processing*, reflecting advances in early forms of computer science being made at the time. In such a model, information is perceived, encoded, processed somehow (something we now call thought or, more technically, *cognition*), and the result is acted upon. The intervening processes, this new approach argued, could be reverse-engineered by conducting experiments. A great number of studies using this paradigm swiftly followed, many of which are still important today. For instance, Miller (1956) observed that people could remember only between five and nine items they had just seen, but also realised we can recall thousands of items of data from memory. This suggested to researchers such as Broadbent that memory consisted of two systems – what we now know as working (or short-term) memory, and long-term (storage) memory (Broadbent, 1957). Gradually, ideas around this cognitive approach to psychology gained ground. By 1967, the first major book out-lining the approach (cunningly named 'Cognitive Psychology') had been released (Neisser, 1967), and it wasn't long until the approach dominated the field. Social psychology was not left behind by this movement: the ideas of social information (e.g. our memory for social events) being observed, processed (i.e. perhaps being altered by the stereotypes we hold about the actors involved), and then leading to a response (perhaps biased judgements about the cause of the behaviour) became (and remains) a common model – termed the *social-cognitive approach*. Equally, attempts to identify linear processes and mechanisms underpinning social thinking and behaving rapidly became the standard paradigm in the field.

The, 1950s, '60s and '70s were also characterised by the increasing dominance of American social psychology. Large amounts of research funding were poured into the US university system, and US social psychologists set a research agenda for the discipline which they perceived as important to their own society at the time. It was also arguably one of the most productive eras of the discipline – as you'll see from the frequency with which work conducted in this period appears in this volume. A whistle-stop tour includes researchers such as Asch and Milgram who undertook pioneering work into social influence, making significant advances in our understanding of con-formity, obedience and minority influence. Festinger combined new theory and the experimental methods to explain why and how we are driven to make comparisons between ourselves and others. Simultaneously, Schachter undertook pioneering research on how small groups function together effectively (or not!). Finally, Gordon Allport's ideas on the role of contact in reducing intergroup con-flict formed some of the most impactive social psychology work ever undertaken on *contact theory*. Ideas around what allows 'optimal' intergroup contact were used to guide the end of racial segregation in the US and have since been applied to post-conflict situations. We will come across many of these topics in more detail in the chapters that follow.

Although it may have been a halcyon period for social psychologists in these areas, it was not all good news. While these topics thrived, other areas struggled. This US cognitively led approach to understanding the social mind usually took an individual-based approach, ignoring the collective elements of human experience. 'Groups' were often seen as collections of individual-level processes interacting with one another, in contrast to the idea that groups have special properties of their own. This challenged (and marginalised) preceding work by people like Wundt and Lewin and slowed down work by European theorists along this line. The methods used during this phase of the discipline were also fairly narrow in scope. Lab-based, experimental studies from a broadly social–cognitive perspective dominated academic journals, often drowning out other voices and ideas.

CRITICAL SPOTLIGHT: WHO WERE THE ALLPORT BROTHERS?

Gordon Allport was born November 1897 in Indiana. He undertook his first degree in 1919 in philosophy and economics. He later focused on social psychology, and spent time with European psychologists in Berlin, Hamburg and Cambridge. On his return to Harvard he developed arguably the first university course on the subject, became editor of the *Journal of Abnormal and Social Psychology* and, in, 1939, became the president of the *American Psychological Association (APA)*. His 1954 book *The nature of prejudice* (Allport, 1954b) outlines many social psychology concepts that revolutionised the field, and still provide guiding principles today. Gordon was not the only social psychologist in the family. His older brother, Floyd Henry Allport, born in 1890, also help shape the field with his own work (for instance, *Social psychology*, Allport, 1924). Floyd's research mostly explored public opinions, attitudes and morale. His legacy also includes being one of the pioneers of the scientific method in the discipline. He also served as an editor on various journals, including the *Journal of Abnormal Psychology and Social Psychology*, and was a member of the Board of Directors of the APA between 1928 and 1930.

THE FIRST CRISIS IN SOCIAL PSYCHOLOGY

As we've seen, social psychology in the post-war period was dominated by experimental psychology, and the rise of the cognitive/social-cognitive approach more generally. Moreover, generous US funding in this area also led to it being mostly US scholars who set the research agenda. However, while mainstream social psychology focused on more and more complex (and arguably abstract) experiments, outlining more and more complex (and equally abstract) cognitive systems, other ways of viewing social psychology were developing. Academics such as George Mead and the 'Chicago School' and, in Europe, sociologists such as Alfred Schütz were bringing concepts around sociology into the realm of psychology. Mead (1934) observed that understanding a person's reactions to the world required understanding how they related to it in ways hard to capture in experimental settings. Schütz, meanwhile, drew on ideas around '*phenomenology*' to highlight that individuals' cognitions and rationality is driven by local cultural influences. This, they argued, made any attempt to pin down 'universal' and 'permanent' psychological processes (the goal of experimental psychology at the time) futile. Until the early 1970s these two forms of social psychology developed in parallel, rarely speaking or even acknowledging the value of the other. However, this situation changed radically in the early 1970s – during the *first crisis in social psychology*.

The first crisis of social psychology revolved around fundamental questioning of the experimental method. Influential works such as Kenneth Gergen's (1973) critique of the field challenged the idea that experimental social psychologists investigated the world in a neutral, value-free way. Gergen also challenged the idea that social psychologists could identify universal and unchanging psychological processes. Rather, he argued, social psychology was developing models of behaviour which were specific to particular social times and places. He also argued that the experimental culture generated a model of psychology which reflected only the worldview of the people running experiments – primarily affluent, white, male Americans. Other authors, such as Harré and Secord (1972), argued that social psychology's position of *realistic positivism* (i.e. an understanding of reality based only on scientifically demonstrated, measurable data) was doomed to failure, as people's thoughts and behaviours are dynamic, complex and, most importantly, self-aware. Similarly, Potter and Wetherell's (1987) work on *discourse analysis* argued that the systematic analysis of any 'text' can be used to understand people's *own* accounts of their *own* behaviour, and that such accounts are the only meaningful understanding one could have. In essence, many critical commentators at the time argued, each individual had their own 'psychology' and attempts to measure general principles in the lab were thus completely inappropriate.

These criticisms and new methods divided the social psychological community. They also led to the development of a number of new *qualitative* methods of study which were based on a variety of data sources (emphasising the importance of people's talk and other communication), and which, crucially, allowed theories and interpretations to arise from the data instead of the more traditional hypothesis–testing approach. They also, perhaps inevitably, lead to a schism within the discipline. On one side, those endorsing the new philosophical positions and techniques argued that their perspective gave voice to various minority groups ignored by conventional psychology and also reflected postmodern thinking and ideas around the nature of reality. On the other hand, the experimental camp saw the new wave of qualitative psychology as unsound and in danger of bringing the whole discipline into disrepute. It was not really until the end of the 1990s that these forms of psychology learnt to co-exist in a meaningful way. Even today, many social psychologists ground themselves in either the quantitative or the qualitative traditions and often have little to do with the other perspective.

EUROPEAN SOCIAL PSYCHOLOGY AND SOCIAL IDENTITY

While these debates rumbled on, another revolution in the discipline was more quietly emerging. Working in the UK in Bristol, two psychologists, Polish-born Henri Tajfel and his doctoral student John Turner, had developed an experimental task, the *minimal group paradigm* (Tajfel 1970, discussed further in Chapter 2) which showed that people randomly placed in arbitrary groups (such as group 'X' or 'Z') would discriminate between their own group and other groups. From this and other related research, Tafjel and Turner argued that individuals were attempting to generate a sense of *positive distinctiveness* between themselves and others through psychological identification with the group they were placed in. The fact that this occurred in such abstract conditions, Tajfel and Turner argued, suggested that using social identity to feel good about oneself was a fundamental social process. This principle was further developed in their seminal work creating the social identity theory (SIT; Tajfel and Turner, 1979). SIT gave a motivational explanation of how groups interact in situations where one group is of lower status, and speaks to the psychology of prejudice and social conflict. An accompanying theory (self-categorisation theory, SCT; Turner et al., 1987) attempted to describe the cognitive underpinnings of how and why these identities arise psychologically. Although SIT and SCT are explored later in this volume (see Chapter 2) it's also worth noting their historical significance.

Since its inception almost 50 years ago, the idea of *social identity* has developed into a more all-encompassing perspective which describes within-group behaviours, approaches to leadership, conflict reduction techniques and, recently, how to harness the power of groups to help people overcome traumatic events and illness. From a historical perspective, Tajfel in particular can be seen as a pivotal figure in the field. Arguing against abstract conceptual research for its own sake, Tajfel suggested that social psychologists should attempt to tackle pressing social issues. He was also a founding member of the European Association of Experimental Social Psychology in 1966 (now renamed the European Association of Social Psychology). The influence of the idea that social identities and groups have emergent psychological properties which affect individuals' cognition also widened the field of social psychology theoretically, challenged the US dominance of the time and did much to reinvigorate research in Europe.

1980s–PRESENT: CONTEMPORARY SOCIAL PSYCHOLOGY

What happened after the first crisis? The tumult surrounding the field in the 1970s and early 1980s of course settled down, and social psychology continued to thrive (albeit still perhaps as two somewhat cautiously co-existing sub-disciplines). These debates, and a re-energised and increasingly productive European research base, resulted in a far more diverse range of methods and perspectives emerging in the 1980s. It could also be argued that these factors also pulled social psychology more in the direction of 'softer' sciences – less concerned exclusively with numbers and demonstrable truths, and increasingly considering postmodern approaches to experience.

Interestingly, the next major paradigm to emerge in the field of social psychology – *social neuroscience* – was a shift *back* towards realist approaches to understanding behaviour. Social neuroscience is often regarded as being founded by John Cacioppo and Gary Berntson in the early 1990s (Cacioppo & Berntson, 1992). It drew on ideas around *evolution* to argue that humans are an innately social species. As a result, the perspective argues, our neurological systems (our brain and central nervous system) should have evolved to support us in social behaviours. Social neuroscientists use techniques such as *functional magnetic resonance imaging* (fMRI) and *electroencephalography* (EEG) to map the various areas in the brain that activate during social behaviours or cognitions. From these relatively simple bio-logical structures, it is argued, the rich and complex social behaviours we observe emerge. Social neuroscientists attempt, in a similar way to those using social-cognitive paradigms, to infer how these complex processes arise from the simpler building blocks.

In contrast to the rise of social cognition, the advance of social neuroscience did not significantly change the way the majority of social psychologists approached their field. Rather it added a new set of tools and, perhaps more importantly, highlighted the interplay between the biological and the psychological. However, the approach is not without its critics. For many social psychologists, the observa-tion that a particular neural pathway or area may activate when, for instance, we engage in social competition or experience social rejec-tion is of dubious value. Critics argue that attempting to pin down social behaviour to a set of neurological processes represents a step back from understanding the nuances of human behaviour – even relative to the *positive realism* era of the 1950s. Furthermore, many social neuroscience tools are used in laboratory or very medical-like environments. For instance, fMRI experiments involve participants lying with their head in a large device which spins magnets around their head while powerful relays generate magnetic fields which are subsequently measured. During this (very noisy!) process, participants are asked to imagine social interactions. Critics suggest these settings will produce results which are not analogous to the reality of people's psychological functioning.

Even for quantitative psychologists, these low levels of *ecological validity* (how much a technique reflects real-life experience) raise questions about their ultimate utility in understanding social behaviour 'in the field'. Despite these concerns, social neuroscience continues to thrive. It today attracts large amounts of research funding and the mass media has also presented some of the more 'sensational' findings to the general public, raising the area's profile considerably (but, perhaps, not always accurately!). As new tools and techniques develop which allow for more fine-grained and ecologically valid measures, it will be interesting to see if more traditional social psychology becomes more willing to adopt the approach more widely.

THE SECOND CRISIS OF SOCIAL PSYCHOLOGY?

Where does the field stand now? Social psychology is still, as science goes, a young discipline. Although it has come a long way from Triplett's work on cyclists and fishing reels, it also still has a way to go before it is fully mature. Indeed, as I write this, social psychology is experiencing what may prove to be its *second crisis*. There is increasing pressure on scientists working in university contexts to achieve 'ground-breaking' science in a 'publish or perish' environment. Unfortunately, it appears this has led to some investigators cutting corners on the quality of science they produce – by manipulating statistical methods to achieve significant results, by ignoring findings that did not fit in with the ideas being tested or, in some extreme cases, by systematically falsifying data. Social psychology as a discipline was drawn into this debate in a stark way in 2011 when the mass falsification of research findings by a prominent psychologist (Diederik Stapel) was discovered. Investigation into Stapel's work revealed that dozens of papers he wrote were based on false data – including work published in top-rated journal *Science* which claimed to show increased racial biases being experienced in 'messy' environments. The resulting backlash has included a major re-examination of how social psychologists conduct analysis (and to what extent they should state publicly in advance what they expect to find, instead of writing about results retrospectively). It has also led to attempts to systematically replicate major studies in the discipline. This in itself has led to worrying results, with some prominent projects suggesting only 36 per cent of attempted replications were successful (Open Science Collaboration, 2015). Some findings originally heralded as ground-breaking in their theoretical significance (for instance, that participants make less-severe moral judgements when they have just washed their hands, or that reducing perceptions of free will makes people more likely to cheat on their partners) have struggled, and questions have also been raised about some of the discipline's most influential paradigms. How will this influence social psychology as a discipline? It may well be that the eventual result of this second crisis is positive: it may encourage new methods, more rigorous science and more confidence in findings. Equally, it may be to the field's detriment if it stifles exploration and slows progress. Ultimately, it is too early to say what the long-term impact will be; tomorrow's historians of the discipline will have to be the judges.

WHAT METHODS DO TODAY'S SOCIAL PSYCHOLOGIST USE?

Before we begin to discuss the specific theories and research which make up social psychology, it is worth exploring the ways research is undertaken, and the role of *research ethics*. As we've seen, social psychology has embraced a variety of these over its development. One important result of the first crisis in social psychology was a re-evaluation of the methods used in the pursuit of understanding, and the philosophical positions which underpin them. It also highlighted a need to appreciate and recognise diversity and brought non-cognitive approaches back to the fore of the discipline. Generally, in social psychology the usual distinction between these methods is between *quantitative* and *qualitative* methodologies. The former revolves around numbers and typically employs empirical methods to 'boil down' complex behaviours or psychological constructs into measurable forms. It then applies *inferential statistics* to draw conclusions about what is being observed (i.e. takes a realist/

empiricist philosophical approach). In contrast, qualitative methods usually consist of more-subjective narrative analysis of data, which typically include speech or language which is produced in a naturalistic or unconstrained manner. It typically takes a more *postmodern philosophy* approach, which argues against the idea of absolute 'truths'.

QUANTITATIVE METHODS

Perhaps the most characteristic method in the quantitative toolkit is the *experiment*. Psychologists identify a hypothesis – for instance that changing factor X will result in a change in outcome Y. They then contrive a situation where only factor X (and nothing else) is changed (an 'experimental condition'), and a situation where the change is absent ('a control condition'). For instance, an investigator may see if seeing pictures of one stimulus (cute puppies) versus another (ill children) influences a behaviour (giving to charity). To try and ensure nothing else changes between conditions, this sort of research usually takes place in a laboratory setting or other controlled environment. The experiment is undertaken on multiple participants and then statistical testing is undertaken to decide if any differences between condition are due to the manipulation, or just down to chance. Measurements taken in experiments are very diverse: they may include questionnaires measuring attitudes, actual incidences of a particular behaviour, response times to different stimuli, cardiac reactivity or levels of neural activation in different areas of the brain (to name but a few). A related approach to experimental studies is that of *non-experimental surveys* or *observation studies*. In these, a number of factors are measured and links between them tested. So, an investigator may hypothesise a link between the levels of identification a person has with one group and the levels of bias they show against another. They would then survey these characteristics amongst numerous people and examine how strong the relationship is. In *observational studies* investigators can also go into the field, observe the frequency of actual behaviours and see how often such behaviours go together. Although such methods are easier to administer (they often require less control and are usually less intensive in terms of research staff time) they have a major drawback – you can never tell which direction causation runs in observed relationships (for instance, does identity cause bias, or bias cause identity, or do they both affect each other?). These sorts of methods usually require the collection of new data, but they can also be conducted on *archival data* (for instance, by looking at economic records and use of racial slurs in the media to try to establish links between stress and racism). Recently, access to publicly held data with tens of thousands of records is becoming more common, allowing for tests across large populations to be undertaken.

QUALITATIVE METHODS

In some ways, qualitative methods are the very opposite of those described above. Where quantitative datasets can include the population of an entire country being analysed at once, qualitative methods often focus on small samples (of a dozen or even fewer for some forms). They generally identify a broad area of interest rather than a specific hypothesis. In interview/focus group studies, participants from a relevant population discuss their thoughts and views on the topic, often in a 'semi-structured interview' format. As well as interviews, qualitative investigators also utilise other sources of 'talk', including transcripts (for instance, police interview transcripts) and publicly available online material (for instance, online forums or social media). Data may also include different types of media (such as visual images shown in adverts). Depending on the theoretical approach taken, the actual analysis is undertaken in different ways. Generally, the investigator is expected to be guided by the themes that emerge from the data, rather than their own expectations of what they should find. Beyond that, approaches vary. For instance, in *grounded theory*, the analyses of a large number of different forms of data are collated and a new theoretical model of how emergent trends link is constructed. *Interpretative phenomenological analysis* involves discussing the underlying meaning of people's talk and is usually undertaken on interview data. In contrast, *thematic analysis* can be more guided by theory, interpreting emerging themes in terms of their links with a particular existing approach. The benefits of a qualitative approach are that it avoids the issues of realism we discussed earlier and recognises the existence of multiple 'truths'. It also provides a richer insight into people's experience than do a series of numbers. However, the results of a given analysis are open to interpretation, and the philosophical underpinnings of this approach make findings harder (or impossible) to generalise from.

It is easy to see these methods as oppositional camps (and, unfortunately, this is a trap which researchers themselves often fall into!). However, one thing qualitative and quantitative methods have in common is that they both require adherence to a methodology which is reported transparently when the results are presented. In quantitative methods, this may involve following the rules around experimental design and statistical analysis in a particular area. In qualitative methods, it involves open reflection on the role of the self in the research processes and adherence to the steps of analysis laid out in the method chosen. Happily, more and more psychologists are coming to realise that the most robust attempts to understand a given phenomenon draw on the strongest elements of both approaches – in a way which is complementary rather than oppositional.

CRITICAL SPOTLIGHT: ONE QUESTION – DIFFERENT METHODS?

Often, a combination of qualitative and quantitative methods provides the best approach. For instance, to test the role of social identity in addiction recovery, researchers have used qualitative techniques to explore how identities around addiction and recovery develop, and quantitative measures to test the effects of developing new identities on subsequent relapse and recovery rates.

THE ETHICS OF SOCIAL PSYCHOLOGY

Psychology is a science which uses human participants as its primary source of data. As such, it is important that we consider how the discipline respects the rights of the people it studies, through the practice of *research ethics*. Ethics in the study of human behaviours (and humans in general, including medical trials) was brought to the fore as a result of the post–World War II Nuremberg trials – where scientists who had conducted highly distressing, damaging and at times fatal experimentation on prisoners were brought to justice.

As a result, codes of conduct such as the *Declaration of Helsinki* were developed to govern research on humans.

Similar to the rest of the psychology discipline, social psychologists now follow comprehensive *codes of ethical conduct* alongside the Helsinki declaration. These govern investigators' behaviour and provide guidance on how to make judgements to ensure ethical practice and vary by country. In the UK, the most commonly used guidance is the British Psychological Society's code of conduct; in the USA it is that of the American Psychology Association. The majority of psychology ethical codes of conduct revolve around similar principles such as *respect* (recognising the dignity and worth of all, with a particular respect for the autonomy, privacy and dignity of participants); *competence* (only undertaking work one is competent to do safely and effectively); *responsibility* (and social responsibility) for one's own actions and the outcomes of the research process; *a duty to maximise benefit and minimise harm* through the research process; and *scientific integrity* in the planning, conduct and reporting of research. The development of these codes, and the introduction of research ethics committees (which review all research conducted by academics to ensure it is ethically sound), helped to ensure that the rights of participants are systematically protected, but were not without mishap. Some past studies have, despite ethical controls, led to behaviours which by today's standards are viewed as ethically problematic. Important examples include Milgram's infamous study in which participants believed they had administered severe electric shocks to other people, with the distress and guilt that resulted, and Zimbardo's prison simulation study, in which participants who became 'prisoners' were harried by fellow participant 'guards' to the point of psychological breakdown (see Chapter 6 for a discussion of both of these studies).

Modern ethical practices have taken account of learning from these experiences and, as a result, are generally now much more robust and span the entire research process. As we've seen in the experiences of the first and second crises in social psychology, it is not just during the data collection phase itself that research ethics come into play. How investigators choose which question to ask, and how they approach the issue methodologically, all feeds into how the study will be conducted and what ethical issues are raised. More recently, the importance of scientific integrity – both in the form of transparency in methodological reporting and statistics at an individual researcher level, and in the editorial and pre-registration norms which the discipline as a whole adopts – has grown further. Ethics in research remains a dynamic subject – in the same way that Zimbardo's and Milgram's research was acceptable at the time, but is viewed ambiguously now, the norms and codes of today may look absurd in fifty or a hundred years' time. Subjects such as online rights to privacy (are your social network posts fair game for researchers?), so-called 'labour crowdsourcing' research (which may offer inappropriate incentives to vulnerable people) and work on behavioural genetics are just a few of the areas which may pose particular ethical challenges for today's scholars. Psychologists have worked (and will continue to work) together to agree acceptable (and unacceptable) ways of researching, drawing on best practice from other disciplines (for instance, medicine).

CRITICAL SPOTLIGHT: THE DECLARATION OF HELSINKI

The Declaration of Helsinki reflects the key principles outlined in the *Nuremberg Code*. The Nuremberg Code was developed following the prosecution of various scientists who undertook horrific, inhuman experiments and sterilisation of unwilling human participants – most notably Nazi scientists experimenting on prisoners, concentration camp detainees and other vulnerable populations. The Declaration of Helsinki itself revolves around a number of basic principles, including the right to make informed decisions about whether or not to consent, special care over potentially vulnerable participant groups, the importance of informed research planning, careful risk assessment and ongoing independent ethical oversight. At the time of writing, the declaration was in its seventh revision. Until around the year 2000, it was widely used as the basis for ethical practice guidelines internationally. However, it has recently been challenged by alternative formulations, such as the *Good Clinical Practice* guidelines, and the *EU Clinical Trials Directive*. Part of the shift has been that while the Declaration of Helsinki outlines general principles, modern research has developed more prescriptive standards for researchers to adhere to.

CHAPTER SUMMARY

As this chapter has shown, social psychology is a dynamic discipline with a rich history. The focus of the discipline has changed over time – moving from a concentration on individuals to groups and back several times. The confidence social psychologists have in themselves and their discipline has also waxed and waned. Early experimentalists heralded a new, scientific way of understanding the complexities of people, and the cognitive revolution brought new tools to bear to help aid the accumulation of data. However, these approaches have also led to great uncertainty, with critics arguing that experimental realism can never fully encapsulate the full gamut of human behaviour, and proposing new, less empirically led methods. More recently, quantitative social psychologists have again begun to question the methods they use, this time with concerns about how repeatable their work is, and how they approach scientific integrity.

Throughout these changes, there are some central features which, it could be argued, most social psychologists would agree on. For instance, Lewin's idea of social psychology as an interactive process – suggesting that no-one can exist psychologically in a vacuum – is widely recognised to be fundamental. The importance of these features can be seen in the way that they affect all areas of our thoughts and behaviours – shaping our perception of the world, the way we process information and, ultimately, the way we behave. I hope that, as you progress through this book, you appreciate how the studies and theories you read about have been shaped by the various events, individuals and movements we have discussed in this chapter. I also hope you make links between them and your own experience – your own personal 'social psychology'.

KEY CHAPTER POINTS

- Social psychology is the study of how our thoughts, feelings and behaviours are affected by the actual, imagined or implied presence of others.
- The area has been of general interest to scholars since Plato and Aristotle, and more formally since the late 1800s.

- Social psychology encompasses both qualitative and quantitative approaches. These methods, in particular quantitative ones, have faced challenges – particularly during the first and second crises of social psychology.
- Social psychological research is governed by a set of ethical codes on conduct which aim to protect participants from harm and ensure scientific integrity.

SUGGESTED FURTHER READING

- Kruglanski, A. W., & Stroebe, W. (eds) (2012). *Handbook of the history of social psychology*. New York: Psychology Press.
- Gergen, K. J. (1973). Social psychology as history. *Journal of Personality and Social Psychology*, *26*, 309–320.
- Open Science Collaboration (2015). Estimating the reproducibility of psychological science. *Science, 349*(6251), aac4716.
- Banyard, P., & Flanagan, C. (2006). *Ethical issues and guidelines in psychology*. New York: Routledge.

SELF AND MOTIVATION

THEME OVERVIEW

In this theme we begin to look at what can be thought of as the 'building blocks' of social psychology. In the first chapter of the theme, 'Understanding the self', we consider how social psychologists conceptualise selfhood. In doing so, we highlight the tension between individual- and group-level accounts. We see this theme re-emerge when we examine how our self-esteem may (or may not) be tied to others' evaluations of us. This in turn has direct relevance for the study of how our online and offline selves differ. This chapter concludes with a critical examination of the idea of a wholly conscious, free-willed 'self', with a discussion of free will and automaticity. In the next chapter, 'The ways we think', we move our discussion to core cognitive processes which influence social behaviours. We examine ideas around rationality, how our relationships with other people influence our own motivations and how the self-control we display in interpersonal interactions can wax and wane. We also consider where 'thought' itself resides by examining recent evidence into embodied cognition, and how our thinking and behaviour is influenced by the culture we grow up in.

2

UNDERSTANDING THE SELF

WHAT IS THE 'SELF'?

What makes you *you*? Take five minutes and list whatever comes to mind.

What did you come up with? Was it a set of values you hold, or a list of behaviours or emotions? Did you mention social groups you belong to or activities you enjoy? Was it influenced by what others think of you or how positive you feel about yourself? Or maybe who you aspire to be? Is everything on the list representative of your current self, or does it also represent past or future versions of you? In all likelihood, your list reflects a mixture of all of the above, and a range of other things. If you undertook the above exercise it may also have left you feeling a little unsatisfied – perhaps you listed a number of things which described you, but also failed to capture the essence of *you*. If so, you are in good company. Psychologists have long argued over what makes up the self (or even whether such a thing exists at all), and the popularity of different definitions has varied over time. For instance, Mauss (1938; see Mauss, 1985) highlights that at some periods of history (for instance, in pre-classical times) the 'self' seemed to be understood solely by reference to narratives about the world. From such a perspective, people are seen as having a role to play in the 'story' but little independent meaning beyond that. Ancient Egyptian views of the self separated out the physical and a more fundamental 'shadow essence' (which we could see as being similar to a soul). They also argued that the shadow could persist only as long as the body was preserved through mummification. Later, Roman philosophers suggested the self was seen to be governed by a personality 'type' which fixed how one would think and behave – and assumed one's behaviour was directed towards fulfilling one's inevitable destiny. Religion has also influenced the view of the self – for example Christianity's view of a moral self, or Buddhism's rejection of the idea of a permanent self existing at all. It's also a popular literary subject – Oscar Wilde's character Dorian Gray temporarily avoided staining his self with his misdeeds by transferring the sin to a portrait, and science fiction has long explored what makes a self a self (with Arthur C. Clarke's murderous artificial intelligence, HAL 9000, suggesting that it is not just people that do bad things to one another!).

More contemporary psychological attempts to understand the self tend to veer away from the more esoteric side of these debates, but also represent a diverse set of opinions as to what makes you into you. This chapter will look at key social psychology accounts of the self – examining perspectives which primarily revolve around ideas of *self as an individual being* and *self as part of social structures or groups*. We will also explore how our self-esteem (the extent to which we feel favourable towards ourselves) influences, and is influenced by, our sense of self. Finally, we'll question that a self as a conscious, truly self-aware agency has meaning by reviewing evidence suggesting that much of our behaviour is unconscious and uncontrollable.

THEORIES OF SELF: INDIVIDUAL-LEVEL ACCOUNTS

Conceptualisations of self have often revolved around whether the self is an individual concept ('individual self') or one tied up with social relationships within groups ('collective self'). Psychologists also explore whether we have 'one self' or 'many selves' and also whether these constructs always guide our behaviour, or only influence us on occasion.

PSYCHODYNAMIC VIEWS OF THE SELF

A classic way of understanding the self as an individual-level concept is via *psychodynamic theory*. Psychodynamics was developed principally by Sigmund Freud, working with others, in Vienna between the late 1880s and his death in 1939. The psychodynamic approach argues that the self is split into three aspects – the *id*, the *ego* and the *super-ego* (Freud, 1920). The id is part of the self which contains our basic desires and drives, such as nourishment and sexual and aggressive tendencies. The id has no rational aspects and demands immediate responses to its (often multiple) demands. The id interacts with the other two aspects of the self – the super-ego and the ego. The super-ego is almost the polar opposite of the id – acting as a moral compass, and as a critic of the id's desires. Finally, the ego acts as a negotiator between the id, the super-ego and reality. It tries to meet the needs of the id, while considering the drives of the super-ego and minimising long-term harm to the self. Unresolved conflicts between these structures are thought to cause mental illness, such as depression and anxiety. It is argued that the super-ego and ego are the only the parts of the self that are open to conscious inspection, and even they have a large proportion which resides in the unconscious or 'pre-conscious' sections of our psyche. In clinical contexts, classic psychoanalytical techniques such as *free word association* and *ink blot tests* aim to give therapists a clue as to which unresolved conflicts reside in the unconscious and help to coax them into the conscious realm where they can be resolved. Psychodynamics is generally in decline as a popular model of understanding the self, as is psychoanalysis as a treatment technique. However, the work of theoreticians such as Freud has made a lasting contribution to social psychology – in particular highlighting the important role of the unconscious in our behaviour. It also lay the groundwork for *trait-based models of personality*.

TRAIT-BASED MODELS

Other individual approaches to understanding the self can include looking at traits which define people – and can guide our interactions with others. One way of doing this is by arguing that we have various dimensions of personality, each varying between individuals. For instance, the *P-E-N model* (Eysenck & Eysenck, 1974; 1977) suggests personality varies on three dimensions: *psychoticism/socialisation, extroversion/introversion* and *neuroticism/stability*. Similarly, the *OCEAN model* identifies *openness to experience, contentiousness, agreeableness* and *extraversion* (see McCrae & Costa, 1987). These trait-type models can also be more specifically linked to types of social behaviour or attitudes. For instance, Theodor Adorno's work on *authoritarian personalities* (Adorno et al., 1950) and, more recently, Bob Altemeyer's ideas about *right-wing authoritarianism* (Altemeyer, 1981) argue that some people are more inclined to endorse discriminatory beliefs than others. Such individuals also follow strong leaders more readily and are more conservative. Other lines of research looking at traits as part of the social self consider the extent to which people tend to be *pro-self* versus *pro-others* in their outlook and behaviours (see Van Lange et al., 1997); and how we view the causes of our own and others' behaviours (attribution theory, which is explored in the *social relationships* theme). Levels of empirical support for these approaches vary – some commentators, for example, highlight the fact that so-called 'traits' often have low test-retest reliability (for instance, my score on a personality measure may fluctuate over relatively short spaces of time, or between situations). However, the idea that we have particular traits which make up our self continues to be a dominant discourse in the field.

THE SELF IN RELATION TO OTHERS

Most accounts of the self recognise that the way we perceive ourselves is often linked to how others view us, and both these constructs can guide our cognition and behaviour. Perhaps the strongest form of this argument is made by the *symbolic interactionism* school (e.g. Blumer, 1986; Mead, 1934). This approach argues that our reality, including our sense of self, is based on a shared understanding of what objects (including people) mean. So, one person's behaviour could be categorised as 'terrorist' by one set of people, and 'heroic' by another. Applied to self, the ways we think and behave can also vary in meaning. For example, doing something risky with little thought could be regarded as either 'bold' or 'foolhardy'. Thus, our understanding of ourselves is based very much on social interactions with others and the extent to which they shape our interpretation. In particular, symbolic interactions approaches argue, we draw on the 'reflective appraisals' of others' opinions to generate our sense of self. This process is also referred to as the *looking glass self* (Cooley, 1902). Evidence supporting this approach is widespread. For instance, research conducted in India suggests that watching Western male stereotypical figures in films influences male movie-goers' self-perception and their interactions with women (Derné, 1999). The way others act towards us has also been shown to have long-lasting effects. In a famous experiment on *self-fulfilling prophecies*, experimental psychologists Robert Rosenthal and Lenore Jacobson showed that telling teachers that a sample of their young students (randomly selected) had 'unusual potential' led to these children being treated differently, and subsequently developing a higher IQ than their peers (Rosenthal & Jacobson, 1966). Although the idea of such a *looking glass self* may make intuitive sense, and has a wide range of empirical support, it does have some caveats and limitations. Most notably, it appears that the way we think people perceive us is more important than how we are actually perceived (Shrauger & Schoeneman, 1979). Also, as we will discover when we discuss self-esteem, whom we choose to take seriously when we think about how others see us, and how we respond to negative evaluations, is complicated – we do not simply allow all negative (or positive) evaluations to shape our sense of self.

SELF-DISCREPANCY THEORY

Another way of understanding how our concept of self influences us is Higgins' (1989) *self-discrepancy theory*. This argues that we hold three variations of our self-representation – our *actual self* (how we see ourselves at the moment), our *ideal self* (how we would like to be) and our *ought self* (the self we think we should be, often driven by external evaluations such as social norms). Higgins argues that when we feel our actual self is out of kilter with our ideal or ought selves we act to reduce the gap. If I feel, for instance, that I am not being sufficiently kind (or assertive, etc.) relative to how I would like to be, or to how others think I should be, I can act more in that way.

The idea of different forms of individual self is also picked up in *elaborated self-awareness theory* (Carver & Scheier, 1981), which argues that we also have a *private* and *public* self which we can be aware of. The private self consists of what we think ourselves (i.e. how we are thinking or feeling privately). The public self reflects how aware we are of how others may see us (for instance, through what we publicly say or do). These levels of awareness change what standards we use to guide our behaviour. You could think of this as influencing which of our 'actual', 'ideal', and 'ought' selves has the most influence on us at any given time.

Of course, most of us do not wander around constantly dwelling on our sense of self while we think and behave, and social psychology recognises this. Indeed, some theorists argue that when we are in groups, we may engage in a process known as *deindividuation* which leads us to act with less or no reference to our self. This can lead us to behave more anti-socially. Both being in a group and feeling anonymous can encourage deindividuation. For instance, psychologist Edward Diener and colleagues (Diener et al., 1976) showed that children on a trick-or-treating tour (where children in fancy dress call at people's houses at Halloween asking for sweets) more often took advantage of an opportunity to steal money or candy when they thought they were anonymous (i.e. wearing a mask). This effect was particularly pronounced if they did not know the adults in the situation. Similarly, ideas around *automaticity* (which we explore in more depth later in this chapter) suggest that we often behave in social situations according to *situational schema* – set 'scripts' which tell us how to behave (for example, when going to a restaurant, one usually waits for a table, agrees with the one offered, orders some food, eats and pays the bill, usually without much thought, or reference to the self). We may have social schema about a variety of behaviours (how we respond to criticism, what we do when we first arrive at work, etc.). So, for much of the time, our self may be largely irrelevant! Of course, another way of looking at this is that our self is actually more a collection of these relatively automatic ways of behaving than it is anything else.

Although they have different foci, the above accounts all have one thing in common – they assume that the self is something which resides largely within the individual. This *bottom-up approach* can be contrasted with other accounts of the self, so-called *top-down approaches*, which suggest that our self is more closely tied to our relationships with others. It is to these group-level accounts that we now turn.

THEORIES OF SELF: GROUP-LEVEL ACCOUNTS

What groups are you a member of? Are any of these important to you? How do they make you feel when you think of them? On reflection, do these group memberships form part of your self? The accounts of self we have looked at so far have assumed that people generally consider the self as being mostly contained within (and defined by) individual-level characteristics (i.e. traits) and evaluations (how others perceive us as individuals). However, as the exercise above may have revealed, much of our idea of self is tied up with the groups we are a part of – our *social identities*. Psychologist Susan Fiske argues that we choose to be a part of a group to fulfil *core social motives* comprising *belonging, understanding, controlling, self-enhancement* and *trust* (Fiske, 2010). But how do these collective identities operate, and what effects do they have on our sense of self? One way of understanding this is via *social identity theory*.

SOCIAL IDENTITY THEORY

Social identity theory (SIT) was developed by Henri Tajfel and John Turner in the 1970s and '80s to explain intergroup relations (see Tajfel and Turner, 1979). SIT rests on three assumptions. First, it assumes that we want to feel good about ourselves. Second, it assumes that aspects of our self are tied up with the groups we are members of. Finally, it argues that we can feel good about ourselves on the basis of positive comparisons between our own groups (ingroups) and others (outgroups). When groups are low in status, they may not have opportunities to engage in such *positive differentiation* in obvious ways, and this motivates thought and behaviour. Briefly, SIT argues that when we are in low-status groups, we make a judgement as to whether we can use a *personal mobility* strategy and simply leave the group (i.e. if boundaries between our own group and others can be crossed, are *permeable*). If boundaries are seen as *impermeable* (i.e. we cannot move from one group to another) group members look to change the status of the group (to generate positive differentiation). If group members can perceive an alternative to the status quo, they may engage in *social competition* – actively trying to change relative status through social action, civil disobedience, peaceful protests, violence etc. If group members cannot imagine a future in which they are equal (or superior) to other groups then they may engage in *social creativity* strategies which allow positive differentiation despite apparent status differences. Such strategies include changing the value of dimensions used for comparison (e.g. 'money isn't everything'), finding new dimensions ('we are not a rich group, but we are honest!') or finding a new comparison outgroup ('we may not be the richest, but we do better than these folk over here'). SIT argues that by conceptualising intergroup relations in this way, the approach can be used to understand why, how and when a group engages in the various strategies (personal mobility, social competition or social creativity) it outlines.

SELF-CATEGORISATION THEORY

SIT provides a description of why social identities are important to people, and some of the mechanisms which underpin intergroup relationships and behaviour – particularly around possible status changes for groups and their members. In this sense it is a very motivational account of social behaviour. It does not, however, really discuss how, at a cognitive level, a particular social identity is selected at any given time. Nor does it provide a more general understanding of social categorisation. These aspects of social cognition are described in *self-categorisation theory* (SCT), developed by John Turner and colleagues (Turner et al., 1987). One key principle of SCT is the idea of *levels of abstraction*. The self can vary on a dimension between 'self as I' (a low level of abstraction), 'self as ingroup' (my own group relative to an outgroup – a moderate level of abstraction) and, at the highest level of abstraction, 'self as a human'. At each level of abstraction, more people are considered part of the self. The level of abstraction at which we self-identify is dictated by what makes most sense in the situation we find ourselves in, and a number of other factors. These include *perceiver readiness*, *comparative fit* and *normative fit*. SCT recognises that identities are not created from nowhere – they are a product of our experience. As such, some identities (those which we feel more favourable about, have used more often or meet our current needs or goals) are thought to be more accessible to us: we are said to have higher *perceiver readiness* to use them. *Comparative fit* refers to the discriminatory power of a particular categorisation: we look for groupings which maximise differences *between* groups, while minimising differences *within* groups. Finally, *normative fit* is the extent to which people's behaviours fit with our expectation of how members of a particular group behave – essentially we use our stereotypes (see Chapter 5) to guide decisions of how we categorise people into 'us' and 'them'.

THE COGNITIVE EFFECTS OF CATEGORISATION

Once an identity is activated, a number of cognitive and behavioural effects are likely. One common effect is that we perceive differences *between* groups as greater than they actually are. Simultaneously, we also perceive differences *within* groups as being less pronounced than they really are. We also see ourselves as more interchangeable with other ingroup members, see the world from the point of view of the group, and are more likely to experience deindividuation (see Postmes & Spears, 1998). These effects can also influence how we see and remember the world. For instance, Duncan (1976) showed Caucasian American students a video of an interaction between a white and a black actor. One ambiguous moment in this interaction was perceived as an intentional 'shove' more often when the 'shover' was black than when they were white. In terms of memory, we are better at remembering ingroup members as individuals than we are outgroup members (Van Bavel & Cunningham, 2012). We also distort our memory to fit our beliefs about social groups. For instance, Nelson, Biernat and Manis (1990) showed men pictures of women and men of various heights (on average, they were the same height). They then asked the participants to estimate how tall the males and the females were on average. Men estimated that the women were shorter than the men. More surprisingly, this effect was sustained even when participants were (i) told groups were the same height and (ii) offered a financial incentive to be accurate!

Since their inception, SIT and SCT have evolved into more of a social identity *perspective* rather than a single theory. Early empirical evidence for SIT included the minimal group paradigm, which appeared to show evidence for a motivation to engage in positive differentiation (see the Critical Spotlight on the minimal group paradigm for more on this). More recent research involves both experimental and correlational work, in both the laboratory and the field. The idea that we have meaningful social identities has been applied to diverse real-life domains, such as riots (Reicher, 1996), workplace management practice (Ellemers, De Gilder & Haslam 2004; Hogg, 2001), conflict reduction (Bar-Tal, 2000), addiction recovery (Frings & Albery 2016), litter dropping (Grasmick, Bursik & Kinsey, 1991) and many more. It has also been used to understand group processes such as ingroup dissent (Marques, Abrams & Seródio, 2001), the development of group identity amongst children (Abrams et al., 2003) and the collective experience of emotions (Bar-Tal, Halperin & De Rivera, 2007).

CRITICISMS OF SIT

The social identity perspective is arguably one of the most influential approaches in modern social psychology and has driven both thinking and applied practice for over four decades. However, it is not without its critics. One major criticism of the social identity perspective and SCT is that they may have more explanatory than predictive power. This means they are good at explaining why something happened in light of the theory but weaker at predicting what will happen in a given situation. Another weakness is that some aspects of the perspectives (such as the self-esteem/identity link; see Rubin & Hewstone, 1998) have received mixed support.

EVOLUTIONARY PERSPECTIVES ON GROUP-LEVEL SELF

The social identity approach is not the only approach which understands the self at a group level. Evolutionary accounts of psychology argue that natural selection favours a tendency towards *kin altruism* (helping those whom one is genetically related to more than others), which enables and encourages group co-operation. Moreover, humans are highly social creatures, who rely on groups which function effectively (i.e. allow people to exchange favours and share risks and rewards) to survive. Evolutionary selection processes have therefore favoured individuals who can function well in groups. This evolutionary perspective can be used to explain our ability to undertake tasks which are important for group function (such as using reasoning to detect people who cheat in deals) with less effort than undertaking the same task in an abstract setting (Cosmides & Tooby, 2005). It also explains the ever popular pastime of gossip as an exchange of social information about trustworthiness (Dunbar & Dunbar 1998), humour as a form of 'social grooming' (Polimeni & Reiss, 2006) and many other social behaviours. It also suggests that the readiness of people to identify with ingroups (and favour them relative to outgroups) may be driven by evolutionary pressures (such as kin altruism). One limitation of much evolutionary theory is that although it can be explored experimentally (for instance, by giving people logic tasks, either in the abstract or presented as scenarios where they must identify cheaters), you can only use the results to infer evolutionary processes. You cannot, unfortunately, go back in time and watch the processes themselves! The problem this raises is around *falsifiability* – you can argue that process X is a product of evolution, but you could also argue that A, B or C were, if they were present. For instance, there are differences in the preference for being found funny vs. finding things funny observed between men and women. Men seem to prefer women who appreciate humour, while women prefer men who produce it. This has been attributed to mate selection processes (Bressler et al., 2006). However, one could also imagine an evolutionary explanation for a lack of difference, or a reverse pattern of findings. It is important to note that critics of social identity approaches have levelled the same criticism at that paradigm, and advocates of both approaches would argue that such falsifiability is present to some extent: both approaches rest on foundational principles which can be tested and they both can be used to develop effective interventions and to understand events with a good level of reliability.

Although SIT and evolutionary approaches have many differences, they also both stress the importance of social groups in normal psychological functioning. In doing so, both highlight that the way we feel about ourselves (our *self-esteem*) can be seen as an inherently social process. But how exactly does the way we feel about ourselves interact with our social relationships?

CRITICAL SPOTLIGHT: THE MINIMAL GROUP PARADIGM

The *minimal group paradigm* (MGP) was one of the experiments on which social identity theory was built. It aimed to explore the minimum conditions required for intergroup group behaviour. In its early forms (e.g. Tajfel et al., 1971) it involved separating people (initially school children) into arbitrary groups (for instance, those who preferred images by modern artists such as Klee and Kandinsky). They were then asked to give points from a selection of choices to another member of their group, and a member of the other group. The points would be exchanged for cash, and participants did not know who else was in the same group as they were. These point rewards were paired – so giving X points to your group would lead to a member of the other group also being awarded Y points. The number of points on each side of the pair varied, so participants could choose to be *fair* (giving equal points), aim for *maximum joint profit* (highest total number of points, irrespective of who got them), *maximise ingroup profit* (to get the most for the ingroup, regardless of outgroup points) or try to generate *maximum difference* (to get as many points possible *more* than the other group, regardless of total points gained). They could also elect to use an *ingroup favouritism strategy*, a combination of the latter two approaches. The results from this (and other studies) suggest that people engage in positive differentiation even when they do not directly benefit from generating a difference between their own group and others in terms of material gain (recall that they gave points to unknown members of the groups). The MGP seems a fairly robust methodology, having been replicated among different age ranges and cultural backgrounds, when changing the basis of group membership, and in many other variations.

SELF-ESTEEM AND SOCIAL SELVES

INDIVIDUAL AND SOCIAL SOURCES OF SELF-ESTEEM

Sometimes, we feel great about ourselves. Other times, we feel we are not good enough. We may feel positive about some aspects of ourselves (maybe our intelligence) but bad about another (maybe our looks). These self-evaluations are often referred to as *self-esteem*. Festinger (1954) observed in his *social comparison theory* that we are motivated to maintain positive self-esteem and can aim to do so by seeking to make comparisons with people we see ourselves as superior to (*downwards comparisons*) while avoiding those against people we feel inferior to (*upwards comparisons*). We also tend to overestimate our good points, feel we have more control over events than we actually do, and have an inflated sense of optimism (a set of traits which Sedikides and Gregg (2007), call a *self-enhancing triad*). Generally, across most populations, people have moderate to high self-esteem (e.g. Baumeister, Tice & Hutton, 1989). However, contrary to what you may expect, low-esteem does *not* seem to be linked to things like aggression (Baumeister, Smart & Boden, 1996). Similarly, high self-esteem doesn't automatically mean people are pleasantly confident (indeed, they can also be arrogant and highly self-absorbed – see Kernis, Grannemann & Barclay, 1989).

BIRGING AND CORFING

We've already seen the importance of group membership for our sense of self, and this seems to translate to self-esteem. If our groups do well, we can benefit from this positive differentiation, despite perhaps not being directly involved in the group's success. Such *basking in reflective glory* (BIRGing) has been experimentally observed. For instance, Cialdini looked at American football fans at US universities with a strong involvement in the sport (Cialdini, Borden & Thorne, 1976). On a series of Mondays following a big game, researchers went into lecture halls and counted the number of people wearing uni-branded apparel. Following a win, more students wore such clothing. In their second study (published in the same paper), Cialdini's team also rang students and asked them to describe the previous day's game (if they had seen it). When the team had won, people used 'we' ('we did well') more than when the team had lost ('they did badly'). This suggests people were highlighting their affiliation with winning, but not losing, teams. The opposite effect to (*cutting off reflected failure*, or CORFing) has also been observed in other studies. Boen, Vanbeselaere and Feys (2002), for instance, observed that voters who displayed party political signage on their windows and lawns were much quicker to take it down if their party lost!

SOCIAL CREATIVITY AND SELF-ESTEEM BUFFERING

Taken together, the above evidence suggests that we use our positive group identities to our advantage to maintain self-esteem. It also suggests that how others perceive our group (or, at least, how we think others perceive our group) can dramatically affect our sense of self. One implication of this is that if we are in mostly low-status groups, we do not have opportunities to draw on the perceived worth of our groups. This in turn may be related to lower self-esteem. Interestingly, this does not always appear to be the case: work by psychologist Brenda Major and colleagues suggests that individuals in low-status groups have a wide range of levels of self-esteem, and that the variation between individuals in the same group often exceeds the variation between groups (see Crocker & Major, 1989). Why might this be?

Social identity theory would explain this effect by arguing that when individuals cannot move between groups (i.e. the boundaries between them are impermeable) and when they can see no likelihood of their low status relative to a dominant group changing, they are likely to engage in *social creativity* strategies. These provide the opportunity for positive differentiation, but at a price – they also reduce the motivation to engage in *social competition*. Being a member of a low-status social group can also provide opportunities to understand negative events in ways which are less damaging to our sense of self. For instance, Sherman and colleagues (Sherman et al., 2007) showed that teams of losing sports players typically rated their degree of control over the outcome as being low (i.e. they blamed the situation for the loss) relative to winning teams – presumably to protect their self-esteem. However, when losing teams were able to publicly place value on other dimensions of being in the team (camaraderie, humour etc.) before making the ratings, this defensive tendency subsequently disappeared (as self-esteem needs had been met in other ways). Likewise, Testa, Crocker and Major (1988) showed that unattractive women who received negative feedback on an essay from a male marker did not experience self-esteem loss when they believed the marker had seen them (presumably attributing the poor mark to discrimination rather than ability). These buffering effects do not suggest that discrimination between groups is OK, but does highlight how adaptable people are in managing in difficult situations.

As well as (sometimes) being a reflection of the groups we are in, self-esteem may also affect the way we behave towards other group members. From a social comparison or a social identity perspective (such as above), self-esteem is a fairly dynamic concept which may not have a lot to do with how positively we should really see ourselves. However, having some link between reality and our self-esteem may be important. For instance, *sociometer theory* (Leary & Downs, 1995) suggests we may have evolved a sense of self-esteem to facilitate functioning in a group (which, as humans, we need to do to survive). Sociometer theory argues that if we behave contrary to group norms, the group negatively evaluates us. Such evaluation serves to lower our self-esteem, which in turn causes us to change the behaviour and hence remain in the group. This model can be contrasted against the previous approaches we have discussed in that it suggests that (i) our esteem may be an accurate perception of how others see us and (ii) it is primarily an individual-level (as opposed to a social-level) system.

The individual-level and group-level accounts of the self we have discussed here represent the 'classic' approach to understanding the self, and many have been developed over decades. While most of these perspectives are still thriving, they have all had to account for two important developments in recent times. The first is rapid changes in technology which have resulted in the growing importance of the internet, and the idea of *online selves*. The second is the development of ideas around automaticity which challenge the very notion of a volitional self. It is to these two ideas which we now turn.

ONLINE VERSUS OFFLINE PERSONAS

How we construct our self may well be changing. Since becoming widely available in the 1990s, the internet has significantly changed the way we connect with others. In particular, it has presented new opportunities and methods to interact with other people (email, instant messaging, social network sites, online gaming and forums, to name but a few). Psychologists are still getting to grips with what these enormous changes mean – both in terms of existing theory, but also in terms of opportunities to develop new approaches. In this discussion, we look at two such modes of communication – online forums and social networking sites – and explore some of the theory and evidence they have generated.

Online forums about particular topics are a popular form of communication. Anyone can join a public forum and post about a topic they are interested in and interact with other like-minded people to discuss it. Two interesting features of these groups are that they (i) are often anonymous and (ii) have fairly permeable boundaries (i.e. people enter and leave the group fairly easily). One way of understanding the effects of such features of a group is through classic accounts of anonymous group function – such as *deindividuation* (Diener et al., 1976; see also above and Chapter 6). This perspective would suggest that people using forums under a pseudonym are likely to also experience a lack of *self-regulation*. This can lead to an increased likelihood of people undertaking socially undesirable behaviours – 'flaming', 'trolling', 'spamming' and general online nuisance-making are all examples of such behaviours which you may have encountered yourself. However, perhaps more nuanced understandings of such behaviours are needed. Psychologists such as Lea and Spears (1991) and Reicher, Spears and Postmes (1995) argue in their *social identity model of deindividuation effects* (SIDE) that, far from relatively anonymous communication leading people to lose all sense of identity, online communication could make people focus *more* on their social identities. For instance, a lack of personal information makes people fall back on group-level information and adopt these sort of identities easily. Individual-level anonymity may also allow group members to express identities and challenge norms in a way impossible when people are more easily identifiable (and, as a result, potentially subject to sanctions).

One topic the SIDE model has been applied to is how communication methods made possible by the internet may facilitate groups attempting social change. Since early work in this area, the internet revolution has been shown to have at best mixed effects upon civic involvement – including politics and campaigning causes. On the one hand, displaying political affiliations and making political comments to a large number of people has never been easier. Early research on engagement with the National Geographic Society (NGS) website suggests that people's online interactions often run alongside face-to-face and telephone communication. However, people who engaged with the NGS only via the internet were not particularly committed to the NGS online community (Wellman, Boase & Chen, 2002). In contrast, Kende et al. (2016) suggest that users' social activity on social media sites is a strong driver of intentions to engage in collective action, and Alberici and Milesi (2013) show that increased inter-action in political forums have a similar effect. To date no research has conclusively shown that these intentions successfully translate into actual action (or, more specifically, the conditions under which they do or do not). For instance, levels of social media activity seemed to spike significantly immediately before major developments in the 2010 'Arab Spring' (in which a number of democratic movements across the Middle East gained momentum). Although it appears this increased online activity may have mobilised protestors, it is also clear that numerous people involved in those social communication activities did not themselves actually engage in 'real', offline political activity (Eltantawy & Wiest, 2011).

In more everyday use, social network sites such as Facebook, Twitter and Instagram provide opportunities for social interaction, but they also require us to present the self in a much more conscious (and accountable) way than do forums. Such online interactions can be incredibly beneficial: for instance, Bliuc et al. (2017) show that online self-help can be a powerful driver of personal change for people battling addiction. More generally, Tosun (2012) also observes that social network sites facilitate the maintenance of long-distance relationships that would otherwise be impossible to sustain a mean-ingful way. However, the quantifiable nature of our interactions (in terms of the number of friends, likes, retweets etc. which we can accrue) can lead to people feeling pressured into being strategic about what information to put forward – generating a desire to pre-sent a self which is acceptable to others (Enli & Thumim, 2012). For some, this can lead to the sense that one is being 'inauthentic' (Davis, 2012). Internet use can also lead to social isolation from one's imme-diate family and smaller face-to-face social circles (Kraut et al., 1998).

Similarly, perceptions of how others use social networking sites can also lead to problematic, even addictive, use (Marino et al., 2016).

This area of social psychology is still very much in its infancy, but is developing rapidly, with many new accounts of theory and evidence being published every year. However, this new field faces the challenge of not only developing new theoretical frameworks but also having to cope with rapidly changing phenomena: social networks and ways of communicating change regularly, and things that seemed like they would be around forever (for instance, social interaction platforms such as MySpace and Secondlife) can rapidly be replaced by new technologies, or evolve into new and unexpected niche communities.

CRITICAL SPOTLIGHT: MAKING A FIRST IMPRESSION ONLINE AND OFFLINE

In Chapter 4 we will see the importance of making a first impression. We will discover that some traits, such as warmth, intelligence and attractiveness, contribute to making 'a good first impression'. We will also see that a good (or bad) first impression can have huge consequences on how people interact with you in the future. We all know the importance of sending an impressive-looking CV, turning up for a job interview (or to meet your new partner's parents!) in a positive mood, and looking at least fairly presentable. However, we may not spend so much time thinking about how we present our online persona. The ways we interact with social networks, the things we blog about and the comments we make online all form part of our *digital identity*. In general, many of these things are also publicly available. Your potential employer (or in-law!) may well receive their first impression of you as a result of what Google throws up when they type in your name ... How happy are you with what will they find?

SOCIAL BEHAVIOUR, FREE WILL AND AUTOMATICITY

In the final part of this chapter we will ask an important question about free will: are we in control of our selves, or do our selves control us? In essence, what extent of free will can we claim to have?

One way of understanding this question is through the role of *traits* (at an individual level) or processes such as *social norms* and *conformity* (at a group level). We can see our behaviour as being influenced by these factors and, at times, they can make us behave in ways we may prefer not to, despite our attempts to resist (see Chapter 6). However, it can also be argued that, for much of the time, we are in control of the way we behave and these processes have little or no effect on us. But what if our sense of control was largely an illusion?

The *implicit cognition* approach (also referred to as *automaticity*) makes an argument that we have little control over our behaviour, positing that up to 95 per cent of our behaviour is unconscious and occurs automatically (see Bargh & Chartrand, 1999). Automatic processes such as these can be understood by models such as the *associative-propositional evaluation* (APE) model (Gawronski & Bodenhausen, 2011). Briefly, APE argues that sometimes we behave as a result of reflective conscious processes (explicit associations). These often rely on proposition relationships (if …, then …). However, APE (in line with most other models of cognition) also argues that our mind is made up of nodes of information which are connected to one another. Sometimes (and many authors would argue mostly) we rely on these connections (*implicit associations*) to make decisions for us without the need for conscious reflection. This system has been referred to as a *perception–behaviour expressway* (Dijksterhuis & Bargh, 2001), as it links seeing and doing directly, and it all occurs very quickly. To give an example of associative processes in action, we can think of a personal weakness of my own – ice cream. It is bad for me. However, I also find myself eating it from time to time. Why? From an APE point of view, I may have a node for 'ice cream', which is also connected to an attitude ('yum!') and a behaviour ('eat!'). When one node is activated by a *stimulus* (i.e. the ice cream node is activated when I see an ice cream truck), it activates the relevant *cognitions* (yum) and also activates the *behavioural enactment* (eat) with little or no conscious intervention. It's worth noting that 'ice cream' may also be attached to other nodes (e.g. 'unhealthy', 'avoid'). If the pathway between 'ice cream' and 'eat' is more well established (in technical terms, has a lower *activation threshold*) than the 'ice cream/avoid' path, I will likely eat some. If the latter path is stronger it may win out and I won't. If I decide to eat, another set of nodes, linked to the behaviour of buying and eating an ice cream come into play. This set of activations is known as a *behavioural enactment sequence*. In this case, I go to the truck, ask for an ice cream, pay and eat. Such sequences occur without thought and, once started, are hard to control. To give another example, when walking or driving along a route you usually use for a particular destination, you don't pay much attention to route planning. Moreover, once you set off to a familiar destination, you must concentrate quite hard to divert yourself to another! In the ice cream example, this aspect of enactment sequences also suggests that once I have started the sequence (i.e. gone to the truck) it will be hard to stop myself making a purchase …

What is the relevance of implicit cognition to social psychology? Importantly, these implicit processes also apply to social behaviours. For instance, nodes which represent social categories ('black individual') may also be linked to stereotypic information ('aggressive') and behaviours ('avoid', 'be defensive'). From this perspective, prejudicial, potentially conflict-increasing behaviours can occur unconsciously, even in people who may wish to avoid them. Authors such as Bargh argue that this implicit association route dominates much of our day-to-day behaviour (including social behaviours) and is actually very difficult to overcome even if we want to (see Bargh & Williams, 2006). This also suggests that, sometimes, it may be better to measure concepts such as intergroup bias using implicit rather than explicit methods. The influence of these ideas is such that we will come across evidence for the automaticity of social behaviours in virtually every chapter of this book. Examples include research showing that priming white participants with faces of African Americans can lead to greater levels of hostility (part of the stereotype for this group) when faced with a mild provocation (Bargh, Chen & Burrows, 1996); that implicit attitudes to minority groups predict the quality of interpersonal interactions (McConnell & Leibold, 2001); and that implicitly measured social identities are a predictor of behaviours such as alcohol consumption (Frings, Melichar & Albery, 2016). The implicit/automatic approach also has some important implications for the idea of self. For instance, if much of our behaviour is automatic, is there such a thing as the self? Or is our self a combination of our automatic and more reflective systems working at different times?

CRITICAL SPOTLIGHT: REPLICATION OF AUTOMATICITY RESEARCH

Work on implicit cognition has not been without its critics, in particular around the issue of replication. For instance, Bargh, Chen and Burrows' (1996) finding that priming people with old-age stereotypes leads them to (automatically) walk slower has been the subject of a number of replication attempts. One of these, by Doyen et al., (2012), suggests that the effect may be driven by the unconscious social influence of the experimenters, rather than priming *per se*. Bargh responded to this by arguing that other studies have replicated this effect and also that the general principles of priming are well established by a variety of research teams. However, as we have seen in our discussion of the replication crisis (see Chapter 1), these debates are ongoing.

CHAPTER SUMMARY

In this chapter we have focused on how social psychology understands the idea of 'self' and an important associated concept – self-esteem. In both these domains we have seen that the field broadly divides into approaches which understand these concepts at an individual level ('self as I') and those which understand them at a group level ('self as a member of a social category'). What both these levels of analysis have in common is that they recognise that our self is usually defined in comparison with others (either directly or via social norms and standards). We've also seen that our understanding of the self may have to change in the near future – the presentation of multiple 'selves' online and offline, and the idea that much of our behaviour may be automatic, both challenge and complement our existing understanding of these areas.

KEY CHAPTER POINTS

- The self can be understood as an individual- and group-level psychological construct.

- Most individual-level accounts focus on comparisons between the self and others, or self and standards.
- Group-level accounts focus on the importance of social identities (aspects of the self which are tied up in group memberships) or evolutionary processes.
- Our self-esteem can also be driven by individual and group processes.
- Our self may not have as much free will as we might think!

SUGGESTED FURTHER READING

1. Abrams, D., Frings, D., & Randsley de Moura, G. (2005). Group identity and self-definition. In S. A. Wheelan. *Handbook of group research and practice* (pp. 329–350). Thousand Oaks, CA: Sage Publications.
2. Amichai-Hamburger, Y. (2017). *Internet psychology: The basics.* New York: Routledge.
3. Brown, R., & Capozza, D. (eds) (2016). *Social identities: Motivational, emotional, cultural influences.* New York: Psychology Press.
4. Bargh, J. A., & Chartrand, T. L. (1999). The unbearable automaticity of being. *American Psychologist, 54,* 462–479.

3

THE WAYS WE THINK

HOW RATIONAL ARE WE? THE ROLE OF SOCIAL-COGNITIVE BIAS

As we have seen, the idea of a 'self' and the concepts which relate to it are fundamental components of social psychology. However, to understand social interactions fully we also need to understand the core concepts around how we think – including models of cognition, biases and motivational processes. We also need to consider the effects of culture and language effects on our thinking processes, and the relationship between mind and body. We start this journey by challenging an idea which we might hold quite dear: the concept that we are 'good' at thinking in the first place!

Some people think of themselves as rational, thoughtful and able to make good judgements in most situations. Others may see themselves as more impulsive, and unwilling or unable to think things through. However, in reality, all of us are affected by so-called 'cognitive biases' to a greater or lesser extent. A cognitive bias is an error in thinking which happens in a reasonably common and predictable way. Much of the initial work on cognitive biases was conducted by Amos Tversky and Daniel Kahneman (e.g. Tversky & Kahneman,

1983). These psychologists identified a number of biases which affect our everyday thinking and, subsequently, our behaviour. One such bias is the *conjunction fallacy*. Consider the following, and then answer the question:

> Linda is 31 years old, single, outspoken, and very bright. She majored in philosophy. As a student, she was deeply concerned with issues of discrimination and social justice, and also participated in anti-nuclear demonstrations.
> Is it more probable that (i) Linda is a bank teller or (ii) Linda is a bank teller and is active in the feminist movement?

Tversky and Kahneman found that most people who read this scenario thought that it was more probable that Linda was both a bank teller and an active feminist. It appears that rather working out the actual probabilities (logically, it's always more likely someone is going to be a bank teller than that they are both a bank teller and *also* fit some other category) we rely on a *heuristic* (a cognitive shortcut which we use to make thinking easier). In this case the heuristic is around *representativeness* – Linda seems to *represent* option two more than she does option one. These cognitive biases are thought to act automatically and also to be very hard to prevent. Interestingly, although many biases involve judgements with little social content (for instance, the *planning fallacy*, which suggests we consistently underestimate task completion times, or *framing effects*, where we are more attracted to identical arguments couched in terms of avoiding loss than we are to those couched in terms of achieving a gain), many of those identified are tied up with social cognition. For instance, *optimistic bias* gives us a tendency to think we will be more likely to receive better outcomes and less likely to incur negative ones than are other people (Weinstein & Klein, 1996). The *false consensus effect* represents a tendency to assume other people agree with our position. The *authority bias* is a tendency to assume that those in authority (including sportspeople and scientists endorsing products on television) are accurate and trustworthy. Finally, the *fundamental attribution bias* (which we explore in Chapter 4) suggests that we consistently underestimate the effect of situational factors on other people's actions (and overestimate such effects on our own behaviour). The use of *stereotypes* (see Chapter 5) can also be seen as a bias. In social settings this can manifest as a bias towards seeing traits in others that we expect to be there, even if they are not in reality. It can also lead to *'belief in a just world'* – a way of understanding the world which suggests that people deserve the situation they find themselves in: for instance, 'poor people are poor because the lazy'. Social-cognitive biases can also affect interpersonal interactions. For instance, the *shared information bias* reflects a tendency for members of the group to focus more on information they have in common than on information that only some group members possess (even if the former is arguably of more use in the discussion).

This list of cognitive biases only scratches the surface of the array of systematic errors that affect the ways we think. Some psychologists argue that these heuristics are fundamentally problematic. Indeed, it's difficult to see a context in which a tendency to place the blame on people for their own situations (ignoring the social context they are in) would be socially just. However, it should also be recognised that heuristics are important for everyday functioning. As we don't have the time or capacity (or motivation) to examine every situation in intricate detail, heuristics provide a reasonable 'best guess' which, in many situations, suffices. You may also wonder how we get through the day making so many cognitive slip-ups! Again, the extent to which cognitive biases are automatic or preventable is the subject of much debate in psychology. As we will see in the next section, some models of cognition argue that in different situations the impact of any given bias may be greater or lesser. They also argue that we can, to some extent, reduce their impact by being motivated (i.e. to be accurate). However, perspectives around automaticity also argue that, even with the best will in the world, we are unlikely to be totally free from these biases. This has important implications when considering the extent to which interpersonal and intergroup interactions may be shaped by the biases we hold. To understand the circumstances under which we are most likely to be affected by biases, it is worth looking at so-called meta-theories of cognition which offer a general perspective on how much control we have over thought processes. How then do we conceptualise our *irrational self*?

UNDERSTANDING THE IRRATIONAL
SELF: MODELS OF THINKING

Prior to the 1980s, a commonly held assumption was that people were fundamentally *rational actors*. For instance, Heider (1958) argued that individuals are essentially *naive scientists* – attempting to understand their world (in particular, their social world) through the generation and systematic testing of hypothesis ('naive theories') against reality. Heider and others assumed that we did this in a relatively unbiased and rational way. These ideas were largely based around how we understand the causes of others' and our own behaviours (which we discuss fully when we look at attribution theory; see Chapter 4). Subsequent studies of people's attribution of causes of behaviour revealed that, perhaps unsurprisingly in hindsight, these processes are as prone to bias as any other. This, combined with the myriad other examples of biased cognition outlined by Kahneman and Tversky, challenged the idea of rational actors. In response, Susan Fiske and Shelley Taylor (Fiske & Taylor, 1982) introduced the idea of the *cognitive miser*. In contrast to the naive scientist who attempts to accurately deduce the state of the world, the cognitive miser tries to find the most simple and efficient way to understand the situation. They do this by relying on a number of heuristics and cognitive shortcuts, in an attempt to avoid expending cognitive energy unnecessarily. Fiske and Taylor also argued that such a strategy was ultimately rational given the enormous quantity and diversity of stimuli we need to process every second. Importantly, they also argued that this tendency is present not only in routine and unimportant situations, but also in contexts where the stakes are high and we are more motivated (at a conscious level) to be accurate. This assumption itself proved problematic, and resulted in later work in this area arguing that we are in fact *motivated tacticians*.

MOTIVATED TACTICIANS

In contrast to the ideas of the naive scientist (we are *always* rational) and the cognitive miser (we *always* rely on cognitive shortcuts), the concept of a motivated tactician argues that we fall between the two. When we are both willing (i.e. motivated, usually in pursuit of the goal) and able (the cognitive task is within our ability and other task demands are not too high) we expend more effort on attempting to be more accurate in cognition. As such, we should be less prone to systematic biases. If we are unwilling or unable to exert this cognitive effort our cognitive miser comes into play – we expend the least effort by relying on heuristics and shortcuts. As well as making sense of the fact that we are sometimes analytic and sometimes not, this approach is also important because it brings the concept of *motivation* into the picture. Whether we choose to expend energy or not is driven by how desirable (or undesirable) a goal or outcome is. The goals which dictate the amount of energy we expend can also depend on what we want to achieve. If we are looking to confirm our beliefs about a particular issue, we are unlikely to expend much energy. In contrast, if we wish to uncover some 'truth' or to be accurate, we expend more. This concept has important implications for social psychology. For instance, *majority group members* are typically interested in confirming their beliefs about the status quo, so are unlikely expend much energy thinking about issues which may challenge those beliefs. Similarly, if we find interactions with people from another group potentially stressful, this may impact our ability to move beyond the stereotypes we hold and prevent us from having an authentic interaction with the person in front of us.

Limitations of the motivated tactician approach

One implication of the motivated tactician paradigm is that, if we are willing and able, we can avoid cognitive biases. However, more recent work around the concept of *automaticity* (the idea that much of our behaviour is uncontrollable and/or unconscious; see above) suggests this may not be the case. For instance, even people who want to have unbiased views towards minority groups in their society have been shown to implicitly hold negative attitudes. Perhaps more importantly, these attitudes have been shown to affect subsequent behaviours (i.e. interpersonal interactions; see Greenwald et al., 2009). Likewise, the challenges a situation puts upon us may affect us in ways we are unable to control (e.g. Blascovich et al., 2001). Small behavioural 'nudges' can also impact our behaviour, even when we are making decisions of high personal value (Sunstein & Thaler, 2008). So, in summary, while it is likely the level of cognitive miserliness which we display will vary from situation to situation, it is unlikely we will ever be truly 'rational actors'.

COGNITIVE DISSONANCE

One further reason the idea of being a motivated tactician is important is because it highlights the important influence of *motivation* on social-cognitive processes. This idea itself draws upon a number of pre-existing core concepts. Of particular importance is the idea of *cognitive dissonance*, developed by Leon Festinger. Cognitive dissonance is best illustrated with an example:

Find a pen and pencil, and rate on a scale of 1 (*strongly disagree*) to 10 (*strongly agree*) each of the following question:

(1) It is important that we feed the world's hungry children.
(2) it is important we have adequately supplied blood banks to support health services.
(3) Avoiding sugary and fatty food is good for me.

The chances are your total score is pretty high – these are things people mostly agree are important. Now answer the following three yes/no questions:

(1) I've given a meaningful sum of money to a children's charity this month.
(2) I give blood regularly.
(3) I have not eaten any sugary or fatty foods this week.

If you only got one or two yeses (and especially if you have none!) then you probably feeling a slight sense of unease about yourself right now. This is because one belief that you hold about an aspect of yourself (I believe that giving blood is important) is *dissonant* with another (I have not given blood). When we experience such dissonance we are motivated to reduce or eliminate it, and there are a number of ways we can do this. We can rationalise away the discrepancy (i.e. I'd love to give blood, but I cannot because ...). However, in many situations this simply is impossible. In these cases, we need change either our behaviour (i.e. we actually give blood) or our attitude (we come around to the idea that giving blood is unimportant). In this way, our behaviour and attitudes are driven by a motivation to reduce cognitive dissonance.

Cognitive dissonance has been demonstrated in many empirical studies. For instance, using an *induced compliance paradigm*, Festinger and Carlsmith (1959) asked participants to do a set of boring tasks (such as turning a peg through a small number of fixed intervals) for an hour. The tasks were designed to generate negative feelings about the activity. Once the task was over, the participants were asked to speak to a *confederate*. Participants believed this confederate was another participant, but they were actually an actor following the experimenters' instructions. Participants were given the goal of persuading the confederate that the tasks were, in fact, interesting. One group of participants were paid what was (at the time) a significant amount of money ($20), while participants in another group were given a nominal sum ($1). Finally, a control group did not speak to anyone. Once participants had completed this phase of the study they were finally asked to rate how positive or negative they actually felt about the tasks. The participants paid a nominal sum rated the task more positively than those given large sums of money or those who did not speak to the confederate. The experimenters argue that this demonstrates cognitive dissonance: the behaviour 'I told someone the task was good' is dissonant with the attitude 'I don't think that was good'. To reduce dissonance, the nominal participants *had to* change their attitude towards the task. No dissonance was generated in the control condition. In the $20 condition participants could simply justify their behaviour – 'I was given $20 to tell someone the task was good' – and therefore participants in this condition did not feel that they needed to change their attitudes. Similar results have been shown in other studies. For instance, Aronson and Carlsmith (1963) studied groups of children, assigned to one of two experimental conditions. All the children were left in a room with several toys, including one which was highly desirable. In one condition they were told that if they played with that toy they then would be severely punished. In the other they were told that a mild punishment would result. Remarkably, all the children avoided playing with the toy. In a later stage of the study, when children were told they could play with any toy they wanted, those in the mild punishment condition were less likely to want to play with the forbidden toy. The explanation here is that the threat of a mild punishment by itself was insufficient for the children to justify their self-regulated behaviour – so they instead devalued the object.

As you can imagine, cognitive dissonance has been widely used in applied settings including marketing, prejudice reduction and health behaviours. A common marketing tool is to first encourage people to generate a cognition ('I need a clean bathroom'). A behavioural opportunity is then presented in relation to which *not following through on* would generate dissonance with the cognition ('Buy SuperCleaner!'). Similarly, making people aware of their own *hypocrisy* (a form of dissonance) has been shown to affect diverse behaviours – for example, reducing intergroup prejudice and increasing condom use (Stone et al., 1994; Son Hing, Li & Zanna, 2002). From a group psychology perspective, cognitive dissonance can also change the perceived value of being in a group. For instance, Aronson and Mills (1959) made joining a discussion group either easy or difficult by having participants read sexually obscene or non-obscene words from a list as part of a group initiation. They then asked participants to listen to other members of their (newly joined) group having a very boring discussion about animal mating behaviours. Those in the 'difficult initiation' condition rated the discussion as being more interesting than those in the 'easier initiation' condition. This finding (and similar replications) may explain why some groups engage in the often questionable practice of 'hazing' of new group members – both to test their commitment to joining the group, and to quickly establish loyalty.

Cognitive dissonance is important because it suggests we don't always have a lot of control over the thoughts we have and the decisions we make. We have also already seen that this level of self-regulation seems to vary across situations. One model which attempts to understand how this operates is the *ego-depletion* perspective.

EGO DEPLETION

Another factor which dictates how much we are influenced by social-cognitive biases is the amount of self-control we can bring to a situation. One very influential way of understanding self-control is via the idea of *ego depletion*. Developed by Roy Baumeister and colleagues (e.g. Baumeister et al., 1998), *ego-depletion theory* argues that self-control is very much like a muscle. We can use it effectively for a set amount of time; after that it will become exhausted (we are 'ego depleted'). At this point we have much lower levels of self-control. The 'muscle' of self-control then needs to rest before it can be used again. One implication of this is that if we exert self-control in one domain, we later have less available in another. Baumeister et al. (1998) demonstrated this experimentally by having people resist the temptation to eat chocolate. Individuals asked to resist subsequently persisted for less time when asked to complete a frustrating puzzle task. The general principle of ego depletion – that exerting self-control in one context leads to a lower level of self-control in subsequent one – has been replicated in a number of different contexts, including social ones. For instance, Xu, Bègue and Bushman (2012) asked participants to suppress their emotions while watching a video about slaughtering animals for food. They then induced a sense of guilt by getting the participants to subject other people to loud unpleasant noises when they made mistakes in a subsequent game. Following the game, the participants were given a chance to offer money to another participant or give to charity (both of these are seen as measures of prosocial behaviour). Participants who initially saw the video felt less guilty about the loud noises, and donated less money than control condition participants. The authors argue that this is because the ego depletion experienced during the video made participants less able to experience guilt. This effect seems to be particularly pronounced amongst people who are more focused on themselves (*pro-selfers*) than those who typically think more about others (*prosocials*) (Balliet & Joireman, 2010). Ego depletion has also been linked to less-effective executive cognitive function in social settings. Richeson and Shelton (2003) showed that when white minority participants interacted with a black confederate they subsequently did poorly on a Stroop task (a measure of cognitive control). This suggests that unfamiliar intergroup interactions may result in ego depletion. This is important if one considers that, when in such a state, people are likely to show less restraint in their behaviour – including the care they take around such interactions. More generally, ego depletion has also been shown to reduce people's ability to resist persuasive communication (such as marketing). For instance, having too many choices can lead to ego depletion and subsequently also to a strong reliance on heuristics such as 'low price = good value' or 'high price = high quality' (Baumeister et al., 2008). The processes underpinning ego depletion are not completely clear; however, many theorists argue it is linked to *blood glucose* in the brain being consumed and requiring replacement. In line with this, some research testing this hypothesis has shown that ego depletion can be reversed by consuming glucose – such as by drinking lemonade (Gailliot et al., 2007).

Criticism of the ego-depletion paradigm

The ego-depletion paradigm has been criticised from a number of angles. The idea that it is a process driven by glucose depletion has been questioned by research which showed that merely tasting (but not actually consuming) sweet drinks can reverse ego depletion – suggesting it is a motivational rather than a metabolic process (Molden et al., 2012). However, advocates of the approach argue that this may be because your depletion is not like an on/off switch (where we are either depleted or not). Rather, we may be in situations where we become partially depleted and, as a result, reduce our own self-control attempts to avoid total depletion – holding some in reserve for high-motivation situations (Baumeister & Vohs, 2007). Another issue is around how reliably observed the effect is across different laboratory groups (part of the *replicability* issue facing much of social psychology). Some *meta-analyses* (systematic reviews of all literature on a given topic) suggests the effect is fairly robust across different studies, while others using a different methodology suggest it is not (Carter & McCullough, 2014; Hagger et al., 2010). Cross-laboratory efforts to replicate the effect systematically have also not been successful (Hagger et al., 2016). This latter effort has, perhaps inevitably, been itself criticised due to the methodological design. Although there are still questions as to how robust the findings are and under what circumstances ego depletion appears, it seems fair to say that the concept (in some form or other) is an important psychological mechanism, and one that has direct relevance to social cognition. It also highlights the potential importance of interactions between our brains and our wider body in guiding social behaviour. This topic is one that is the focus of a particular subfield of social psychology – embodied cognition.

CRITICAL SPOTLIGHT: EGO DEPLETION VERSUS MINDFULNESS MEDIATION

Ego-depletion theories suggest that self-control is like a muscle which can be depleted, but it is also one that can be trained. One way of developing a stronger sense of will (or to allow ourselves to self-regulate for longer before we experience ego depletion) is to practice *mindfulness*. Mindfulness involves attempting to stay in the present and experience it fully, instead of drifting off to the past or planning and worrying about future. Some studies have shown that engaging in mindfulness training (for instance, meditation) can counteract self-control depletion and improve self-regulatory processes (Friese, Messner & Schaffner, 2012; Masicampo & Baumeister, 2007). A good example of this is in the realm of dieting. Ego-depletion research suggest that if we exercise self-control in one domain, we may be less able to control our subsequent eating. So-called 'mindful eating' training programmes which lead people to concentrate on the experience of eating appear to help them cut down the amount they eat (see, for example, Grossman et al., 2004). This could be in part because, over time, they increase *self-control*.

EMBODIED COGNITION

Where in your body do you think that you think? Many people assume that the act of cognition takes place exclusively in the brain. This concept is reinforced by the focus of disciplines such as neuroscience, which show different areas of the brain increasing in metabolic activity when we think about different things, and different regions appearing to be associated with different functions such as language, abstract thought etc. However, the field of *embodied cognition* argues that a full understanding of thought requires consideration how our entire organism affects how we think and behave. Drawing on philosophers such as Kant (see Carpenter, 2008), embodied cognition argues that the body has various sensorimotor inputs, which themselves interact with the wider environment. These combine with the information-processing functions of the brain to generate cognition and behaviour. For instance, a widely cited study by Strack, Martin and Stepper, (1988) – which you can easily replicate in your own home – shows that holding a pen between one's teeth (which activates the same muscle groups as smiling) makes us feel happier (and encourages us to rate comics as funnier) than holding it between our top lip and nose (activating the same muscle groups as frowning). In terms of visual search, participants asked to point at objects were less able to pick a target out of similar objects which differed in their orientation than were those who were asked to physically grasp the objects. This suggests that the physical grasping motion influenced ability to process information (Bekkering & Neggers, 2002). Similarly, Scott, Harris and Rothe (2001) show that participants better remembered the key points of a story when they were asked to physically act the tale out in groups. Social psychology also often involves ideas related to embodied cognition. Ackerman, Nocera and Bargh (2010) undertook a series of experiments showing that incidental *haptic (touch) sensations* influenced a number of social judgements. For instance, reviewing a CV placed on a heavy (versus a light) clipboard made potential job applicants seem more serious in the eyes of appraisers, touching a rough versus a smooth jigsaw made interpersonal interactions seem more difficult, and holding hard objects made people less flexible during negotiations. It also appears that embodied cognition is not just limited to one's own body: taking account of our surroundings (including other people) can happen in a similar way. For example, when participants in a study by Vacharkulksemsuk and Fredrickson (2012) self-disclosed with a research partner, they engaged in more *behavioural synchrony* (unconscious mimicking of one another's behaviour which gradually leads to synchronisation in terms of the type and pace of movements) and also experienced greater levels of positive emotion.

Embodied cognition is still a fairly young subdiscipline in social psychology, and there are a number of potential concerns, limitations and future questions. One concern is around replicability (around work on priming, such as in Ackerman, Nocera and Bargh's 2010 study). Moreover, the difference between cognitive priming and actual embodied cognition is difficult to define. For instance, the 'pen between teeth' study by Strack et al. could represent the role of muscles as *part* of cognition. However, the mind's *awareness* of the sensation those muscles generate could just be considered brain-related activity. There are also numerous questions to be addressed as the field develops. For instance, it is unclear whether everyone experiences embodied cognition in the same way (and if some people rely on it more or less than others). Equally it is not unknown whether the way we engage in embodied cognition changes over our lifespan. A final, and perhaps most significant, challenge to those investigating embodied cognition is identifying the precise mechanism through which bodily input (i.e. haptic stimulus) affects behaviour (see Meier et al., 2012 for a fuller discussion). Nonetheless, this developing field has already shed light on a variety of phenomena, and forces social psychologists think more widely about how the person exists as a whole, within a complicated and dynamic social and physical context. The first of these aspects, the importance of *social context*, is something that has been widely recognised by psychologists studying the role of culture in social cognition and is also the next focus of our discussion.

THE ROLE OF CULTURE

The idea that thought may not be solely played out in the mind highlights the complex interactions between the mind and other systems. As we will see in this section, another system – *culture* – seems to be an incredibly important influence on our thoughts and behaviour. We all have some idea of what 'culture' is, and many of us are lucky enough to travel to different countries where we get to experience new cultures first-hand. However, it has also proved curiously difficult to pin down an agreed definition. Most definitions argue that culture is a collection of beliefs and practices held in common by a social group – usually at a national, ethnic or at least regional level (although of course we can also think of smaller 'subcultures'). Psychologist Hofstede provides a neat definition by suggesting that culture is 'the collective programming of the mind that distinguishes the members of one group or category of people from another' (Hofstede 2001, p. 9).

Working within this definition, one way of understanding differences between cultures is to consider the extent to which a culture is *individualistic* (i.e. the main unit of analysis is the individual, who is considered to have agency on their own and to be responsible for their own actions and outcomes, and is fairly autonomous) versus *collectivist* (in which people are seen as more interdependent, having less independent agency, and as a result being less individually responsible for their own welfare and outcomes). These ideas also influence how we think about the concept of self.

Triandis (1989) looked at the way different cultures understand the self in terms of their private, public and collective selves (see Chapter 2 for a fuller discussion of these ideas). Triandis rated various cultures on the basis of where they feel they sit on each of three dimensions: *individualism–collectivism, tightness–looseness* (how strongly social norms are held and enforced), and *cultural complexity*. Triandis observed that the more individualistic the culture, the more often people thought of themselves in terms of private self and less frequently they did so in terms of a collective self. Use of collective self was linked to increases in cultural collectivism. Amongst people with a more individualistic self, collectivism is particularly increased when the culture as a whole perceives an external threat or feels itself in competition with others. Triandis argues that differences in cultural outlooks may well be due to social influences during childhood and suggests that how we understand the self can influence other social-cognitive processes and behaviours.

A classic demonstration of how culture (in particular, collective versus individualistic cultures) can affect social cognition is in the study of *attributions* (see Chapter 4). Joan Miller (Miller, 1984) observed that when describing stories of pro- or anti-social acts, North American adults (who live in an individualistic society) tended to describe the cause of those acts as being down to the person. In contrast, Indian Hindus (living in a more collectivist culture) were more likely to attribute the behaviour of the characters in the story to the situation therein. Interestingly, when Miller tested participants who were younger (8 years old and also 11 years old) she observed no difference between the groups. The difference in attributional style only began to become apparent amongst groups of participants aged around 15 – and it continued to increase with age. This suggests that the differences in how we understand others' behaviours are both culturally bound and developmental. Importantly, it also suggests that the effects of culture may become stronger as people become adults.

Collectivism also seems to influence how we relate to one another, especially with regard to accepting difference and encouraging conformity. Because collectivist cultures perceive people as inter-dependent, they may also value *conformity* more than individualistic cultures do. For instance, one of the most influential cross-cultural psychologists, John Berry, showed that differences in the way social groups collected food influenced conformity. The Temne people of Sierra Leone (who rely on a single crop which must be harvested in one short period every year, thus necessitating co-operation between large numbers of people) showed much higher levels of conformity than did a sample of Inuit people from Canada (where people gather food individually or in small family groups) (Berry, 1967). More gen-erally, Bond and Smith (1996) showed that levels of conformity were higher amongst participants from non-Western cultures than amongst both US and other Western participants. However, it's worth noting that non-Western participants had much greater within-group vari-ation. As a result, many non-Western participants showed the same level of conformity as, for example, participants in the US sample.

Differences in a desire for consensus can also lead to people being prepared to accept contradiction more or less readily. For instance, Peng and Nisbet (1999) presented Western and Chinese participants with sets of statements which were apparently contradictory. Western participants tended to polarise their attitudes towards one or the other (exaggerating the difference between the two). In contrast, the Chinese participants were more prepared to accept both ideas moderately (reducing the difference between the two). In a similar study, Choi and Nisbett (2000) expanded on this idea by showing that Korean participants were less surprised when somebody behaved contrary to their expectations than were American participants.

The effects of culture on social behaviour are so strong that they can also affect how we perceive our own mental health, and even what we consider to be a mental health issue in the first place. As a result, some mental health problems can be entirely absent in one culture, but prevalent in another. A classic example of this is 'Koro', a mental health issue observed amongst men in Asia (with its first medical reference in 1865 in China). Those experiencing Koro become highly anxious about the fact that their penis is shrinking and worry that it may disappear (see Mattelaer & Jilek, 2007). So-called 'epidemics' of Koro have been observed in various countries, such as Singapore (in 1967) and in Africa (in the 1990s). In contrast, Koro is almost unknown in the Western world. Interestingly, perhaps as geographical boundaries begin to matter less in a more connected world, variations of Koro have more recently been observed more widely (Chowdhury, 1996). Not all disorders are as apparently unique as Koro – *depression*, for instance, appears to be present in most cultures, although the way it manifests itself can be different, and the prevalence rates vary widely (Bromet et al., 2011). Moreover, as will see in the penultimate chapter of this book, on social psychology and applied contexts, the impact of even pervasive mental health issues such as depression can be affected by social interactions (in particular, the social connections we have with one another).

Although researchers are increasingly aware of the importance of culture in understanding a wide variety of the subjects studied in social psychology, we should not make the mistake of assuming every aspect of thinking differs from culture to culture. For instance, evolutionary approaches argue that there are core 'cognitive modules' which evolved early in our development as a species – and are independent of culture (see Cosmides & Tooby, 2005). Similarly, research suggests that there are a number of core emotional expressions (such as happiness, sadness, anger, fear, disgust and surprise) which are recognised across cultures. However, some work also suggests that the physical expression used to convey particular emotion varies between cultures (Ekman and Friesen, 1975). We should also avoid falling into the trap of assuming that someone from a given culture will think or behave in a stereotyped way: within any group there will be important individual differences. Indeed, it is only when the variation *between* two groups is much larger than the variation *within* a group that we can seriously start discussing cross-cultural differences.

Finally, although most of the work above compares cultures, we should not conceptualise cultures as entities separate from one another. The increasing migration of people and information means the world is more closely interconnected than at any time in the past. Given this, social psychology also considers what happens when

THE WAYS WE THINK

people from different cultures meet and interact (*intergroup psychology*) and what happens when people move one culture to another (*acculturation psychology*). These topics are dealt with in the next chapter.

In summary, culture appears to be an important factor influencing the way we think and behave in a variety of ways. As we saw in our brief history of social psychology, even the very choice of questions asked by researchers is influenced by where they come from – differences between US and European research groups have been discussed, but also increasingly relevant are the ways in which research emerging from Asia differs in perspective. More generally, as the above studies suggest, fairly fundamental thought patterns (which we may have assumed to be universal) also vary quite significantly depending on which group of people we study *within* a culture. This is a problem for social psychology, as it may well be that the research findings we generate are actually tied to particular cultural and social milieus. This effect is compounded by the fact that most psychological research is undertaken in universities, amongst samples of reasonably affluent (or at least socially mobile) young adults, and thus it may not even be a whole culture that is being represented. This has led Joseph Henrich and colleagues (Henrich, Heine & Norenzayan, 2010) to go as far as to say that behavioural science faces a fundamental problem because the samples used, in contrast to the majority of humans alive today, can be classed as 'WEIRD' (White, Educated, from Industrialised societies, Rich and living in a Developed nation).

LANGUAGE AND SOCIAL COGNITION

One important issue in the study of culture is the role of language in social cognition. The question of whether features of our language affect the way we think is the subject of much research. The *Sapir-Whorf hypothesis* (also known as the *principle of linguistic relativity*) argues that language determines, or at least influences, the way we think and the decisions we make (see Koerner, 1992). There is a good body of evidence for this assumption – for instance, aboriginal peoples whose languages have a limited vocabulary to describe counting ('one', 'two', 'many') can struggle with numerical tasks. Language also affects the way people think of themselves in relation to others in terms of space (and ability to not get lost!), and the richness of the language for describing colours also seems to affect our ability to differentiate between them (e.g. Berlin & Kay, 1991). These discussions are important, as they also speak to the extent that we can generalise our understanding of any particular set of social-cognitive processes over both culture and time.

CHAPTER SUMMARY

In this chapter we have discovered that we may not be as good at thinking as we may assume. The extent to which our decisions and attitudes can be considered 'accurate' can be significantly affected by a number of biases. The level of impact these have on us is partly predicted by the level of motivation that we experience at a given moment – which in turn could be constrained by other factors (such as the amount of self-control we have recently exerted). We've also seen that our cognition is influenced by factors outside of our brain: the study of embodied cognition, the importance of language and the fact that psychological processes appear to differ from culture to culture are all important things to consider when trying to under-stand 'the ways we think'.

KEY CHAPTER POINTS

- We are not always rational thinkers – instead we are motivated tacticians, affected by cognitive biases.
- We can also experience motivational effects driven by psycho-logical and possibly biological processes.
- Cognition takes place in the whole body, not just the brain.
- Culture and language can have significant effects on how many psychological processes express themselves.
- Much research is conducted on participants who can be classed as 'WEIRD' (White, Educated, from Industrialised societies, Rich and living in a Developed nation).

SUGGESTED FURTHER READING

1. Fiske, S. (2018). *Social cognition: Selected works of Susan Fiske*. Oxon: Routledge.

2. Baumeister, R. F., & Tierney, J. (2012). *Willpower: Why self-control is the secret to success*. London: Penguin.
3. Eccleston, C. (2016). *Embodied: The psychology of physical sensation*. Oxford: Oxford University Press.
4. Henrich, J., Heine, S. J., & Norenzayan, A. (2010). Most people are not WEIRD. *Nature, 466*(7302), 29.

THEME SUMMARY: SELF AND MOTIVATION

In 'Self and motivation' we have explored a number of ideas which are fundamental to understanding social psychology. We have also seen that there are contrasting understandings of many concepts we may have taken for granted. For instance, questions about what makes up the 'self', the degree of rationality we have, and the level of free will we possess are all contested topics. We've explored the fact that thoughts and motivations can be understood in various ways, and also seen how our cognition is shaped by external forces. What all the material in this theme has in common is the effects it has had on the discipline of social psychology. Each development has changed (or is likely to change) the direction the discipline is headed in. Taken together, they also provide a set of assumptions which guide the questions researchers ask, and the measures they use to explore them. Indeed, as you read the following chapters you will see many of the issues and ideas discussed here reappear.

SOCIAL RELATIONSHIPS

THEME OVERVIEW

As we have already seen, people are very social animals. Our sense of self is tied up with the groups we are a part of, and our social contexts appear to deeply influence the way we think and behave. In this theme we take a tour of key concepts which explain how we relate to each other on an individual and group basis. The 'Self and other people' chapter will explore in more depth some of the mechanisms which govern how we relate to others on an 'interpersonal' (i.e. one-to-one) basis. We'll look at how we understand what attracts us to others, how we understand others' behaviour and how we respond to situations where we need to co-operate. The 'Self and groups' chapter will look at how groups function, exploring topics such as the way groups form, the key features of groups and how groups relate to one another. We'll start by looking at a psychological activity we engage in almost constantly: the efforts we make to understand why other people behave in the way they do (and why we do too!).

SOCIAL RELATIONSHIPS

SELF AND OTHER PEOPLE

PERSON PERCEPTION AND IMPRESSION FORMATION

One of the initial ways we engage with other people is by evaluating what we think of them. Consider a time you made a judgement about someone which was absolutely wrong. Also, think about times you've tried to make a good first impression. Do you think you are good at judging people's character? Do you usually make a good first impression?

Being good at making fast, reasonably accurate judgements about people is important for a variety of reasons. Such evaluations are used in a variety of situations, including deciding whom we should trust, date and employ. Accurate impressions allow us to predict others' likely future behaviour. In contrast, poor judgement can land us in all sorts of difficult situations! Social psychologists have studied how we form impressions and make judgements broadly in two ways. Early research began by looking at how we process *impression-related information*, and the *weighting* that we give to different types of data. Later work focuses on how we process limited information very rapidly and, often, automatically when forming first impressions.

Early research in this field suggested that we seem to place more weight on some aspects of an individual than others. So-called *central traits* have a much larger impact on our judgement than more *peripheral traits* do. Solomon Asch's (1946) *configurable model of person perception* was tested by presenting participants with a list of attributes describing a fictional person. All participants were presented with words such as 'energetic', 'assured', 'talkative', 'ironic', 'inquisitive' and 'persuasive'. In addition, half were given the word 'cold' in the middle of the list, while the other half given the word 'warm' (in the same spot in the list). Participants were requested to rate how happy and reliable this fictional person was. Participants in the 'warm' condition rated the fictitious person as more happy and reliable than did those in the 'cold' condition. Swapping over other words (such as 'blunt' and 'polite') led to similar but far smaller change in evaluations. From this, Asch deduced that some (central or 'cardinal') traits have a greater impact on our judgements than do other (peripheral) ones – with warm/cold being a particularly important dimension. Other work, for instance Susan Fiske and colleagues' work on the *stereotype content model*, also highlights the importance of warmth and intelligence as central traits (see Chapter 5). Being *physically attractive* also seems to have a '*halo effect*' in which we assume physically attractive people also have other positive traits. Dion, Berscheid and Walster (1972) asked people to view photos of averagely attractive, less attractive or more attractive individuals. Attractive individuals were rated as, amongst other things, having more socially desirable traits, more likely to have happier lives, less likely to get divorced, and likely to be more professionally and socially successful. Quite a lot to judge from a single photo!

Although research had made it clear that some traits are more important than others, it still remained unclear how these pieces of information are combined. '*Algebraic*' *models of impression formation* suggest that we give people scores on various dimensions (for instance, how intelligent or honest they are; Anderson, 1965). These dimensions can be both positive and negative. We can then combine these pieces of information in different ways. For instance, we can use *summation* by adding positive traits and subtracting scores for the negative traits to end up with a single judgement score. Alternatively, we may take all the scores and simply form an *average* of them.

Interestingly, these two models may produce different outputs. For example, imagine we have some extra information which is mildly positive about an individual whom we generally feel very positive about. This would make us feel more positive if we summated the scores. However, counterintuitively, this new positive information makes their *mean score* go down! The above models also do not really take into account the idea of central or peripheral traits. As a result, the *weighted averaging* model argues that we take each trait and decide how important it is to us, both generally and in a given situation. We then weight important traits more or less strongly when calculating the average. Interestingly, because we generally have a *negativity bias* (a tendency to attend more to negative information) we usually place quite a strong weighting on negative information. Of these three models, the weighted averaging model seems to have received the most support (see e.g. Singh & Simons, 2010). However, none of them really tells us how we assign weightings to the different dimensions, or the effects that the *order* in which we perceive information can have on our judgements. Such computation is also a cognitively demanding process and the extent to which these systems are automatic isn't really considered (see below). This latter point is highly relevant because often the speed with which we make judgements appears to be particularly important when forming *first impressions*.

FIRST IMPRESSIONS

We form first impressions very quickly – making judgements on some traits (extroversion and intelligence, for example) in as little as five seconds. Some experimental research suggests that the longer we spend making judgements (up to a tested five minutes) the more accurate we are, but a good trade-off between speed and accuracy is achieved after 60 seconds (Carney, Colvin & Hall, 2007). We also seem to draw inferences from facial appearances in as little as 100 milliseconds, are highly sensitive to evidence of traits such as being psychopathic and are reasonably good at judging someone's sexual orientation from even fairly minimal sets of cues (Gillen, Bergstrøm & Forth, 2016; Rule, 2017; Willis & Todorov, 2006). Other traits around which we form first impressions rapidly include conscientiousness, honesty and aggression (e.g. Borkenau & Liebler, 1992). These impressions are not always unbiased, however – the timescale in which they take place suggests their formation is largely an automatic process and, as such, is vulnerable to many of the systematic errors attached to social cognition. For instance, we seem to be highly affected by information presented to us first, moderately so by information presented most recently and least affected by information in between (i.e. we experience *primacy* and *recency* effects; Asch 1946). We also make use of judgements we hold about categories of people (i.e. stereotypes) to make inferences about people which are not warranted by the information we have (see Chapter 5). Finally, we can be affected by irrelevant primes – holding a warm versus a cold beverage prior to making a judgement has been linked to evaluating as people as being more formal/cold, for example (Williams & Bargh, 2008).

How much do first impressions stick? Interestingly, while early accounts argued that first impressions are very difficult to reverse (e.g. Tetlock, 1983), some more recent work (e.g. Mann & Ferguson, 2017) argues that even automatically formed first impressions can be altered shortly after they have been formed. Of course, once we have made a good impression, people still get to know us better and their evaluation can always change over time. The study of ongoing relationships – in particular, interpersonal attraction and relationships – is what our discussion now turns to.

INTERPERSONAL ATTRACTION AND RELATIONSHIPS

Relationships obviously aren't all about first impressions. Social psychologists have investigated why we feel more attracted to some people than others over the long term, and how intimate and nonintimate interpersonal relationships develop. We'll examine this by looking at *physical predictors of interpersonal attraction* (and *evolutionary explanations* for why they may exist), psychological effects which may explain interpersonal attraction, theories which predict whether relationships will blossom and, finally, social psychologists' views of a particularly powerful emotion – '*love*'.

ATTRACTION

We have already seen that we make judgements about people on the basis of their looks very quickly. But what makes an individual attractive? It seems that faces which are symmetrical are perceived as more attractive than asymmetrical ones. Indeed, studies using computer-generated faces which vary in levels of symmetry and averageness show high correlations between these factors and perceived attractiveness (e.g. Grammer & Thornhill, 1994). This is known as the *averageness effect* (Winkielman et al., 2006). While different cultures may favour variations in things like physical adornments (e.g. beards), a desire for average faces seems culturally universal amongst humans. Interestingly, there are also seemingly universal preferences for body types. Men seem to prefer women whose waist-to-hip ratio is 30/70 (Singh & Young, 1995; Singh et al., 2010). This general hourglass shape is also preferred by women judging men (Crossley, Cornelissen & Tovée, 2012).

EVOLUTIONARY EXPLANATIONS

Why are we attracted to people in this way? The *evolutionary approach* to interpersonal attraction understands facial symmetry in terms of genetic fitness – people who have 'average' faces are likely to have more genetically diverse heritage (which in turn may make them more likely to be able to combat disease and generally be biologically resilient). More broadly, the factors that we pick up on around attractiveness may also signal that a person is healthy and fertile. From an evolutionary point of view, such *reproductive capacity* should be more important for men than for women. Women, in contrast, may well be more interested in how well a male can provide for their offspring (given that females can only have a small number of children over their lifespan). Indeed, Buss (1989), using a sample of over 10,000 participants, presents evidence supporting an argument that women value cues associated with resources, while men focus on cues around fertility. There is other diverse support for this evolutionary explanation. For instance, women seem to find men with characteristics signalling genetic fitness more sexually attractive when they are at the most fertile point in their ovulation cycle. Interestingly, this effect only applies to so-called 'short-term mating prospects' and not to more long-term ones (Gildersleeve, Haselton & Fales, 2014). Men also seem to be more attracted to women who are at their most fertile. Miller, Tybur and Jordan (2007), in a study including the results of over 5000 lap dances, show that men give strippers who are ovulating larger tips (on average) than when the dancers were not. However, there is also some evidence which challenges this account. For instance, some recent work suggests that the average preference does not seem to be present in non-human primates (Tomeo, Ungerleider & Liu, 2017).

PSYCHOLOGICAL FACTORS

Clearly, we are not all gorgeously average in our looks, and we don't all radiate signals of perfect genetic fitness. Neither, it is likely, will our partners reach such lofty heights. So, what factors determine how we decide who we want to spend time with? In particular, how does the psychology of interpersonal attraction play out in the context of romantic relationships?

You may have noticed that quite often members of couples seem to be roughly as attractive as one another. You may also have experienced the painful feeling that that somebody is 'out of your league'. The *matching phenomenon* shows that people typically seek out close relationships with people who have more or less the same level of physical attractiveness as themselves. This has been observed both in correlations between existing couples and also in simulated dating encounters (e.g. Berscheid et al., 1971; Murstein, 1972). It has also been reported amongst same-sex close friends (Cash & Derlega, 1978). So, how can it be that sometimes someone who is seemingly 'stunning' ends up going out with someone who appears quite plain? One explanation is that we also display *compensatory factors* – a highly attractive individual may value some particular aspect of a partner strongly, and this can make up for a relative lack of physical attractiveness. Gender differences may play a specific role here; research suggests that when publicly displaying ourselves (for instance, on dating websites) we sell our strong points and also make clear what we are looking for. In line with an evolutionary perspective on interpersonal relationships, men appear to advertise their resources, and ask for looks ('Rich Banker Seeks Stunning Blonde'), while women advertise looks and seek status ('Gorgeous Gal Seeks Professional Male') (see Buss & Schmitt, 1993).

CRITICAL SPOTLIGHT: EVOLUTION OR GENDER ROLES?

Are differences we can observe between genders due to evolution, or the result of socially defined roles with little biological basis? The traditional evolutionary perspective on love and mating makes an argument that men and women display different attributes because they have different reproductive capacities and requirements. For women, producing children is costly (they have to carry the pregnancy for nine months and physically give birth). Women can also only carry one pregnancy a time. This means they can only have a certain number of children over their lifespan. In contrast, men can, from a physical point of view, have as many children as they can find mates for. From this perspective, women seek resources as they wish to maximise investment in their (fewer) offspring. In contrast, men attempt to secure as many mates as they can, with the highest genetic fitness possible. Thus, the argument goes, we display what the other gender seeks. Other perspectives have challenged these assumptions – in particular, *feminist psychology*. This approach argues that differences in such displays are not due to innate gender differences but in fact reflect the narrative of patriarchal (male-dominated and -favouring) society. Endorsing biological explanations for mating behaviour (which have also been extended to theories that rape is an evolutionary adaptive strategy; see Thornhill & Palmer, 2000) can, from this perspective, be seen as a method of maintaining these discriminatory worldviews. These (both well-developed) stances have traditionally been very opposed to one another's basic assumptions about why society is the way it is, and it is only relevantly recently that attempts to find common ground have been made (see Smith & Konik, 2011).

Alongside looks, other psychological factors come into play when evaluating others. Differences in attractiveness can also be diluted by the effects of *mere familiarity* – we are most likely to be friends with people we are close to physically (have close proximity to). For instance, Festinger, Schachter and Back, (1950) showed that, amongst university housing for married couples, people were friends with those in their block, but less likely to name a friend in other (very close) buildings. This can be, in part, attributed to there being more opportunities for contact (see Chapter 5), and anticipation that we will see a certain person again (which generates liking; Darley & Berscheid, 1967). It is also because we generally like things more if they are familiar to us (see Zajonc, 1968). Indeed, once we know someone well, we are more likely to end up in a close/romantic relationship with them (this is known as the *propinquity effect*). We also like people who are similar to us in terms of attitudes and who appear to reciprocate our own liking – as long as we don't feel that they like everyone indiscriminately (Dittes & Kelley, 1956; Eastwick et al., 2007; Newcomb, 1956).

Some factors which influence how much we like someone have nothing to do with the person themselves! In a famous study, male passers-by were contacted and asked to approach an attractive female experimenter by crossing either a very safe and stable or a very shaky, unstable and fear-inducing bridge (Dutton & Aron, 1974). The experimenter asked participants to complete questionnaires which included writing stories about 'Thematic Apperception Test' images (which allow participants to generate stories about ambiguous social situations). Participants who crossed the unstable bridge were more likely to include sexual content in their stories and were also more likely to try to initiate what the researchers describe as 'post-experimental contact' with the experimenter. In this experiment, and two others, Dutton and Aaron argue that participants experience a sense of physiological and emotional arousal as a result of crossing the bridge. Rather than recognising this arousal as fear, participants misattributed it as being arousal generated by the experimenter, resulting in increased attraction!

WHAT KEEPS RELATIONSHIPS WORKING?

Once a close or romantic relationship is established it can be deepened and maintained in a number of ways. One important factor is the level of *self-disclosure* between individuals. Appropriate levels of self-disclosure can generate both trust and intimacy in relationships (Baumeister & Bratslavsky, 1999). We also seem to stay in relationships if we feel that we are getting out as much as we are putting in. This consideration is exemplified in *social exchange theory* (e.g. Kelley & Thibaut, 1978). This approach argues that we evaluate the quality of our relationship in terms of the rewards we get from it, the costs associated and whether or not it is a relationship (i) we think we deserve and (ii) that could or could not be bettered. Social exchange theory argues that a relationship is a constant exchange of costs and rewards in various domains, the net of which we use to calculate whether or not it is satisfying. We also base these calculations on our comparison with previous relationships we have had, and relationships that we feel could potentially exist elsewhere. Although this approach may seem somewhat mercenary, it has received a considerable amount of empirical support – with findings usually showing that a favourable analysis predicts relationship satisfaction and resilience (see Rusbult & Van Lange, 2003). The degree of equity in a relationship also seems to be important. *Equity theory* argues that, alongside absolute costs and values, we are looking for a relationship where what we get out is related to what we put in. Ideally, this *cost/reward ratio* should be similar for both individuals. Generally, when this is the case people seem more content (Adams, 1965). Interestingly, some work on distributive justice in general suggests that women seek tend to seek *equality* (where both people get the same out, no matter what they put in) whereas men seek *equity* (in which expected outcomes should be related to inputs) (Major & Adams, 1983).

WHAT'S 'LOVE' GOT TO DO WITH IT?

One particular emotion which is almost inseparable from romantic relationships (and the subject of innumerable songs, poems and speeches) is *love*. Psychologist Elaine Hatfield (see Hatfield & Rapson, 1993) argues that love can broadly be categorised as *passionate love* (involving intense emotions and 'symptoms' such as physical arousal) and *compassionate love* (which is deep but less physically arousing). Compassionate love is thought to arise from passionate love and is generally considered to be more stable. Other authors argue that love can be split into *eros* (passionate, consuming and sexual), *mania* (featuring jealousy and insecurity, and sex as reassurance), *ludus* (in which love is a game, sex is for fun and commitment is low), *agape* (unconditional love), *pragma* (in which partners think logically about one another) and *stogre* (in which companionate love is achieved without the need for passion) (see Hendrick, Hendrick & Dicke, 1998). The course of love seems to vary by culture. In 2012, for instance, divorce rates in Belgium were 2.81 divorces per 1000 people, more than double the rate observed in Singapore (at 1.3/1000). These differences may be due to whether people are focused on collective goals or individual ones (see Chapter 3). One particular cultural practice that differs is how one chooses a spouse. In many cultures, people fall in love then choose to marry their partner as a result (love marriages). In others, marriages can be arranged. Some evidence shows that ratings of love are higher in love (relative to arranged) marriages in the early years, but drop from between two and five years onwards. In contrast, ratings of love in arranged marriages are initially lower, but after between two and five years they equal or exceed levels of love seen in love marriages (Gupta & Singh, 1982). This may be in part because conceptualisations of 'love' differ amongst these different groups – in particular over the idea that love 'grows' slowly rather than 'appears' at first sight.

ATTRIBUTION THEORY AND BIASES

We have seen how we decide what we think about other people – but how do we evaluate how they behave? We all try to understand the reasons that people behave in the way that they do. We usually think we're pretty good at this. We also think that we have a reasonably good idea of why we ourselves behave in the way we do. For instance, you may know that your work colleague is always late because they simply don't care about the inconvenience this causes others. You also know that the reason you flunked a particular test was that you had a terrible cold which made you unwell and unable to concentrate. These sorts of judgements are known as *attributions*, and their study is an investigation of *attributional theory*.

MODELS OF ATTRIBUTION

This body of work was initiated by Fritz Heider and Marianne Simmell (Heider & Simmell, 1944), who showed participants a short animation in which geometric shapes (two differently sized triangles and a circle) moved around the screen, coming in and out of a rectangular box. You can easily watch this this film yourself by searching on the internet for 'Heider Simmell animation'. When asked to describe the contents of the film, the participants usually explained how a large triangle chased the small triangle and the circle, after the large triangle had had its rest disturbed. They also assign the shapes emotional states such as joy, fear or anger. Clearly, the actual shapes themselves didn't experience emotion, or have a motivation. However, participants were quick to assign these even when given such minimal stimuli to work with. From these observations, Heider developed his *naive scientist theory* (see Chapter 3). In particular, Heider argued that we make an attempt to attribute behaviour to causes which are either *internal* (i.e. due to the person) or *external* (i.e. due to the situation or circumstance). He also argued that we attempt to understand behaviours in this way in an effort to both predict what is likely to happen in the future, and maximise the chance that we can exert some control over the situation. As we typically look for a stable set of explanations, we are more likely to prefer internal (person-based) attributions to external (situational) ones. For instance, understanding that someone's tardy behaviour is due to some feature of theirs makes the future more predictable (they will be late next time). It also offers more interventions, which increases control (invite them to arrive early, or just don't invite them!), than the alternative explanation. If we accept that someone is late because something out of their control occurred, it's hard to know how to respond next time. Jones and Davis (1965) built on these ideas in their *correspondent inference theory*. This model argues that people seek to make an internal attribution by drawing on three sources of information: (i) the extent to which people can *choose* how to behave, (ii) the extent to which the behaviour is *expected* in the social context and (iii) the extent to which people appeared to *intend* the consequences of the behaviour. Under this model, freely chosen, unexpected and apparently intended behaviour lead to a dispositional (internal) attribution.

Kelley's *covariation model* takes these ideas a bit further (Kelley, 1967). The covariation model argues that we use three sources of information in a rational way to understand causation in social situations. These sources comprise *consensus* (whether other people behave the same way in similar situations or not), *distinctiveness* (whether the individual behaves in this way in many situations or just in this specific one) and *consistency* (whether an individual behaves in this way all the time). To give an example, consider a situation in which 'Jo turns up late for an exam on Friday'. If most people turn up late for that exam, consensus is high and we may assume the lateness is to do with the situation. Distinctiveness may be high if Jo is late for all events, or low if it is only for this exam. High distinctiveness would lead to an internal attribution. Finally, if Jo is late for every exam, consistency is high. In contrast, if Jo is late only for this exam, consistency is low. We use this information in combination to make a causal attribution. For instance, if consensus and distinctiveness are low and consistency is high (Jo is the only one late, Jo is late to everything and Jo has been late to exams before) we make an internal attribution – it is something about Jo. If all dimensions are high (everybody was late for the exam, Jo is not late to everything and Jo is always late for exams) it is something about the general category of event (e.g. maybe the exam venue was tough to find). Finally, if consensus is high and both distinctiveness and consistency are low (everybody was late, Jo is not late to other events and Jo has not been late for an exam before) we think it's something about the specific situation (perhaps public transport broke down that day). Early tests of the covariation model suggested people tend to see causes of behaviour as being internal more often than they should – a bias subsequently described as the *fundamental attribution error* (see below). This may have been observed simply because early research did not present enough information. For instance, if we don't know Jo well, or we don't know about others' past behaviour, we will struggle to make an attribution. Indeed, later research suggests that, when given sufficient information, people are actually pretty good at undertaking covariation analysis, and often come out with the sort of attributions that the model predicts (e.g. Cheng & Novick, 1990; Sutton & McClure, 2001). However, it is still not explained why we seem to have a general preference for internal over external attributions. One explanation is that, outside of a lab context with perfectly packaged information, we have a tendency to automatically jump to internal attributions rather than seek out more data.

This suggests that, in contrast to naive scientist approaches, we are at best *motivated tacticians* when it comes to attributions (see Chapter 3). This idea was explored in Gilbert's 'two-step model' of attribution (Gilbert, 1989). This approach argues that when presented with a behaviour, we make a spontaneous attribution that the cause is internal. If we are cognitively overloaded or not really motivated, that is about as much as we think about it. However, if we are not cognitive busy (or highly motivated to be accurate, with sufficient capacity) we may think about the situation a bit more – and this deliberate processing may result in our making a more situational attribution. One benefit of this approach is that it recognises that our will and ability to make accurate attributions are limited. As such, we'd expect attribution to be affected by a number of systematic errors.

ATTRIBUTIONAL ERRORS

The most important systematic error we make in attribution is the *fundamental attribution error*. This error was well demonstrated in a study by Jones and Harris (1967). Participants in this study were presented with essays which were either pro or anti Fidel Castro (the communist leader of Cuba at the time, and as such a controversial figure). Participants were asked a simple question: how much did the essays actually reflect the writer's views? However, experimenters manipulated an aspect of the situation: half of the participants were told that the author could convey whatever opinions they wanted in the essay. The other half were told that the author had been told which position to take and had no freedom to disagree. In the free-choice condition participants (perhaps unsurprisingly) felt that the pro-Castro essays were written by a pro-Castro author and the anti-Castro essays by an anti-Castro author. However, in the no-choice condition the same pattern was present – participants thought that those who'd written pro-Castro essays were more in favour of Castro than those who had written anti-Castro essays (albeit to a lesser extent than in the other condition). This effect occurred despite the fact these participants knew the author had no choice! The classic explanation of this study is that participants made a fundamental attribution error. However, critics of this interpretation suggest that this pattern of results may be due to other reasons. For instance, participants may have expected writers to refuse to author essays that were against their opinions – particularly on controversial subjects. However, many other studies have shown evidence for the fundamental attribution error, particularly when people are pressed for time or cognitive capacity (see Gilbert & Malone, 1995). Other work in this area has also extended the fundamental attribution error to groups. The *ultimate attribution error* reflects a tendency to understand events – particularly negative ones – to have been caused by groups of people rather than situations. Becker, Wagner and Christ (2011) showed that many participants of their (German) sample blamed the 2008 economic crash either on bankers and financiers, or on immigrants. Those expressing the former view also showed a positive relationship between their level of worry about the crash and anti-Semitic attitudes (drawing stereotypes to do with Jewish populations and financial activity). In contrast, highly worried participants who attributed the crash to immigrants were more prejudiced towards that group. However, perhaps encouragingly, a second study which manipulated information in a way which made the *situational* causes of the event more salient reduced the level of bias against these groups.

A related effect is the *actor-observer bias*, identified by Jones and Nisbett (1971). This bias reflects the tendency to see our own behaviour as being more generally due to the situation (external attribution) while others' behaviour is seen as generally due to the person themselves (internal attribution). This may be an effect of *perception*: as an observer we will see the person standing saliently out against the background and behaving; the actor is the centre of attention and as a result we make internal attributions. In contrast, when thinking about our own behaviour the situation is the focus of attention and we cannot actually see the actor at all – leading to an external attribution. A study by Storms (1973) gives credence to this explanation by showing that when people watched a videotape of their own behaviour (i.e. could see themselves as an actor in a situation) there were less likely to make internal attributions about their own behaviour. Although the actor-observer effect is commonly cited in the literature there is evidence from meta-analysis suggesting the effect is not that statistically robust when all studies are taken into account in general – and the effect only really appears when an actor is presented as behaving unusually, when the actor and observer know each other well or when particular methodological devices (such as the coding of free text responses) are employed (Malle, 2006). Malle also observed that whether or not the behaviour was positive or negative had an effect on how we make attributions. This *self-serving attribution bias* has been observed in other studies (e.g. Arkin, Cooper & Kolditz, 1980) – people typically attribute their successes to their own dispositions ('I won the race because I trained hard') and their failures to the situation ('Other people got going before the start gun'). A final bias which we will discuss is the *false consensus effect*. This is the tendency for people to assume others would behave the same way that they themselves would in a given situation. To demonstrate this, Ross, Greene and House (1977) asked participants to wander around their university campus wearing a sign encouraging others to 'Eat at Joes'. Out of the sample, 50 per cent agreed to do it and 50 per cent did not. More interestingly, when asked what they thought others would do, the 50 per cent of people that agreed to wear the sign estimated that 68 per cent of others would also do it. In contrast, the 50 per cent that did *not* agree to wear the sign estimated that 77 per cent of people would also refuse. This suggests that people tend to think others will think and behave the same way as they do. It's worth noting that although these biases appear to be systematic errors in the way we think, that does not make them entirely bad for us. The false consensus effect, for example, allows us to think that our behaviour in a given situation is 'normal' and that the same outcome would be likely to have happened to anybody else. Similarly, the self-serving bias has been shown to be protective of mental health (Beck et al., 1979) and linked to better educational outcomes (McClure et al., 2011). These protective effects seem relatively robust across cultural settings (Fletcher & Ward, 1988).

LIMITATIONS OF ATTRIBUTIONAL THEORY

Attributional theory is an important element in social psychology and remains a vibrant area of research. However, it has also become the focus of criticism particularly around the cultural specificity of much of the research involved. The evidence suggests that collectivist cultures tend to focus less on internal attributions than more individualistic ones do. The fact that majority of research in this area has been done on WEIRD participants also leaves questions around how attributions change over the lifespan, and amongst different demographic groups, open to exploration (see Chapter 3 for a fuller discussion of cultural specificity and WEIRD participants).

CRITICAL SPOTLIGHT: CAN WE CONTROL OUR ATTRIBUTIONS AND IMPRESSION FORMATIONS?

One of the reasons that these two topics are well studied is that they are a regular feature of our day-to-day social cognition. You make many attributions every day and form a first impression of everyone you meet for the first time.

Over the next few days, try to notice when you make attributions about others' (and your own) behaviour(s). When you reflect more consciously on them, do you think you experienced any attributional biases? Similarly, when you meet someone and form a judgement about them, try to later reflect on why you feel the way you do about them – were there some traits which dominated your judgement more than others? Should (can?) you revisit your initial attitude?

Try and keep up this reflection for a couple of weeks: do you notice any change in the number of times these biases crop up? What does this suggest to you about their automatic or voluntary nature? Does your own lived experience support or challenge these theories?

Before we close our discussion on important dimensions which influence relationships between ourselves and others, it is worth briefly discussing two more concepts. We know relationships are driven in part by what people say – but how does the way they say it affect us? We explore this in our discussion of non-verbal communication. Finally, we explore an important example of relationships between the self and others – co-operation – by examining evidence around the concept of social dilemmas.

NON-VERBAL COMMUNICATION

Imagine someone asks you to 'hurry up' with their arms opened welcomingly, and with a genuine smile. Now imagine the same person, saying the same thing, with hands on hips and a scowl on their face. The meanings are clearly different! We all know that *what* we say is often less important the *way* we say things. We also know that we communicate not only through speech but though a myriad of other ways. These non-verbal communications (NVCs) are an important part of our day-to-day social interactions. They may help clarify what we mean when speaking and convey large amounts of information even when we do not. However, they are also a relatively under-researched area of social psychology. Why might this be? Part of the reason is the sheer range of possible forms of NVCs. Our faces alone contain 43 muscles which, in different combinations, can generate huge variation in our countenance – a key source of our non-verbal communication. Hand and body gestures can also vary widely, and their meaning differs enormously not only between different cultures but also within a culture, between contexts. Although the use of NVCs seems to be universal across cultures, their form and when it is regarded as appropriate to express them can vary (for instance, casual, friendly, nonsexual touching is regarded as more as or less appropriate in some contexts and cultures than in others). However, the research that has been undertaken in this methodologically complex field is broadly broken up into the study of facial expressions, gaze direction (*oculesics*), touch (*haptics*), gestures and body movements (*kinesics*).

FACIAL EXPRESSION AND GAZE

Most research on facial expressions in non-verbal communication is based on the idea that there are a number of core emotions which are universally recognised (see Chapter 3). In line with this, we seem to have six basic facial expressions which are linked to the six basic emotions (happiness, sadness, anger, fear, surprise and disgust). These facial expressions are usually pretty automatic and reflect our emotional experience at the time. They can also be both very distinctive and simultaneously pretty nuanced – something as simple as a smile can communicate emotional information which can be distinguished from other emotional expressions from up to 45 metres away. Closer up, we can also differentiate between smiles reflecting experienced joy, smiles being put on despite the fact the wearer is unhappy and even smiles which convey that the wearer (i) is feeling miserable and (ii) has no intention of doing anything about it (Ekman & Friesen, 1982; Hager & Ekman, 1979)! We also use facial expressions (and gaze; see below) as a signal that we wish to take a turn in conversation, or that we are more or less willing to yield the discussion to others (Wiemann & Knapp, 1975).

Alongside facial expression, we are also very aware of where other people are *looking*. Eye contact is an important aspect of maternal infant attachment (e.g. Robson, 1967) and as we age we continue to pay a lot of attention to where other people direct their attention. This is because gaze both reflects social desires and intentions, but also alerts us to important events in our environment (see Ristic et al., 2005). As such, we tend to respond to where people look by matching it in a fairly automatic fashion (Ristic & Kingston, 2005). How we look at others also convey social information – an unwavering stare is often (but not always!) perceived as a signal of dominance or an attempt to intimidate, while breaking a mutual stare can be considered a sign of submission (Dovidio & Ellyson, 1985). In line with this, research also suggests that relatively low-status partners often look at the other person less when speaking than when being spoken to (Exline, Ellyson & Long, 1975).

PHYSICAL POSITIONING

Where we physically stand in relation to other people is also an important aspect of NVC. Hall (1966) identified four distinct zones of personal distance: the *intimate zone*, at 0.5 metres or less away from another person, is generally used by very intimate friends or romantic couples. At this distance we can be very aware of all forms of NVCs being signalled. Both smell and body temperature (themselves NVCs) can also be detected in this region. The *personal zone* (0.5–1 metres distance) is generally used when one close friend speaks to another, and allows touch between parties. The *social distance zone* (1–4 metres) is the zone in which most interactions between acquaintances and relative strangers takes place; it is too far for touch but still close enough for people to maintain eye contact and process many other NVCs. Finally, we sometimes communicate with other people at a *public distance* (4 metres away or more). Hall suggests that this distance is typically used to convey information in and of itself; for instance, a boss may sit further away from their employees, forcing them to concentrate on what's being said and avoiding any impression of intimacy. You may know from your own experience what happens when there is a mismatch between your expectations of acceptable social distance and what the other person tries to engage in! Indeed, we typically take action to avoid what we consider inappropriate social distance by moving away or reducing intimacy in other ways (for instance by looking away or providing less other feedback; Argyle & Dean, 1965).

TOUCH

An important feature of the intimate and personal zones is that they both allow interpersonal touch. The situations in which we feel comfortable touching and being touched vary by context. Touch can also signal a wide variety of aims. It can be used in a fairly *pragmatic* sense – for example, between a doctor and patient. It can have a *formal social function* (e.g. a handshake), or a *warmer social function* (hugging a friend). You can also aim to *signal love and intimacy* (a passionate kiss) which could be primarily sexual in nature (making love, for instance). As well as the cultural differences discussed above, it also appears there are gender differences in touching. Some research shows that women like to be touched more than men do – but only by people they know. Women are also more likely to perceive a sexual component to the action. Alongside this, it appears that men touch women more frequently than the other way around. However, these findings have sometimes been contested (see Stier & Hall, 1984, for a review). It also seems that touch can influence *compliance* with requests, generate social bonds and strengthen romantic relationships – whether or not it is noticed, or recalled (Gallace & Spence, 2010). Touch can also, of course, be used as a form of violence.

GESTURES

Amongst all NVPs, gestures are perhaps the most *culturally specific*. While some gestures (such as displaying a number of fingers to indicate a quantity, or to point the way) are pretty universal, others can be more culturally specific and, potentially, the source of much confusion! Shaking one's head from left to right and back is, in the UK, a pretty clear sign you are saying 'no'. In contrast, the same gesture in India means 'yes'! This variation is slightly surprising, as gestures are one of the earliest forms of communication that we acquire as infants, and pre-human species' use of gestures (possibly driven by dexterity developed via tool use) suggests they were used for communication long before language (see e.g. Bradshaw & Nettleton, 1982; Meltzoff & Moore, 1989). While we typically think of gestures as being something done with hands, arms or heads, they also involve things. For instance, whole body gestures, such as changing posture, also seems to convey social information – for example, erectness of posture seems to serve as an indicator of dominance or success in humans (Weisfeld & Beresford, 1982).

One interesting feature of NVC is *mimicry*. Mimicry can take place in terms of matching gaze patterns, gestures and posture, and it is an important facilitator of social interactions (Gueguen, Jacob & Martin, 2009). How well we understand others' NVCs is important too. Given the importance of NVCs in understanding behaviour and guiding interactions, those that excel at decoding NVCs tend to benefit, and those with impairments in this domain do not. For instance, those high in *non-verbal sensitivity* tend to gain in various ways, including building better rapport and being more socially successful (DiMatteo, Friedman & Taranta, 1979; Edwards, Manstead & Macdonald, 1984). There is evidence that women are better at processing NVCs than are men – but also that most of us improve as we get older (e.g. Hall, 1978; Zuckerman et al., 1980).

This chapter has explored how we evaluate others when we meet them, the factors which encourage us to enter relationships with them and how we understand their behaviour. To conclude our exploration of how the self relates to others, we now turn to a more practical topic – how (and when) we choose to trust (and co-operate) with others.

SOCIAL DILEMMAS

Imagine you are being questioned by the police, along with another person. You need to decide whether to confess to the crime or not, and know the other person being questioned is making the same decision. If you both stay quiet, you will both receive moderate sentences. If you confess and the other person stays quiet, you receive a very light prison sentence, while the other receives a sentence longer than both moderate ones and the short one combined! Equally, if you stay quiet and they confess, they get the light sentence and you the extraordinarily long one. Whether you are innocent of the crime or not is irrelevant. Think about this – what would you do?

In many situations, *co-operating* with another person can lead to the best overall outcome (in the above situation, a moderate total number of years). However, it can also lead to a risk that you will receive a poor outcome if the other person doesn't follow suit. The above scenario (also known as the '*prisoner's dilemma*') and related situations are called *social dilemmas*. Similarly, the '*tragedy of the commons*' (Hardin, 1968) describes a situation in which a resource (common grazing land) can support a limited number of livestock per farmer and still replenish itself. Each farmer allocates slightly more animals than their share (but only one or two extra – 'surely that won't hurt?'). Over time, the grazing space is destroyed, and no-one can use it. Examples of real-life social dilemmas include *resource conservation* (if everyone conserves/limits use of replenishing resources they can be sustained, while overuse will extinguish them), *collective action* (not being vaccinated may avoid slight risks to the self, while benefiting from 'herd immunity'; however, if everyone does this, immunity is lost) and *public good dilemmas* (where everyone puts in an amount of resource into a shared pot, which pays out more to everyone if a threshold is reached – taxes being an example). In many social dilemmas, observed levels of co-operation are very low (depending on the balance of costs/benefits outlined). In essence, people are behaving routinely in suboptimal ways. Why might this be?

Early accounts of people's behaviours during social dilemmas drew on economic perspectives such as *game theory* (Von Neumann & Morgenstern, 1944), which argues that people in such situations (called *actors*) are essentially *self-interested* and *rational*. So, why do we not always choose to co-operate with others for the best outcome? Although the total number of years collectively served in a social dilemma may be lowest when we co-operate, we are also aware of the *sucker's outcome*, which is the greatest cost (or lowest reward). Moreover, in case of renewable resources, co-operating defers our gain now for one in the future (which, if the resource exhausts, may never materialise). As (game theory assumes) we work on the basis that others will be attempting to maximise gains and minimise losses, it makes sense for us to do the same.

The *structure* of the game can also influence how people behave. For instance, if we have *perfect information* (for instance, we know what others are planning to do, how much of a resource is left and what will be left in the future once others act) we can plan our behaviour to be more sustainable, as the need to maximise immediate gains decreases. However, if any information is missing (*imperfect information*) co-operation will be low. Perfect information is rare. In many real-life situations (how much carbon the atmosphere holds, levels of aquifer water reserves underground, fish in the sea, etc.) it can be hard to know what the 'pool' is from which people are drawing. Also, people's motives and behaviours are not always shared freely. *Infinite* games also encourage co-operation. When all actors in a game have a long-term stake in a resource, it is more likely to be managed well. For instance, in shared fisheries, if all fishermen are going to stay from season to season, all have an interest in maintaining stocks by avoiding overfishing (see Ostrom 1991). Importantly, they can all also be sure others also have the same goal. The introduction of new actors can be disruptive to such systems. Indeed, once people see that stocks are reducing, levels of co-operation between actors drop rapidly.

Psychological influences are also important in increasing co-operation. As you may have guessed, a lack of trust between actors is a major cause of non-co-operation. Having a chance to communicate can build trust, which, in turn, increases co-operation (Balliet, 2010). This effect is more likely, and much enhanced, when people see all actors in a dilemma as being in the same group (e.g. a fishing collective or association) and when they have a leader who can allocate outcomes and ensure *contracts* between parties are policed. Individual differences in psychological processes also influence outcomes. So-called *pro-selfers* (who, as the name implies, look more to their own welfare, and see people as independent) do not co-operate as much as *prosocial* folk (who look to others' welfare and see more interdependence; see Kelley & Stahelski, 1970). Experimental evidence shows that the presence of people who *consistently co-operate* in social dilemmas raises overall levels of co-operation amongst others (Weber & Murnighan, 2008).

While much of this continues to involve pen-and-paper measures, or real groups playing out games, recent work using fMRI scanners (which reveal neural activity in the brain) is also starting to link co-operative behaviours to specific regions of the brain, increasing the levels of analysis available to researchers. The overall picture is mixed. Given the importance of social dilemmas in many large real-life problems, it is unfortunate to recognise that co-operation is not the norm. However, it is also encouraging to observe many situations where it is achieved, and that psychologists are gradually mapping out the optimal conditions to encourage it.

CHAPTER SUMMARY

In this chapter we have focused on various aspects of social psychology which explain how we (as individuals) relate to other people. We've seen how we perceive others and how particular traits strongly influence first and enduring impressions of them. We've explored how we understand the causes of other people's behaviour, and also how we interpret social meaning from non-verbal communication. Finally, we've explored an important aspect of interpersonal relationships – trust and co-operation. Throughout all of these topics, we've seen that social judgements are driven by different motivations and automatic and reflective processes. I hope this chapter has also highlighted just how complicated things that we take for granted (meeting someone for the first time, giving someone a high five) can be from a psychological point of view. This level of complexity gets even greater in our next chapter – as we scale up from an individual- to a group-level analysis.

KEY CHAPTER POINTS

• We use various sources of information to make judgements about people, but weight some more strongly than others.

- Relationships between people can be explained from cognitive, motivational and cultural perspectives.
- We understand others' (and our own) behaviour as being driven by disposition or circumstance (internal and external attributions).
- A key form of communication, non-verbal communication is important but relatively poorly understood by psychology.
- Trust — studied through social dilemma research — appears hard to sustain, but potentially benefits everyone when achieved.

SUGGESTED FURTHER READING

1. Dwyer, D. (2000). *Interpersonal relationships*. London: Routledge.
2. Gilbert, D. T., & Malone, P. S. (1995). The correspondence bias. *Psychological Bulletin, 117*, 21–38.
3. Depaulo, B. M., & Friedman, H. S. (1998). Nonverbal communication. In D. T. Gilbert, S. T. Fiske, & G. Lindzey (eds), *The handbook of social psychology* (pp. 3–40). New York: McGraw-Hill.
4. Ostrom, E. (1991). *Governing the commons: The evolution of institutions for collective action*. Cambridge: Cambridge University Press.

5

SELF AND GROUPS

DEFINITIONS OF GROUPS

As we saw in 'Understanding the self', the groups we are in and the social identities that result from them are incredibly important in our psychological lives, fulfilling social motives in changing the way we see the world. This chapter explores some of the key principles in group psychology, in particular focusing on how we interact with one another. However, before we can do this, it is useful to have a clear understanding of what a group is. On the face of it this appears pretty simple – we can all think of what a group seems to be. However, a closer examination makes it trickier. For instance, can two people be a group? Do the group members need to know each other? Do I need to know that I'm in a group to actually be a member? These and other questions have led to a number of attempts to define a group. One classic definition by Johnson and Johnson (1987, p. 8) suggests a group consists of

> *Two or more individuals in face-to-face interaction, each aware of his or her membership in the group, each aware of the others who belong to the group, and each aware of their positive interdependence as they strive to achieve mutual goals.*

Several important aspects of this definition are worth noting. First, it seems that Johnson and Johnson argue that we should really know every group member, and have a clear idea who is in and not in the group. Clearly, this is problematic when one starts dealing with larger, fairly diffuse groups: for instance, people may identify as being a 'Mini (car) owner', without knowing others in that group well (or at all). The definition also argues that the key feature of groups is a sense of *interdependency* (i.e. what one group member does affects the other members) and common purpose. But it is possible to think of psychologically meaningful groups where this is not necessarily the case – for instance, people who think of themselves as 'cancer survivors'.

One way around these definitional problems is to think about the features of the group. A key feature is *entitativity* – the sense that things go together (Campbell, 1958). For instance, a flock of birds appears to have entitativity when flying because they travel together, and have co-ordination that hints that the group has a shared goal. In group terms, high-entitativity groups have clear definitions of who is and who is not in the group (i.e. clear group boundaries), often share a clear sense of purpose and have a low level of variability between group members. High-entitativity groups may include families and long-standing friendship circles. In contrast, groups that only come together for a short time or those that are almost entirely task-focused are likely to be much lower in entitativity. Differences in entitativity are likely to affect levels of conformity within a group, commitment to it and possibly levels of identification with it. Psychologist Holly Arrow and colleagues argue that another way of discriminating between groups is to consider common *bonds* versus common *identity* groups (see Arrow, McGrath & Berdahl, 2000). The former are based on interpersonal relationships (i.e. how much one relates to other people in the group), while the latter rely on how much one is attached to the concept of the group itself. Another proposed marker of group membership includes common fate (how much outcomes will be shared) and the presence of social hierarchies and roles (Campbell, 1958; Sherif & Sherif, 1969). Given these disagreements, it is perhaps more useful to have a *general* understanding of what a group is. One attempt to do this comes from John Turner's work (Turner, 1982, p. 15) which simply argues that groups are 'individuals

… [who] perceive themselves to be members of the same social category'.

However one defines a group, it is obvious that they are important in our day-to-day functioning. As such, a number of researchers have explored how groups influence the thoughts and behaviour of their members (which we explore in the *social influence* theme of this book) and also how they interact with other groups. This latter topic is the main focus of the current chapter.

WHAT NEEDS DO GROUPS FULFIL?

We have seen some examples of how we define (or struggle to define) what a group is. However, why do we form or join groups in the first place? One way to understand this is via Festinger, Schachter and Back's (1950) emphasis on *social communication*. Such communication is driven by two pressures – a desire to produce *group locomotion* (i.e. the group achieving its goals) and a desire for *social reality* (a shared understanding of the world). Broadly, communication motivators can also be used to understand why we are members of groups. At a basic level, being part of a group allows one to achieve far more than one could do alone – and this *interdependence* appears to be an important feature of groups (see Rabbie & Horwitz, 1988). Things we take for granted, such as our mobile phones, represent complicated endeavours that a single person will be unlikely to achieve, even if given a huge amount of time. In historical terms, being part of a group allowed early humans to effectively hunt large prey, protect resources and generally look after themselves in a potentially dangerous environment. It is important to note that this goal interdependence is a two-way street – the individual influences the group's goals, and group membership can change individuals' orientation in turn. However, it's unlikely the group membership is based purely on 'getting things done'. Groups also provide considerable emotional support, and an increasing amount of evidence suggests that group membership provides a wide variety of benefits to both psychological and physical health (see Chapter 9). *Social identity* approaches (such as Tajfel & Turner, 1979) and more *evolutionary* approaches such as *sociometer theory* (Baumeister & Leary, 1995) both argue that we draw our sense of self-esteem in part from memberships – with identity approaches arguing that we look for positive differentiation between our own and other groups, and sociometer theory arguing that we have an innate need to belong and that our self-esteem is a mechanism to make sure we behave in ways which keep us within the group rather than being forced out of it. Complementary to this idea is the concept of *optimal distinctiveness* – the concept that we have a need both to feel unique but also to belong. Being part of a group allows us to fulfil the belonging need, while comparisons between and within groups allow us to feel distinct. Social identity perspectives also suggest that being part of a group helps us avoid being in a state of 'subjective uncertainty' about how to understand the world and how to behave (Hogg, Hohman & Rivera, 2008).

GROUP FORMATION AND DISSOLVING

Many groups which we are a part of have existed since long before we were born, and will continue to exist long after we have died. Some of these groups we can join, and some we can leave. Alongside these established groups we may also be involved with groups which are in the process of formation, or in the process of being dissolved. The idea of such a group life cycle is typically perceived as involving '*forming, norming and storming*'.

FORMING, NORMING AND STORMING

Tuckman (1965) argued that groups typically go through a number of stages over their life cycle. Groups initially go through a period of *forming* in which group members focus on group organisational structures and roles. Typically, there is a desire to avoid conflict during this phase. Once people are familiar with one another, the process of *storming* begins. During this phase, conflicts around the purpose of, and roles within, the group are expected. Once these are established, a phase of *norming* leads to a feeling of cohesiveness and mutual support. This facilitates the fourth stage of '*performing*' – characterised by good morale, high productivity, flexibility and harmony. This is where the best work of the group occurs. Later iterations of this model also highlighted that groups can go through a phase of '*adjourning*' (Tuckman & Jensen, 1977). In this phase people adjust to the groups' goals being completed (or to further efforts being futile), and to the group dissolving.

GROUP MEMBER SOCIALISATION

An alternative way of understanding how groups form is to look at how new and established members socialise one another. Levine and Moreland's (1994) model of *group socialisation* understands the development of groups from this perspective. They argue that how people function within a group varies across five phases. The first phase, '*investigation*', takes place before an individual joins the group. Potential group members reconnoitre potential groups. Groups also attempt to recruit new members (if they feel they need to). Once the two meet and someone joins a group, there is a phase of *socialisation* in which the new group member attempts to adapt to the group. The best outcomes for this phase are observed when both the individual makes an effort to socialise themselves and the group has an intensive, formal socialisation programme (see Ashforth, Sluss, & Saks 2007). Once mutual commitment (or another '*acceptance criterion*') has been achieved, groups move on to the *maintenance* phase. Individuals function within the group, negotiating their specific role (which may change). If these negotiations are successful, the member will remain in the maintenance stage. However, if the individual's or the group's commitment to the other deviates to the extent that it reaches a '*diverging criterion*', a phase of *resocialisation* may occur. This is often an attempt by the group to reassimilate the individual and an effort by the individual to reaccommodate to the group. This phase is often rockier than initial socialisation. For instance, Isabel Pinto and colleagues show that new members of a group receive less-negative evaluations for violating group norms than do well-established 'full' group members. If this resocialisation is successful, maintenance reoccurs (Pinto et al., 2010). If a group member leaves, a phase of *remembrance* is also likely. During this phase the group incorporates the individual into its collective story, and the individual reminisces about their time in the group. Although the individual and the group may not have much to do with one another, they may also feel a sense of obligation and loyalty to each other.

INITIATION RITUALS

Many groups employ a formal initiation which prospective members complete before joining the group, and existing members may need to undergo before changing roles. These events can be fairly benign (for instance, a baptism signals joining a church group), slightly demanding (a new member of a sports team may be required to set out equipment) or embarrassing (having a 'best man's speech' made about one when getting married). They can also be very extreme – even at the time of writing, a small number of European student fraternities still require members to take part in fencing duels with live blades and little facial protection, and ritualistic beating and unwanted sexual contact are common initiation requirements when joining street gangs. Making people work hard to get into a group appears to increase subsequent loyalty to it – due to the cognitive dissonance it generates (see Chapter 3). Specifically, we resolve the dissonance generated by doing something unpleasant to get in by valuing the group more. Experimental studies have demonstrated this effect, showing that getting participants to read out embarrassingly sexually explicit passages, or receive electric shocks, as part of joint work-group leads to greater commitment to the group further down the line (Aronson & Mills, 1959; Gerard and Mathewson, 1966). Initiation rites are an example of *social norms*, which we will now explore.

SOCIAL NORMS

One of the key ways in which groups generate shared understanding and influence group members is through *social norms*. We all know how to behave correctly (most of the time, even if we don't do it!) because we have knowledge of the social norms of the group. Social norms can cover both attitudes and behaviour, and are usually something that we will be reasonably conscious of. Some seem to be found in almost all cultures (taboos against incest being a classic example) while others are fairly culturally specific (for instance, British customs around waiting in line differ from those found in other countries – which can lead to frustration when these two groups meet!). Norms can be described as *descriptive* or *prescriptive*. Descriptive norms describe how group members behave and think about a particular issue. Prescriptive norms (also known as *injunctive* norms) described shared opinions about how group members *should* behave (Cialdini, Reno & Kallgren, 1990). Norms can also be generated in relatively spontaneous and unconscious ways. For example, Cialdini, Reno and Kallgren (1990) had participants seated in an area which was either covered in litter or not. In the littered area, participants in some conditions also witnessed other people contributing to the mess. Cialdini hypothesised that people would generate an injunctive norm about littering behaviour *from* the environment which would affect their behaviour *towards* it. In line with this, when the littering norm was signalled by a messy environment, participants themselves were more likely to litter. This was especially the case when the participant saw another person littering beforehand (presumably validating the norm that the participant generated from the environment). Although some norms are clearly signalled in this way, others are held, but relatively unspoken. For instance, imagine what would happen in your next seminar if you arrived at the class to find a single person whom you did not know sitting and waiting for the session to begin. Now imagine that from amongst all the available chairs, you selected the one next to theirs, sat down and did not speak or make eye contact. This behaviour would likely make both you and the person who you sat next to feel very uncomfortable! These so-called '*hidden norms*' make up a large part of our social behaviour, and are the focus of a field of study known as *ethnomethodology* (Garfinkel, 1967).

One way to understand these hidden norms is through the idea of *social schemas*. Schemas are learned collections of connected information about a given topic (see Bartlett & Burt, 1933). Social schemas include the various ways people behave in social situations. For instance, if dining at a formal restaurant, you typically wait to be seated; a waiter then takes your jacket and gives you a menu. You then request courses to eat (in a particular order – no dessert first!), eat, request the bill, pay it and then leave. Such schemas are commonly held, cover diverse situations, and affect the way we think, behave and perceive our role in society (in particular around gender roles; see Bem 1981). The majority of groups have a set of well-defined social roles; these describe how various people and subgroups are supposed to (and are permitted to) behave. Lecturers and students, for example, have different functions and expectations associated with their roles in an educational context. In a workplace, the content and method of how a senior boss and a junior employee work will be different, as will acceptable communication styles. Interestingly, research generally suggests that when people understand, accept and behave in line with social roles, everyone is generally happier and more productive (e.g. Bettencourt & Sheldon, 2001). However, as will see in our discussion around conformity and obedience (see Chapter 6), such roles can also take on a more sinister turn when they override moral sensibilities, or encourage behaving in ways which are oppressive or even fatal to others. But what other functions do norms have, and can they change?

THE FUNCTIONS OF NORMS

Norms appear to be highly functional devices. By generating shared meanings for social objects and events and by providing clear ways to behave, norms reduce subjective uncertainty (which, as we have seen, is one of the key needs for the group to address). They can also facilitate productivity for both the group and the individual. For instance, sports teams may hold norms about being on time for training, being physically fit, being highly motivated during both training and matches, and respecting one's teammates. All these behaviours contribute to better group performance in this context (Munroe et al., 1999). Similarly, Frings and colleagues (2016) show that members of peer support groups such as Alcoholics Anonymous identify norms which facilitate good outcomes for group members (being respectful, maintaining confidentiality) and minimise poor ones (sexually predatory behaviour, poor turn-taking). Of course, social norms needn't increased productivity – norms encouraging people not to work *too* hard, for instance, will actively reduce outputs. Similarly, the contents of social norms can be divisive both within and between groups (as we will begin to see when we discuss stereotypes and stigmatisation below).

CAN SOCIAL NORMS CHANGE?

Norms function because they are socially shared and generally agreed upon. As such, changing norms can be problematic for the group – potentially increasing subjective uncertainty and lowering group locomotion. However, groups whose norms never evolve will inevitably stagnate and often fail. Behaviours which once seemed to be completely normative (for instance, slavery) become completely unacceptable, while the unacceptable can become normative (for instance, using your boss's first name in many workplaces). As will see in Chapter 6, group members often go to great lengths to ensure that group norms are maintained, and those who fail to meet injunctive norms are brought swiftly back into line or expelled from the group. However, we will also explore a body of research which shows that groups at times encourage change, and how minorities within groups can change group norms. We'll look at these processes initially through the lens of a particular type of group norm which defines how we think about other group members: *stereotypes*.

STEREOTYPES

Perhaps one of the most important social norms that groups hold surrounds their views of *other* groups. Such *stereotypes* are influential preconceptions which affect our evaluations of and the beliefs we have about members of a particular group. These in turn affect our behaviour towards members of that group. The *stereotype content model* developed by Susan Fiske and colleagues (SCM; Fiske et al., 2002) argues that stereotypes can be categorised according to where they fall on two dimensions – first, how *warm versus cold* the group is perceived to be, and second, how *competent versus incompetent* they are. This creates a taxonomy of four different sorts of stereotype, each of which makes different cognitive and behavioural outcomes more likely. A group can be seen as being both low in competence and in warmth (i.e. cold). This *contemptuous stereotype* might include groups such as the homeless and drug addicts, and elicits behavioural responses such as avoidance and emotional responses such as disgust. The opposite of this is groups who are seen as high in both warmth and competence. An *admiration* stereotype is usually reserved for one's own group and close allies. Emotions such as pride and co-operative behaviours are likely responses to people in these groups. Between these two extremes are situations where warmth is high and competence is low, and where warmth is low and competence is high. The former of these is a *paternalistic stereotype*. It is often applied to groups such as the elderly, the unemployed and, in some studies, homemakers, and elicits feelings such as pity and condescension and behaviours including helpfulness. Despite its (on the surface) positive tone, such a stereotype is also quite disempowering! When we perceive people as being low-warmth/high-competence, we see them from the point of view of an *envious* stereotype. Historically, this has often been applied to ethnic groups such as Asians and religious groups such as Jewish people. Envious stereotypes are usually associated with envy and resentment, which can translate into attempts to compete with the group or efforts to hinder their progress.

The SCM has received a good amount of empirical support and is a widely used way of understanding stereotypes. Typically, research has shown that the various stereotypes are linked with the expected cognitive and behavioural effects. However, there are also some limitations and criticisms of the model. For instance, most of the evidence involves self-reporting (which is of course prone to self-presentation biases). It also does not account for other possible dimensions which may be important in understanding stereotypes. The SCM continues to be one of the dominant paradigms for understanding the forms that stereotypes take cognitively. It does not, however, specify the process through which the stereotype actually impacts thoughts and behaviour – a topic dealt with, in part, by ideas around *stereotype expectancies*.

STEREOTYPES AS EXPECTANCIES

Once a stereotype is activated, it can influence the way we understand the world, and how we process and record information. For instance, Nelson, Biernat and Manis (1990) show that gender stereotypes associated with men being taller affect estimates of actual height, even when cash prizes are offered for accuracy! Hoffman and Hurst (1990) show that stereotypes about gender and occupation also affect how we interpret other ambiguous information – usually as a result of falling back on our stereotypes. Stereotypes also change the information we actively seek out or attend to. For instance, if you believe someone is an introvert you may ask questions during a job interview which will reveal that tendency (Snyder & Swan, 1978). They can also affect what we remember. For instance, we recall instances of stereotypic associations such as 'attractive-stewardess' more easily (and overestimate the frequency with which they occur more readily) than we do non-stereotypic ones such as 'serious-waitress' (see Hamilton & Rose, 1980 and other work on such *illusionary correlations*).

SELF-FULFILLING PROPHECIES

The expectancies associated with stereotypes can become self-fulfilling prophecies. For instance, Rosenthal and Jacobson (1966) took a class of children and randomly assigned half of them to an experimental condition. Their teacher was told these particular children were 'growth spurters' with high potential. At the end of the semester's teaching, those whom the teachers believed to be more gifted had in fact improved more than those in the control condition! Although no processes were formally tested, it is possible that expectations on the teachers' part led to the 'growth spurters' being paid more attention and given more opportunities to develop and gain confidence (for instance, by being picked to answer questions). This in turn led to these students developing quicker, reinforcing the beliefs which in turn reinforced the behaviours. A good example of how such processes may operate was demonstrated by Word, Zanna and Cooper (1974). In their first study, they showed that when participants interviewed a (confederate) member of a negatively stereotyped outgroup for a mock job, the length of the interview was 25 per cent shorter, and the interviewer sat further from the interviewee and had more awkward speech patterns (speech delays, stuttering, etc.). In their second experiment, the investigators trained the confederate to behave in these ways. They then had these *confederate interviewers* interview actual participants (either using the behaviours or not). Independent raters assessed that the participants mirrored the behaviours of the confederate, and also, in the 'awkward inter-action' condition, rated the participant as less suitable for the job. In essence, both parties in the interaction behaved awkwardly, and this led to a vicious cycle, to the detriment of the minority group member.

We have seen evidence that stereotypes can influence a variety of processes, but how amenable are they to change?

STEREOTYPE CHANGE

Given the importance of stereotypes for intergroup relations, it's unsurprising that they've also been the focus of much research which tries to understand how to change them. Unfortunately, it appears that stereotypes are resilient to change. One example of this is research conducted by Miles Hewstone and colleagues (Hewstone, Hopkins & Routh, 1992) which explored attempts to change stereotypes held by children towards police officers. At the time of the study (following on from periods of intense police action against strikers and various other civil action groups) the image of the police was often fairly negative. One way the police attempted to change this was to employ *police liaison officers* who would go into schools to present a positive example of who the police were. Hewstone and colleagues observed that although the police liaison officers themselves were generally evaluated positively, this effect did not 'spill over' into the children's evaluations of police as a whole. The children effectively *subtyped* the liaison officer into a different category of police officer – with more traits shared with caring welfare professionals than with the police. However, more positively, it also seems that if we can generate more of these subtypes then the general stereotype is applied less widely, and could be considered as being less impactful on our overall behaviour. An alternative approach to *immediate stereotype change* comes from the idea of '*book-keeping*'. Rather than sudden conversion between one set of attitudes and another, we gradually change our belief towards a particular group as we accumulate *disconfirming evidence*. Such information can be provided if groups experience sustained levels of high-quality intergroup contact (see below). Change via book-keeping is slow, not least because (as was seen above) we are quite resistant to observing such evidence (see Hewstone, 1989).

CRITICAL SPOTLIGHT: AUTOMATICITY IN STEREOTYPES

Stereotypes needn't be consciously experienced to affect our behaviour. Research using tasks such as the *Implicit Association Task* (IAT; Greenwald, McGhee & Schwartz, 1998), which measures implicit relationships between a target category (e.g. white or black) and evaluations (positive or negative), shows that these implicitly held attitudes can, at times, be better predictors of prejudice than can pen-and-paper questionnaires (although this claim has been disputed; see Oswald et al., 2013 for a review of the research in this area).

STIGMATISATION AND PREJUDICE

One cognitive outcome of stereotypes is *prejudice*. Think about some group in society which is perhaps marginalised in some way. You will likely be able to generate a number of negative traits which are often associated with this group. These are all examples of prejudice. Generally, prejudice is understood to be an attitude towards a group of people with cognitive (beliefs about the group), affective (feelings about the group) and behavioural (ways of behaving towards the group) components. Allport (1954b, p. 9) defined it as 'an antipathy based on faulty and inflexible generalization. It may be felt or expressed. It may be directed toward a group as a whole, or toward an individual because he [sic] is a member of that group.' As this definition suggests, prejudicial attitudes are generally (but not always) negative in nature. Holding a prejudice about a group often means that when we encounter one of its members we treat them in line with our beliefs, rather than considering the person as an individual. It also makes intergroup-level identities more salient than interpersonal ones. An extreme form of prejudice is *stigmatisation* – in which the perception of an individual is reduced solely to a single negative trait, usually associated with the group membership. People with communicable diseases, physical disabilities and mental health issues are all often stigmatised in Western society.

Prejudice can impact intergroup reactions in a number of ways. In our current discussion we focus on the role of prejudice and anxiety during intergroup interactions and also its effects on attribution processes as two examples.

PREJUDICE AND ANXIETY

In terms of anxiety, prejudice can lead to lower-quality interpersonal reactions, which in itself can lead to reinforcement of the prejudicial belief. For instance, Blascovich et al. (2001) suggest that interactions with stigmatised individuals can generate uncertainty – which makes working or conversing with them threatening. Blascovich et al. demonstrated this in a laboratory context by having white participants interact with confederates. The confederates demonstrated a stigmatising trait (or, in control conditions, did not). In their first study, the confederate had a large facial birthmark (in fact simulated). In the second, the stigmatising trait was racial (being African-American) and socioeconomic (being poor). Importantly, the experimenters used cardiovascular indicators to show when people were feeling threatened by the interaction. In both experiments, interacting with the stigmatised other led to a state of threat. Interestingly (and in line with the *contact hypothesis*; see below), when participants had more experience of interacting with African Americans generally, they experienced less of a threat response. The threat itself led to less positive outcomes during group work, and more stilted conversations between the partners. This is one example of the way that prejudices can become self-fulfilling prophecies (see above).

PREJUDICE AND ATTRIBUTIONS

In terms of attributions (see Chapter 4), Pettigrew (1979) identified the *ultimate attribution error* (UAE) as being particularly problematic for groups which are the subject of prejudice. The UAE represents a tendency to understand negative events associated with an outgroup as being the responsibility of the group themselves, rather than the situation they find themselves in (when compared with judgements made about ingroup members and negative events). In reverse, positive events associated with the outgroup are likely to be seen as circumstantial in cause –either 'an exceptional case', or down to luck or an incredible amount of effort – making a repeat occurrence unlikely. As we would imagine, this is likely to result in outgroup members being perceived as being less competent (bad things are their fault, good things are due to circumstance) and often colder (as negative effects on the self associated with the outgroup are likely to be attributed directly to the group). As we will see shortly, both of these effects make prejudices very difficult to shift once they are established. Clearly, being a member of a group which is subject to prejudice is problematic, but to what extent does it affect core aspects of our self – such as self-esteem – and how does it affect performance?

PREJUDICE AND SELF-ESTEEM/PERFORMANCE

Being a member of a group which has prejudice directed towards it has important implications for our general welfare, psychological well-being and physical health. Our earlier discussion on self-esteem (see Chapter 2) suggests that the link is likely to be complex between how our group is evaluated and our health. For instance, *social identity creativity* and *social identity buffering effects* ensure people can maintain positive self-esteem even when their group is evaluated negatively by others, or lacks in a given dimension. However, groups experiencing prejudice are often of lower socioeconomic status or face considerable social difficulties – both of which factors themselves are linked to poor psychological and physiological health. One particular phenomenon explored in the social psychological literature around prejudice is *stereotype threat*. The original study exploring this effect was conducted by Claude Steele and Joshua Aronson (Steele & Aronson, 1995). They asked groups of African-American and white students to undertake a difficult verbal skills test. For some of the students (in a 'stereotype threat' condition) the test was described as 'diagnostic of intellectual ability'. In a 'non-stereotype threat' condition, it was described as 'a laboratory problem-solving task' that was non-diagnostic of ability. Finally, another group of students was told the test was non-diagnostic but also advised to see it as challenging ('challenge' condition). In the stereotype threat condition Steele and Aronson observed that the African-American students did much more poorly than their white counterparts (even once their actual aptitude, measured by SAT scores, was controlled for). This difference was not observed in the non-stereotype threat conditions. Why might this have been? Pulling together almost a decade and a half of research, Schmader, Johns and Forbes (2008) argue that when we are aware of a stereotype which is relevant to both our group membership and our performance, our worry about confirming the stereotype results in our performing poorly. This generates a state of stress, as efforts are undertaken to suppress negative thoughts and feelings. At the same time, we actively monitor our performance. All these activities detract from our ability to perform well. Since initial research in this area, stereotype threat has been observed in a variety of contexts, across different groups. For instance, activating gender identities has been shown to reduce women's maths aptitude. Similarly, white males doing sports tasks they are stereotypically weak at, relative to other ethnic groups, do poorly when tasks are 'diagnostic'. Some of these studies have observed *social boost effects* – where activating positive stereotypes (for instance, Asians being good at maths) can actually increase performance. While a full review is beyond the scope of this book, interested readers are recommended to explore this area by starting with Nguyen and Ryan (2008) for a thorough overview. One point to note about stereotype threat is that it is *self-reinforcing* – stereotypes generate worry, which decreases performance, which reinforces the beliefs. This makes it another form of self-fulfilling prophecy. As you can imagine, this is not the only process which maintains prejudice, and it is to other such processes that we now turn.

CRITICAL SPOTLIGHT: STEREOTYPE THREAT – SHIFTING THE BLAME?

Stereotype threat research has been instrumental in helping education systems devise fair assessment procedures and highlighting that people from disadvantaged communities may face challenges above and beyond those experienced by others. However, there is also a potentially negative aspect. Focusing on such changes may to some extent level the playing field within academic contexts but may also ignore the underlying causes of the threat. Moreover, stereotype threat can also be misunderstood. If one perceives that opportunities for social advancement are being offered, but people are 'too anxious' to do well, where then does the responsibility lie? As we will see later in this chapter, such 'stories' societies tell themselves about status differences are an important way that intergroup differences are maintained.

HOW IS PREJUDICE MAINTAINED?

Once prejudicial beliefs towards a group are established, it appears that a number of processes come into play which make them difficult to change. Our discussion will therefore now focus on the role of *legitimising beliefs*, and differences in how people understand why the world is the way it is and endorse the status quo.

TYPES OF LEGITIMISING BELIEFS

One common mechanism which maintains prejudice is a set of beliefs which reinforce differences in the status quo. For instance, people high in *benevolent sexism* (see Glick & Fiske, 1996) may believe that women are superior caregivers and more understanding of people, and also that women need nurturing, protecting and generally looking after. If you hold these beliefs, is not a great step to make an argument that women are more suited to some roles (perhaps childcare) than others (perhaps being a CEO of a multinational organisation). Beliefs can also link directly to differences in status. For instance, in a survey of relatively affluent white Americans, Ryan (1971) observed a series of commonly held beliefs about low-status groups – for instance that poor people are just focused on the present, black parents neglect their children (creating a cycle of despair and deprivation), poor people seek self-esteem through gambling, single mothers have 'strange' sexual inclinations and inner-city residents undermine the economic integrity of their neighbourhoods through crime and violence.

These legitimising beliefs can form part of a broader *belief in a just world*. This is the idea that we live in a world in which people 'get what they deserve ... The judgement of deserving is based on the outcome that someone is entitled to receive' (Lerner, 1980, p. 11). In essence, if we receive good outcomes we probably deserve it, and if we receive poor outcomes we probably deserve that too. Legitimising beliefs act to reinforce this idea of a just world. Just world effects have been seen in a variety of arenas, including people's understanding of poverty (Harper et al., 1990), being a victim of sexual violence (Janoff-Bulman, Timko & Carli, 1985) and contracting diseases such as AIDS. These ideas suggest that much of these groups' predicament is down to their own behaviours, and thus the solution must also come from them. Interestingly, it seems that belief in a just world, while generally problematic for low-status groups, seems to be protective for those that endorse it: individuals with just world beliefs seem to experience higher levels of psychological well-being (e.g. Lipkusa, Dalbert

& Siegler, 1996). A further related belief set is the 'Protestant work ethic' (PWE; Katz & Hass, 1988). This is a general philosophy held by a number of Western countries which holds that work has a moral value and that hard work leads to success. A logical extension of this belief is that people who don't succeed in life are generally lazy. As with belief in a just world, levels of endorsement of this assumption vary from person to person – and it has implications for how we view others. For instance, research suggests that those who endorse PWE highly also, amongst other things, demonstrate more prejudice, co-operate less with others and have negative views towards social welfare for the unemployed (Furnham & Quilley, 1989; Katz & Hass, 1988). These effects can also be reinforced by high levels of *social dominance orientation* (Sidanius & Pratto, 2001). This personality trait varies according to the extent that an individual sees hierarchy as preferable and legitimate in organisations and/or social systems, and seeks social dominance over others. High social dominance orientation is linked to more authoritarian and more racist beliefs (e.g. Duriez & Van Hiel, 2002) and research shows that men have higher levels (on average) than do women (e.g. Mast, 2002). What are the implications of these sorts of legitimising beliefs for minority or disenfranchised populations? Unfortunately, legitimising beliefs typically shift much or all the blame for low status or limited opportunity onto the population itself. This has the dual effect of reducing the high-status group's responsibility to rectify the problem ('they bring it on themselves') and can also generate a perception that such interventions are unlikely to be successful ('we could try to help, but …').

THE ROLE OF SOCIAL NORMS AND CONFORMITY EFFECTS

Before we move on from prejudice, it is worth noting that it is, by its very nature, a socially held belief. As such, it becomes part of the norms of society. This means that all the various processes in play which help reinforce norms amongst people also act to maintain a given prejudicial belief. As we will see in the *social influence* theme, group norms are often very difficult to overcome, and standing up against them can carry considerable risks for the individual(s) involved. You can find a fuller discussion of these effects in the following chapter.

CRITICAL SPOTLIGHT: INGROUP LOVE OR OUTGROUP HATE?

As we have seen from work on group psychology, one common device groups use is to generate a positive evaluation of the ingroup relative to the outgroup. One key question is whether this tendency is driven (and/or expressed by) a desire to promote and enhance the ingroup ('ingroup love') or diminish and derogate the outgroup ('outgroup hate'). Psychologist Marilynn Brewer (1999) conducted a review of the social psychological literature to see what the evidence points to. Her conclusion? Most intergroup behaviour is driven by a desire to enhance the ingroup, and drivers such as positive differentiation, sensitivity to threat and distrust can be present without outgroup hate. Although this sounds relatively benign, it's important to note that not getting something (a coveted job, access to education, a smile when passing someone) because another is trying to enhance an ingroup you are not a member of can be seen as functionally the same as being denied it because someone is actively out to get you! Equally, once groups are in conflict, some behaviours are also driven by a desire to derogate the outgroup directly.

MANAGING INTERGROUP RELATIONSHIPS

When groups get along, good things happen. Ideas, customs and practices are exchanged, new friendships can bloom and the world can be a richer place. However, as we have seen, intergroup relations can be highly problematic. Given this, ways of improving such relations have been the subject of much research. The majority of work in this area can broadly categorised as revolving around *intergroup contact*, *attempts to recategorise groups*, or making the *pursuit of positive intergroup relationships* itself normative.

CONTACT THEORY

Poor intergroup relations are characterised by negative/damaging contact between members of each group, and/or by little contact at all. For instance, in apartheid South Africa different ethnic groups interacted almost solely in situations where the power balance was discriminatory (i.e. boss/labourer) or in instances of intergroup conflict (situations involving crime or protest). The apartheid system forced these groups apart from one another most of the rest of the time. While this sounds extreme, many metropolitan areas across the world feature fairly closed local communities which have limited contact with the rest of their societies. While contact between groups can of course increase intergroup tension, much research also shows that, if managed properly, it can be a key ingredient for reducing conflict.

The dominant theoretical approach in this area is *contact theory*, developed by Gordon Allport (Allport, 1954b). This approach argues that contact between two groups can reduce prejudice, reduce intergroup discrimination and improve intergroup relations. It is most likely to have these effects if four key conditions are met. Specifically, Allport argued that intergroup relations should take place in situations where people have *equal status*. When this is not the case the power imbalance makes it likely that the lower-status group will feel (or actually be) relatively exploited. Of course, in the majority of intergroup situations where there is conflict, a degree of status imbalance is present, and changing the status quo is both hard to achieve and unlikely in a short timeframe. However, Allport argues (and subsequent research also supports e.g. Cohen, 1982) that it is within the contact *situation* that status is the important determinant of the level of success. The second factor associated with good contact is the presence of a *common goal*. When people from both groups must work together they become more likely to set aside their differences: as we will see when we review evidence supporting the contact hypothesis, the use of common goals can be a powerful tool to reduce conflict. It's also important to recognise that these common goals require *co-operation* between groups to be present (rather than goals being pursued alone or competitively). Finally, contact theory argues that the contact situation (and its purpose) must *receive the support of higher authorities*. Specifically, authorities must make clear that no prejudice and discrimination will be tolerated and enable the acceptance of positive intergroup contact as the norm. This support can include formal legislation (for instance, employment law preventing discrimination). It can be an explicit part of *political philosophy* (for instance, multiculturalism is an ideology arguing diversity should be celebrated and everyone valued, which feeds into how state services including education in the UK are organised). It can also refer to social and organisational leaders (for instance, work gang bosses and religious leaders) and organisational policies (for instance, formal policies around discrimination or the use of derogatory language). These factors are important as they encourage change in social norms of behaviour which, as we have seen, are a strong determinant of intergroup relations. Indeed, once such norms are established, an individual going against them can find *themselves* the target of derogation.

Contact theory was widely applied during the desegregation of black and white school children in the US school system – a process which started in 1954 and, many argue, is still in its final stages today (as recently as 2016, a Mississippi school district was mandated by court to effectively desegregate its schools). More recent investigations into contact theory suggest that even if actual person-to-person contact is not possible, the principles can still be used to reduce intergroup prejudice. For instance, the *extended contact hypothesis* argues that if someone you know and like has positive contact with an outgroup member, this can 'spill over' into an increase in your own positive evaluation of the outgroup (Wright et al., 1997). Indeed, it may even be the case that even imagining positive interactions with outgroup members can lead to improvements in evaluations (this *imagined contact effect* was first described by Crisp & Turner, 2009).

CATEGORISATION APPROACHES

An alternative approach to contact is to ask group members to think about how they categorise themselves and others and encourage the use of more beneficial categorisations. For instance, making people think less about groups and more about individuals (*decategorisation*) may reduce the effect of stereotypes on interpersonal relationships (see Miller & Brewer, 1984). At a group level, the *common ingroup identity model* argues that if a common identity can be found which both groups have in common, and people can be persuaded to adopt this identity, prejudice can be reduced (see Gaertner et al., 1989). For instance, appealing to a *national identity* may reduce perceived differences between groups on the basis of *social class*. Of course, people are heavily invested in their existing identities and this shift can be hard to achieve. The principles of contact theory come into play here. These approaches seem to be most effective when people can maintain their lower-level identities (known as *subordinate* categorisations) while endorsing the higher-level (*super-ordinate*) identities. This idea is developed in the *mutual differentiation model* (see Hornsey & Hogg, 2000). In contrast to drawing on such levels of abstraction, using multiple identities is a key feature of various *cross-categorisation models* (Hewstone, Islam & Judd, 1993). For instance, in the context of problematic relationships between people in Bangladesh and India who were either Muslims or Hindus, Hewstone, Islam & Judd (1993) observed that highlighting common group membership (i.e. religion) reduced prejudice generated by differences in the other (i.e. nationality). Usually, communality in one category has a greater effect than communality in the other (i.e., religion may reduce cross-nationality bias, but shared nationality may not help with cross-religious tensions).

CHALLENGES TO CONFLICT REDUCTION

Although a number of models have been developed, improving intergroup relationships is not easy. As discussed above, individuals are highly invested in their social identities and any change to norms, superior ingroup status or distinctiveness can generate resistance (see Chapter 6 for how this may be expressed). Even people who attempt to improve their attitudes and behaviours in public may encounter difficulties unless they've also privately endorsed the change. Specifically, attempting to suppress thoughts with which society disagrees (for instance, prejudicial ones) can lead them to get stronger (*rebound effects*; see Wegner, 1989). Contact and cross-categorisation approaches can often also fall prey to '*subtyping effects*' associated with stereotype change (see above).

THE *ROBBER'S CAVE* STUDY

Many of the ideas around contact theory and categorisation approaches were explored in a single seminal study by Sherif and colleagues (Sherif et al., 1961). The *Robber's Cave* study involved taking 11-year-old boys to the summer camp bearing the same name. The study was split into three distinct phases. Before the study began the boys were split (unbeknown to them) into two groups. Each group was bussed separately to locations within the camping area. They were unaware of each other at this point. In the *group attachment* phase, the experimenters had each group of children generate a name for themselves – one group called themselves the 'Rattlers' and another the 'Eagles'. The experimenters helped individuals generate group identity through activities such as creating a group symbol, flag and T-shirts. The children also took part in a variety of games and fun activities. The second phase of the study was to generate *intergroup competition*. During this phase, the children were made aware of the presence of the other group and a number of intergroup competitions were set up (for instance swimming, tug-of-war and camp-building competitions). The winners of these contests received highly valued prizes (including medals and, perhaps somewhat naively given what was to come, pocket knives!). Group competition turned nasty fairly quickly. Group members called one another names, refused to eat with outgroup members, stole prizes that had been awarded to the outgroup during 'cabin raids' and also engaged in clearly identity-relevant behaviours such as flag burning. They generated stereotypes of the other group members, including derogatory attributes (in particular, arguing that all members of the group 'smelled bad'). A number of physical altercations between group members were also narrowly avoided. Interestingly, it seemed that individual group members who wanted cross-group friendships were also derogated.

During the first two attempts the research team had at undertaking this study, the intergroup conflict escalated so far that the experimenters were forced to end the camp (and the experiment) early! During the third attempt, however, participants reached the final phase of the study – *intergroup reconciliation*. During this phase, the experimenters initially devised events which were not competitive (such as firework shows) which both groups attended. Perhaps unsurprisingly, they did little to reduce intergroup tension. Finally, the experimenters set up a number of tasks which required both groups to work together – for instance, preparing the water supply to the camp and rescuing from a ditch the truck that was carrying everybody's food. Undertaking these tasks could be seen, from a contact theory point of view, to be delivering authority-supported, mutual-status, interdependent and frequent contact. Following these tasks, positive evaluations of outgroup members increased and intergroup relations thawed. Seating at meals became less divided by group affiliation (and, in contrast to previous meals, most of the food was eaten rather than thrown around!). Somewhat touchingly, at the end of the camp most of the children travelled back to their home city in one bus, and the children did not sit on the bus as 'Rattlers' and 'Eagles' but as a single group.

The *Robber's Cave* study is an experimental demonstration of many of the processes we have discussed so far in this chapter. Many lessons learnt (for instance, the importance of teamworking and superordinate goals) have both set the research agenda and influenced practical interventions for over 60 years. However, we can also critically evaluate it on a number of fronts. One key issue is that the sample was relatively unique (middle-class 11-year-old boys) and the situation somewhat contrived (many, but not all, real intergroup conflicts involve competition over resources such as prizes, and few involve artificially generated groups with no history). The general model used in the study has been replicated in other populations and settings and findings are generally similar (see e.g. Fisher, 1990), although transporting them to more complex, long-standing conflicts can be difficult (Maoz, 2000), and changes to the set-up of the study can change the outcome significantly (e.g. Tyerman & Spencer, 1983). Finally, from a contemporary ethical standpoint, the study raises questions: it's unclear whether either the children or their parents/guardians could realistically have known what the camping trip held for them, or if the same findings could have generated in a lower-risk/harm way. Setting these issues aside, the study still represents a highly detailed, rich environment which closely resembles actual social situations. Its impact has also been enormous – replications and discussion of it continue to this day, and the original research itself is still a core part of every university course on social psychology.

ACCULTURATION PSYCHOLOGY

Throughout history, people from different cultural backgrounds have been, by choice or circumstance, brought together. Movements of large numbers of people from one cultural context to another have also been common. For example, primarily European pioneers lived along-side and eventually displaced indigenous Americans. This population was in turn joined by others – for instance, the Chinese population living within America increased by around 300,000 between 1849 and 1880, eventually making up around 10 per cent of the population of California. In the UK, large waves of immigration from former Commonwealth countries, and from European neighbours such as Poland, have been a consistent feature of the country's changing demographic. The study of the strategies that people within these cultures use to interact with each other is called *acculturation psychology*.

The dominant model in the study of acculturation is Berry's (1978) *bi-dimensional model* (e.g. Berry, 1997). This argues that immigrants to a culture can decide how much they want to integrate in terms of *contact* (spending time with host-culture members or not) and *cultural maintenance* (the extent to which they maintain their own cultural customs and practices). When people are low in a desire for contact and high in desire for cultural maintenance, they are adopting a strategy referred to as *separation*. This is obviously not a good outcome for intergroup relations, but it is linked to relatively low levels of *acculturative stress* (perceived difficulty and the resultant stress that arises as a result of intercultural interactions). The opposite situation, where high levels of contact and low levels of maintenance are desired, is referred to as *assimilation*. Assimilating individuals discard their old identity and exclusively adopt that of the new host culture. Between these two, *integration* refers to high levels of contact coupled with a desire to maintain one's own customs – the identity of being 'African American' being a good example. Finally, when someone has low desire for contact but also low desire for maintenance they can be described as undertaking a *marginalisation* strategy (which is linked to poor mental health). A given group is thought to have a general tendency towards one of the strategies. However, individuals may also choose a different strategy from that of the group as a whole. A study of 5000 immigrant youths, across 13 countries, suggests that integration is the most frequently used strategy, followed by separation, assimilation and, least frequently pursued, a strategy of marginalisation (Berry et al. 2006).

In the same way that incoming cultures tend to adopt a particular strategy, so the host culture has a particular preference. The host culture can adopt a *segregation* strategy, where there is little desire for contact with, and little expectation of change from, the newcomers (ghettoisation is a good example of the result of this). The host culture can also expect high levels of contact and high levels of maintenance (i.e. *multiculturalism*) or high levels of contact and low levels of cultural maintenance (the idea of *a melting-pot*). Finally, the group can expect immigrants to not maintain their own culture and also have little contact with the host culture – a strategy of *exclusion*. These preferences are usually expressed through legislation (what citizenship entails, people's rights, etc.), custom and practice (for instance, which holidays are celebrated), and social institutions (for instance, schooling practices). When the incoming culture's preference matches with that of the host culture, more harmonious relationships are (generally!) expected.

A related area of study focuses on a phenomenon called the '*acculturation gap*'. Typically, children and adolescents adapt far quicker to a new society than do their parents. This can leave a gap between how acculturated one generation is compared with the next. Given that some estimates suggest around one in five children in the US are from immigrant families, it's important to understand what impact this may have. Larger acculturation gaps have been linked with greater levels of parental conflict, higher levels of drug and alcohol use, and conduct problems (e.g. Schofield et al., 2008; Myers et al., 2009).

LIMITATIONS OF THE BI-DIMENSIONAL APPROACH.

One of the main controversies in this area of research is the legitimacy of using a bi-dimensional model of acculturation (such as Berry's; see Rudmin, 2003). Defining four strategies can be seen as suggesting that no other alternatives exist. It also implies that a given individual will consistently follow one strategy exclusively over a given time, or that they apply the same strategy to all areas of their lives. But, for instance, migrants may display one particular strategy at work and another during their personal lives. Some early research in this area also had some serious limitations. For instance, methodological problems – the practice of taking a 'median split' and then categorising people into absolute categories (rather than higher or lower on a given dimension) – can lead to an artificial reduction in within-group variance. In layperson's terms this means that you may observe apparent differences between groups which are due to the methodology rather than a reflection of reality. Despite these problems, acculturation psychology is a thriving area and Berry's model continues to dominate the field. It has been used to understand large-scale shifts in populations and has influenced the creation of social systems to facilitate effective acculturation. It's also been used to highlight potentially at-risk migrant groups, so they can receive the support they need.

CHAPTER SUMMARY

In this chapter, we have taken an overview of the key areas of group psychology. We have seen that the process of group formation and dissolution can be argued to have stages which involve conflict within groups (a theme we pick up on when we discuss persuasion). We've also seen how psychological processes such as stereotyping and prejudice can keep groups apart. This focus on the more negative side of social psychology is perhaps driven by a desire to address social problems – sometimes at the expense of the study of more positive aspects of intergroup relations. Indeed, many groups do get along harmoniously, and the study of intergroup contact and acculturation both highlight how this desirable state can be achieved. Social groups also play a part in many (if not most) of the other areas of this book. For instance, persuasion and conformity (which we pick up in the next theme) can often involve social norms, and prejudices may feed directly into impression formation (see Chapter 4). When reading (or rereading) other chapters of this book, consider how the group processes we have discussed here may impact the processes under discussion, and ask yourself if any process is completely 'individual'-level in nature.

KEY CHAPTER POINTS

- Groups serve a number of important psychological functions, and social norms are an integral part of their composition.
- Stigmatisation and prejudice is maintained via legitimising beliefs, and has mixed effects on self-esteem.
- Stereotypes can be thought of as expectancies of a group, and can be both self-fulfilling and difficult to change.

- Contact theory argues that key features of a contact situation increase the likelihood of a reduction in intergroup conflict. This is supported by studies including the *Robber's Cave* study.
- Acculturation psychology suggests the level of desired intergroup contact and origin-culture maintenance, and predicts acculturation style and psychological outcomes.

SUGGESTED FURTHER READING

1. Brown, R. (2001). *Group processes*. Oxford: Blackwell Publishing.
2. Bar-Tal, D. (ed) (2010). *Intergroup conflicts and their resolution: A social psychological perspective*. New York: Psychology Press.
3. Nguyen, H.-H. D., & Ryan, A. M. (2008). Does stereotype threat affect test performance of minorities and women? A meta-analysis of experimental evidence. *Journal of Applied Psychology, 93*, 1314–1334.
4. Chun, K. M., Organista, P. B., & Marin, G. (eds) (2003) *Acculturation: advances in theory, measurement and applied research*. Washington, DC: American Psychological Association.

THEME SUMMARY: SOCIAL RELATIONSHIPS

Over this theme, we have explored how people relate to one another. At an interpersonal level, we have looked at how we understand other people's behaviour, how we form impressions and relationships, and how both our verbal and non-verbal behaviour influences others. We have also explored group psychology, examining how groups form and how they guide our cognition and behaviour. We've also examined how intergroup conflict can arise, be maintained and, hopefully, be resolved. A number of threads run through these discussions. We see that people rarely operate as truly independent units – the social norms we carry have a tremendous influence on our lives. We've also seen that we value consistency. Once we have formed a first impression or a stereotype they can be hard (but not impossible!) to change. Across both these chapters, it is clear that social relationships can often be challenging to negotiate – both at an individual and a group level. However, we've also discussed how vital they are – and how we are truly 'social' beings.

SOCIAL INFLUENCE

THEME OVERVIEW

How would you behave if told to do something you fundamentally disagreed with? How do revolutionary movements overturn the opinions of the society they exist in? When you see an advert promoting a new product, how good are you at separating the facts from the marketing spiel? Do others invigorate you to work harder, or do you just blend in and slack off? All of these phenomena can broadly be understood as instances where *social influence* comes into play.

In many ways, the study of social influence encompasses all of social psychology. Recall that the impact of the 'actual, imagined or implied' presence of others is part of how we define the field. In essence, when someone's actions (or something which signifies such actions) changes how someone else *thinks*, *feels* or *behaves*, you can argue social influence has taken place. As such, our discussion of social influence encompasses almost every page of this book. However, we can also narrow the discussion by looking at how people change the intended behaviour of others (which we discuss in Chapter 6, 'Conformity and obedience') and how we are both recipients of, and targets for, people's attempts to change our opinions on a given issue (explored in Chapter 7, 'Persuasion').

Across these two chapters we will explore how, why and when we conform to others' demands, the effects of groups on our performance, how society deals with people who won't conform to the prevailing view and how such minorities can cause major social shifts. We also explore the theory and practice of persuasion by investigating the extent to which we are rational thinkers, how irrelevant information such as mood and colour influence us, and how the science of persuasion is applied to marketing and public policy.

As you read this, consider the sources of social influence in your own life and, perhaps, the ways in which you also exert your own influence on your social world.

6

CONFORMITY AND OBEDIENCE

CONFORMITY VERSUS OBEDIENCE

We can all think of times when we tried to get someone to behave the way we wanted them to. We can also think of times we may have conformed to comply with other people's expectations. This chapter will examine the processes underlying conformity and obedience. *Obedience* is typically defined as following orders from someone in authority. Importantly, when someone is obedient they do not necessarily have to *agree* with the behaviour – rather, they must *comply* with it. Obedience can be a useful process: many organisations require that people do what they need to even if they don't always agree with the actions (consider what would happen if a school full of children could do exactly what they liked!). However, as we will see, it can also lead to people behaving in ways that they feel very uncomfortable with – to the point that their actions clash with their core moral values.

In contrast to obedience, *conformity* is usually seen as behaving in line with the way the group wishes or expects (i.e. the social norms the group has; see Chapter 5). Again, conformity has many benefits: recall that Festinger argued that having a sense of *social reality* (which requires conformity to some extent) is an important part of 'being a group', with all the psychological benefits that come with that.

In this chapter, we'll examine ideas around conformity and obedience by looking at a number of classic studies exploring how people conform, and are obedient to, authorities in groups. We will also look at how groups can influence one to behave differently (for instance, by working harder or becoming more extreme in one's opinions) and how we respond to people who fail to conform. Finally, we will explore how minorities can sometimes not only not conform but also change the social norms of the majority.

CLASSIC STUDIES IN CONFORMITY

SHERIF AND THE AUTOKINETIC EFFECT

One of the earliest experimental demonstrations of conformity was conducted by Muzafer Sherif (see Sherif, 1936; 1937, for a review) and was based on the *autokinetic effect*. The autokinetic effect is a visual illusion where a spot of light in a dark room appears to move when, in reality, it is stationary. Sherif observed that participants typically saw the dot moving when viewing it *by themselves* – usually estimating movement of around 10–20cm. Individuals tended to be fairly self-consistent in their estimates. Sherif then asked people to do the same task in groups. He observed conformity arising naturally: people's estimates tended to converge around a developing group norm. People whose estimate was lower than the norm tended to increase it over time, whereas people who thought the dot was moving a lot tended to reduce their estimate. Sherif argued that this was because, in ambiguous situations, people use social information to make judgements – they conform to what other people are thinking. Interestingly, participants claimed to be unaware of these changes – all also denying that the judgements of the other people had influenced their own when asked at the end of the experiment. There are a few important features of this study which are worth bearing in mind. First, the situation meant that conformity was very likely. There is no 'right' or 'wrong' answer in this study, and it was hard for participants to gauge how well they were doing. It's also interesting to think about the fact that individuals did not solely conform to the view of one other person – instead, Sherif observed a tendency for the group to converge on a group norm. Whether this is conformity or rather some form of *group decision-making* is unclear. However, what this work did show was that people generate and then adjust their behaviour in line with social norms. As such, it was highly influential and prompted many other researchers to investigate the idea of conformity. Most prominent of the subsequent investigations were perhaps those conducted by Solomon Asch and colleagues (Asch, Solomon & Guetzkow, 1951).

THE ASCH PARADIGM

The *Asch paradigm* was developed to demonstrate conformity in situations where the right and wrong answers were unambiguous. Asch had participants look at three lines of (obviously) different lengths. The participants' task was to say which line was the same length as a fourth *target line*. When asked to do this task alone, participants' accuracy rate was greater than 99 per cent – all participants got the task right almost all the time. However, the purpose of the experiment was to see what would happen when an individual participant was faced with several other participants who gave a *clearly wrong* answer. In reality, all but one of the participants in every run of the experiment were *confederates* – effectively acting as stooges who were trained to give the same (wrong) answer in 12 specific trials (out of 18 trials in total). In each trial, the participant was asked to give their answer *after* hearing the wrong responses of the confederates. Asch was interested in how the actual participant responded in these 12 'wrong answer' trials (known as *critical trials*). The results were pretty startling: over the whole study, 36.8 per cent of responses in these trials conformed to the incorrect group; 5 per cent of participants always followed the crowd, 25 per cent always ignored it and the remaining 70 per cent conformed some but not all the time (so 75 per cent of people conformed at some point). Why might people behave in this way?

Asch interviewed his participants to try to understand the motivations for conforming (or not). He identified themes in his participants' responses, including people being highly confident (or not) in their judgements (remember, this task is objectively easy) and wanting to be normative. This latter motivation led to conformity even when participants felt everyone else was being intentionally wrong for some reason. Asch also undertook many variations on his paradigm. For instance, he observed that increasing the number of confederates from one to two or three increased levels of conformity substantially. However, increases above three didn't further increase conformity (in fact, it seems that conformity reduced when the groups got too large, perhaps because the situation became unbelievable!). Asch also observed that having a single confederate who gave the correct answer during the critical trials decreased participants' conformity with those giving incorrect answers – in some instances reducing the number of conforming participants to just 5 per cent (we will see more about the effect of minorities defying majorities later in this chapter). Asch also argued that the conformity rates seemed to increase when the task was made more difficult, when people perceived the confederate as attractive and amongst people with low self-esteem.

Asch's research around conformity *seems* to provide unequivocal evidence that conformity is widespread. At no point in the trial were participants told that they had to conform to what others did, or that the group members were interdependent in any way. It also seems that conformity occurred even when the group members were people that participants didn't know, had spent no time with beforehand and were unlikely to spend much time with in the future. Perhaps most importantly, the study demonstrated a situation in which people conformed to something they knew was not right. However, there are also some important limitations of this study. The social milieu it was conducted in (1950s America) was one in which conformity was relatively highly valued. It also represents an unreal situation – people may have felt their performance during task was unimportant, and as such that the cost of not 'going along with the crowd' probably outweighed the cost of being incorrect. It could be argued that in real-life situations where the stakes are higher, we would expect less conformity. This is an issue we will explore in the next two classic research programmes that we highlight, *Milgram's obedience studies* and the *Zimbardo prison study*.

CRITICAL SPOTLIGHT: NORMATIVE OR SOCIAL INFLUENCE?

Asch understood his paradigm to show that people want to conform in order to garner social approval, and to avoid disapproval or punishment from others. As such, Asch argued, conformity is very much an individual-level response. In other words, conformity is a result of an individual's thinking and actions in relation to other individuals. An alternative way of understanding this is from a social identity perspective. Turner et al. (1987) argue that these conformity effects can instead be seen as a result of *group categorisation* – people see themselves as a group member and, as a result, adopt the norms of the group. This approach would argue that perhaps the task was not as unambiguous as it appeared to researchers and those outside the situation. If this was the case, it is entirely possible that adopting this group norm could also have changed people's belief about what was the correct answer. We'll see how this social categorisation account of group influence can be applied to other classic conformity studies further in this chapter. In the meantime, do *you* think people *believed* that the erroneous line was a different length in Asch's paradigm? Or did they just behave as if they did?

THE DARKER SIDE OF CONFORMITY: MILGRAM AND ZIMBARDO

As we noted above, much early research into conformity was driven by a desire to understand how some individuals who were involved in World War II (on both sides) were prepared to act in terrible ways to fellow human beings. Many war criminals tried for their crimes in the aftermath of this conflict rested their defence on the fact that they were 'only following orders'. The sense of blind obedience to authority was something that Stanley Milgram wanted to explore. Was it possible that the terrible events of that period were, even in part, a result of people just mindlessly behaving in the way they were told to? And, if so, what implications would that have for the way society responds to such individuals?

THE MILGRAM STUDIES

Milgram attempted to address these questions by constructing experimental paradigms during which one individual would inflict (they believed) actual pain on another, at the request of an authority figure (Milgram, 1963). The basic design of the study was that participants first met with the experimenter and another person they believed to be a second participant (in reality, a confederate). In this meeting there were 'randomly' assigned to a role as either a *teacher* or a *learner*. The allocation was fixed such that the participant was always the teacher. The group then moved to another room, where the learner was strapped into something similar to an electric chair; the teacher was informed that this was to ensure they could not escape. The teacher was then escorted to another room, this one containing an impressive-looking (but sham) 'electric shock generator', with a variable voltage dial. The participant was led to believe that the purpose of the study was to test the effects of electric shocks on memory. After receiving a small shock themselves as a demonstration, the teacher read the learner a list of pairs of words. The learner was then required to complete the word pairs when prompted by the teacher. Each time the learner got this wrong, the teacher was required to deliver an electric shock (increasing by 15 volts each time). After every shock, the teacher could hear through the wall the learner's (actually pre-recorded) pained response. Each time a shock was given these responses increased in distress. As the voltage approached 135 volts, the learner began to bang on the wall and complain about a medical condition. Eventually, all noise from the learner ceased (including answers, which the teacher was required by the experimenter to meet with further electric shocks).

How did participants respond to this task? Prior to undertaking the experiment, Milgram asked psychology students how many people they thought would deliver the maximum shock voltage. On average, those surveyed thought only 1.2 per cent of participants would do so. In contrast, most participants delivered shocks up to the 135V level.

At this point, many participants began to question the purpose of the experiment. If a participant queried the effects of the shocks on the learner, they were told that they 'would not be responsible' and to 'carry on' by the experimenter. Whenever participants wanted to halt the experiment, there were given a set of standardised prompts to continue (e.g. 'the experiment requires that you continue' or 'you have no other choice, you must go on'). The experiment only ended when participants had been prompted in this way four times and asked to stop the fifth time, or when they had given a 450V shock to the learner three times. In the initial series of studies using this paradigm, 65 per cent of the original 40 participants delivered a 450V electric shock to the learner. However, all participants questioned the purpose of the study, and many had very strong psychological responses. Milgram reports attempts of participants trying to bargain their way out of the study ('I'll give you the fee I was going to be paid back'), and also participants experiencing severe physical signs of psychological distress including trembling, stuttering, nervous laughter, lip biting and even seizures.

What did Milgram conclude from this? In describing the results of his research, Milgram later described the response of one participant by saying that 'What is extraordinary is his apparent total indifference to the learner' and noting his 'robotic impassivity'. He also argued that his studies showed that 'Stark authority was pitted against the subjects' strongest moral imperatives against hurting others, and, with the subjects' ears ringing with the screams of the victims, authority won more often than not' (Milgram, 1973, p. 76). These views reflect Milgram's *agentic state* interpretation of his findings – specifically, that when people feel that they have been reduced to a tool being used to achieve someone else's ends, they absolve themselves of responsibility for their own actions, and see little opportunity to influence events. Once this occurs, Milgram argues, people become highly obedient. In this way, people are able to do horrific things to one another because they are 'following orders', thinking themselves unaccountable and unable to do anything else. However, other interpretations of these findings have also been offered (see the Critical Spotlight, 'Milgram Misunderstood?').

Regardless of the 'whys' surrounding participants' behaviour during these studies, Milgram's work does suggest that within all individuals is a potential for behaving in terrible ways. However, it could be argued that such effects may not be so apparent in more ecologically valid situations, or in situations where people have the opportunity to discuss and deliberate with others the rights and wrongs of a given action. One study that attempted to explore obedience and conformity, and its effects on individuals' capacity for both 'evil' and 'resistance', in such a context was Zimbardo's (in)famous *Stanford prison experiment* (Haney, Banks & Zimbardo, 1973).

CRITICAL SPOTLIGHT: MILGRAM MISUNDERSTOOD?

Perhaps unsurprisingly, in the half-century plus since Milgram's research was undertaken it has received considerable critical attention, and alternative explanations for the effects have been offered. For instance, in contrast to the situational focus of Milgram, Blass (1991) suggests *personality* plays a role in obedience. The effects have been attributed to so-called *demand characteristics* of research: it could be that participants obeyed the experimenter not because they were obedient to authority but because they felt the experimenter had more knowledge about how the learning was faring – i.e. the experimenter was *trusted* rather than *obeyed*. This may spring from an *enduring belief* that authority figures are usually benevolent (as opposed to malevolent).

More recently, social identity researchers have suggested people may have actively identified with the *goals* of the experiment in the Milgram paradigm. Rather than blind or ineffectual individuals, they become *engaged followers* of the experimenter. These researchers point to evidence gleaned from conceptual replications of the study, and the archives of the experiment itself, suggesting that the participants were much more likely to comply with the request to continue when it was framed as an ideological request ('The experiment requires you to continue', invoking the positive value of science and the participant's contribution to it) than when they were 'ordered' to continue (Haslam & Reicher, 2017; Haslam, Reicher & Birney, 2014). What do these alternative interpretations imply in terms of the accountability of war criminals that we described at the start of this chapter?

THE STANFORD PRISON STUDY

The Stanford prison study is perhaps one of the most infamous psychological experiments ever undertaken. The aim of the study was to see how people behaved in line with expectations surrounding social roles. In the study, 24 male participants were recruited. They were mostly white and middle class. All of them were considered to be psychologically healthy. Half of these participants were assigned to be 'prisoners' and half to be 'prison guards'. The prisoners were dressed in uncomfortable clothes, given a number with which to identify themselves in place of their name, and, after being realistically mock-arrested by the local police, incarcerated in a mock jail built in the basement of the university. Those assigned to the guard role were dressed in prison guard attire (khaki shirts and trousers, dark sunglasses which prevented eye contact) and equipped with batons. Zimbardo himself played the role of 'prison governor'. It was anticipated that the study would last for two weeks. The guards were told that they should not physically harm the participants or prevent them from having food and drink. However, they were encouraged to instil a sense of fear and powerlessness in their charges, to meet their goal of maintaining good order in the 'prison'.

The study rapidly generated extreme experiences for everybody involved. After an initial protest by the prisoners which involved them blockading their cells, the guards escalated the frequency and severity of the disciplinary measures – prisoners were made to defecate and urinate in a bucket (as opposed to using the designated toilets), were roundly abused verbally, had their mattresses removed such that they had to sleep on the floor and, in some cases, had their clothing confiscated so that they were left naked. Push-ups were used as a form of physical punishment, as were demands that prisoners count out loud for hours at a time. The guards also attempted to divide the prisoners by offering better conditions to those who co-operated with the new regime. The prisoners themselves underwent considerable psychological distress: just 36 hours into the study one prisoner became extremely upset and began to, in the words of the research team, 'act crazy'. Although this participant was withdrawn from the study, the remaining prisoners were not, and the study continued. Other prisoners displayed behaviours such as hysterical crying, disorganised thinking and other symptoms of extreme distress, and some were subsequently released. Still the study continued. When a new 'prisoner' was brought into the prison, he almost immediately expressed concern about the treatment of the participants already there. The guards responded by placing him in solitary confinement. In turn, he went on a hunger strike. As the study progressed, the guards became more and more tyrannical and the prisoners (on the whole) increasingly broken and submissive.

Why was the study not stopped? One account (offered by the researchers) is that everybody, including Zimbardo himself, lost perspective on what was going on. Some events support this notion: at one point, the guards believed that a prisoner who had been previously freed was coming back in an attempt to release his fellow inmates. In circumstances which may seem surreal to us now, Zimbardo and the other guards responded by attempting to get the participants who were prisoners moved to an *actual* jail. When this failed, they physically disassembled, transported and rebuilt the prison in a different part of the building, and moved the prisoners! Zimbardo stayed behind to explain to the returning participant that the other 'prisoners' had been freed and the experiment terminated. The situation got even more bizarre when a priest visited the prison, was told the participants were in fact prisoners and suggested they needed to get a lawyer to 'escape'. The priest went on to call the parents of several of the participants, who in turn actually appointed lawyers to go and defend their children! The study was ended six days after it began, but only when a PhD student (Christina Maslach, whom Zimbardo eventually married) objected to the conduct of the study.

How did the participants feel about their experiences, and what are the theoretical explanations for the findings? Following the study, many of the guards expressed surprise and disappointment that they were able to behave in the sadistic way that they had (or had failed to stop others behaving that way). Many of the prisoners reported that the emotional after-effects of the study lasted well beyond the six days it went on for. The traditional explanation for the behaviour of both groups is that participants adopted the various roles that they were supposed to – of guards and prisoners. Additionally, Zimbardo became sucked into his own role as prison governor, which eclipsed his duties as an experimental investigator and, more importantly, his duty of care towards all the participants in the study. This account assumes that participants became *depersonalised* and *deindividuated*, acting out their roles rather than taking responsibility for their own behaviours.

However, this account is not without its critics. For instance, one guard (arguably the most brutal of the bunch) suggested that he had behaved in the way had to give the researchers interesting data to work with (a form of *demand characteristics*). One prisoner has also made similar assertions. Moreover, the lack of scientific control, the role of the chief researcher in the research process (and his influence in directing the guards' behaviour), the small sample size and issues around recruiting people who actively wanted to experience 'prison life' all generate problems when it comes to understanding what the results of the study mean.

BEYOND ZIMBARDO: THE BBC PRISON STUDY

A notable investigation which followed the Stanford prison study was the *BBC prison study*. Undertaken by Stephen Reicher and Alex Haslam in 2006, this TV series attempted to replicate some aspects of the Stanford prison research, but with much tighter ethical controls (for instance, constant monitoring of participants' well-being by an independent panel) and events planned to test specific hypotheses. The BBC prison study played out very differently from Zimbardo's work. In particular, prisoners were offered the chance to be 'promoted' to guard status. This aimed to test the hypothesis, derived from *social identity theory*, that some participants would pursue an individual-based strategy, while others would work collectively to overcome the guards' dominance of them. The study also revealed that the guards experienced considerable discomfort about their roles (a form of cognitive dissonance) – although none felt this way strongly enough to switch places with the prisoners! It also highlighted the power of (seemingly powerless) people to overcome a dominant majority: three days into the study the prisoners engaged in collective civil disobedience which effectively disempowered the guards. There was then an attempt to generate a commune between guards and prisoners, but this failed. At this point new, self appointed, guards decided to take matters into their own hands by increasing the severity of allowable punishments, and enforcing their own rules. The BBC prison study was ended three days after it began to avoid these escalations following the path of the Stanford prison study. Although this study received considerable criticism from Zimbardo himself, Haslam and Reicher argue that this study was *not* a replication of the Stanford study, but also that the events which took place highlight different interpretations of the Stanford study findings – namely that people do not simply 'live a role' but engage in collective behaviours governed by a group's motivations, social norms and identity-based concerns. Haslam and Reicher also highlight the power of minorities, and the fact that identities are *shared* between two groups rather than simply held by one (see Haslam & Reicher, 2007, and Reicher & Haslam, 2006, for the authors' reviews of this research, and Zimbardo, 2006, for his critique of it).

CRITICAL SPOTLIGHT: ETHICS IN RESEARCH

Both the Milgram study and the Stanford prison experiment raise serious questions about the ethics of conformity research. In both cases, the behaviours that participants engaged in, or were subjected to, had a lasting psychological impact. Milgram reports participants writing to him to tell him that their experiences of administering electric shocks deeply affected them – some negatively but also some positively (in that they felt aware of the potential within themselves). Zimbardo observed similar effects in the short term, but also reported that his participants had no long-term adverse effects from taking part in the study.

The main ethical issues around the studies are (i) *informed consent*: it's unclear whether or not participants understood the severity of the experience they were signing up for; (ii) the *right to withdraw*: in both studies it was implied that participants could not stop once the experiment had begun, degrading their right to withdraw; and (iii) protecting the *dignity and well-being* of participants: in both studies it seems participants were placed in harm's way either physically or psychologically.

Lessons learnt from these studies have informed modern psychological ethical practice: truly informed consent, the avoidance of undue coercion or influence to continue taking part in a study, the management and minimisation of risk, and immediate and effective debriefing are all cornerstones of contemporary ethical practice.

SOCIAL INFLUENCE AS A TWO-WAY STREET

Much of the research we have discussed so far has concentrated on group members conforming to a perceived group norm, or a figure of authority. In doing so, it assumes that influence is something which happens *to* group members, without really considering how they themselves affect the group. Indeed, social influence is a two-way street – with people acting as both sources and recipients of attitude-changing efforts (Moscovici, 1976). We will shortly see how groups respond to members who 'break the rules' and also how minority group members can overturn majority opinions (i.e. have *minority influence*). Before that, we'll see how group members can influence one another to become more extreme through the process of *group polarisation*. After reading this section, think back to the Zimbardo prison study – how do you think these theories can be applied to the findings?

GROUP POLARISATION

Group polarisation is said to occur when a group's final attitudinal position is more extreme than one would expect from the original, pre-discussion attitudes of its members. Original work in this area by Stoner (1968) involved participants rating how riskily they would act in a particular situation, and then discussing the issue with other people before rating their risk-taking again. Post-discussion, participants were prepared to act in a riskier manner – an effect Stoner named *risky shift*. Later work showed that this effect could work both ways – group members could become either more or less inclined to act in a risky manner, depending on the initial leaning of the group.

Polarisation also applies to attitudes and behaviours. For instance, Myers (1975) gathered groups of female participants to discuss their attitude towards a number of feminist political issues. Prior to the discussion, the average attitude of the sample was moderately pro-feminist. Participants then met in small groups and discussed the issues, before having their attitudes measured again. The average attitude had become more pro-feminist. Polarisation in behaviours can also be seen in a variety of social psychology experiments – Sheriff's

Robber's Cave and Zimbardo's simulated prison study being good examples of this in action (see above and Chapter 5).

What processes might underpin group polarisation? Research suggests the effects are in part due to both *social comparison processes* and *informational processes*. Levinger and Schneider (1969), in their *pluralistic ignorance model of polarisation*, argued that group members are motivated to express an opinion that is roughly between their actual opinion and where they perceive the group norm to be. It also assumes people underestimate the extremity of the group norm. When someone publicly expresses opinions which are more extreme than those they really hold, other group members listen and, using the new, falsely extreme information, subsequently assume the group norm is more extreme than it actually is. They then make their own contributions, trying to fall near this more extreme new norm. Other group members (including the original group member) follow suit, resulting in a gradual increase in extremity. Essentially, all group members make each other more extreme via their attempts to conform to one another's views! Another form of social comparison process is the so-called '*bandwagon effect*' (see Myers, Brown Wojcicki & Aardema, 1977), in which group members attempt to appear slightly more extreme than the perceived group average. Again, this increases the perceived average, making the next person more extreme again, and so on. Both of these approaches assume that the accuracy of the attitudes is irrelevant – it is a drive to conform which drives effects. In contrast, other researchers have argued that polarisation is a purely informational process, rather than one linked to conformity.

In contrast to social comparison accounts, *information-processing perspectives* suggest that polarisation occurs because when people meet, they exchange ideas and add to the information they have. This process leads people to become more confident and more extreme in their opinions. This approach suggests a few important conditions which must be met for polarisation to occur – namely that information must be meaningfully exchanged, and that this information will be most effective if it is novel to the recipient. One implication of this is that if all members have the same information, little or no polarisation should occur. Generally, this approach has received good empirical support: groups which exchange more persuasive or numerous novel arguments experience more polarisation than those which do not (Ebbesen & Bowers, 1974; Burnstein & Vinokur, 1975). However, not all evidence supports it. For instance, group members often focus on information and arguments of which everyone is aware, at the expense of new information. An informational approach would seem to preclude polarisation in such circumstances. In addition, it seems that even when fairly minimal information is exchanged, polarisation can occur. For instance, Blascovich, Ginsburg and Veach (1975) showed that providing even minimal information on 'who bet what' in a hand of blackjack could led to polarisation. Given this, it seems both social comparison and information processes are likely to play a role in attitude polarisation. Indeed, meta-analysis on the topic suggests there is consistent evidence for both, but also that informational processes seems to have a larger average effect on polarisation than social comparison (Isenberg, 1986). Polarisation research has given great insights into how groups become more extreme, but it generally has one important limitation – namely that it assumes all group members have initial attitudes which roughly agree (technically, we assume they all hold attitudes that are within the '*latitude of acceptance*' of each other; see Chapter 7). Often this is case, but what happens when a member's thoughts or behaviours are well outside the group's social norms?

WHAT HAPPENS WHEN PEOPLE BREAK THE RULES? INGROUP DEVIANCE AND MINORITY INFLUENCE

As we have seen previously in this chapter, group members can exert a significant amount of pressure on individuals to conform to the group. The attitudes and behaviours the group members are expected to conform to are dictated by the group's *social norms* (see Chapter 5). Early work on conformity focused largely on experimental groups; the participants did not know each other prior to taking part, and probably wouldn't have much interaction the future. These groups also often operate in isolation from others. In the real world, however, *social identity theory* tells us that groups make comparisons between themselves and others to generate positive differentiation (see Chapter 5). This differentiation is based on the assumptions that (i) groups can reliably distinguish between their ingroup and an outgroup and (ii) they can reasonably claim to be superior on a given dimension to the outgroup. We see these effects both in the Stanford study and, even more strongly, in the BBC prison study. But what happens when someone *does not conform*? Or, more specifically, what are the psychological results of an *ingroup* member violating ingroup norms and behaving like an *outgroup* member (Marques, Abrams & Serôdio, 2001)? Interactions with such group members (termed *ingroup deviants*) can lead to strong psychological and physiological stress responses (Frings et al., 2012). They also threaten the two important assumptions about groups outlined above. As such, ingroup deviants attract particularly harsh responses. In their research on the so-called '*black sheep effect*' Marques and Yzerbyt (1988) showed that when participants evaluated a target who behaved against the norms of the ingroup, the evaluation was harsher when the deviant was an ingroup (as opposed to an outgroup) member. This research is important because it suggests conformity may often be rooted in social identity (see Chapter 5).

Subsequent research focusing on ingroup deviance suggests that responses to deviance are most extreme when ingroup status is threatened, but also these responses depend on the effects of deviance behaviour in the context it occurs in (being more lenient if the deviance may actually improve the group's image; see Marques, Abrams & Serôdio, 2001; Morton, Postmes & Jetten, 2007) Ingroup deviants may receive communication which aims to restore the deviant's normative status while also highlighting how they differ from the group norms (e.g. Frings & Abrams, 2010). The role of the deviant in the group is also important – for instance, criticism of the ingroup raised by newcomers generates more resistance than does the same criticism from old-timers (Hornsey et al., 2007). One way of understanding this literature is by arguing that deviants are unlikely to prevail in attempts to change group members' minds. However, the field has been criticised for assuming groups are always resistant to change. We can see by simply looking at our society that this is not the case: groups change their attitudes for many reasons. How (and when), then, do deviants succeed? This key question is addressed through the study of *minority influence*.

MINORITY INFLUENCE

In both conformity and obedience research, groups influence individuals to behave in particular ways. During group polarisation, group members generate conformity effects without always meaning to. We have seen that minorities often conform to majority positions with little or no encouragement (i.e. in the *autokinetic effect* and *Asch's line paradigm*). We have also seen that majorities actively seek to make deviants normative. However, with a little thought we can also generate examples of when *minorities* change the *majority* opinion: the suffragettes' battle for women's rights, the US black civil rights movement's fight for emancipation and the UK's somewhat unexpected decision to 'Brexit' from the EU could all be seen as situations in which a minority, with an initially deviant opinion, changed the prevailing attitude. Interestingly, although majorities are typically resistant to change, history shows that they also need it to prevent stagnation and, ultimately, subsequent decline. Although the minorities described above prevailed, many others fall, often forgotten, by the wayside. As you would imagine, social psychologists have been very interested in how *minority influence* operates, and what factors influence success.

Work on minority influence was kick-started by Moscovici in 1976 (Moscovici, 1976). His model outlines five propositions which are important to the understanding of minority influence. The first proposition argues that *every group member irrespective of rank is both potential source and receiver of influence.* This is important as it addresses previous assumptions in the literature which focused on group members who deviate being expelled or marginalised, without affecting the majority. It also challenged the assumption that majorities are *nomic* (i.e. having strong norms and agency) while minorities are *anomic* (having poorly defined norms and a lack of agency). The second proposition suggests that *social change is as much of an objective of influence as social control is*. Moscovici here highlights that some institutions (such as families, churches, educational contexts) favour social influence aimed at maintaining the status quo. In contrast, others minority groups (such as progressive artists) encourage social change. Moscovici also argues that it is only by understanding minority influence that you can understand the processes of social change. His model further proposes that *any processes which generate social change inevitably also involve conflict,* which can be experienced at an *intrapersonal* level (conflict based on uncertainty) or an *interpersonal* level (based on a fear that others perceive us to have a low resistance to influence). Perhaps of most interest to those seeking social change, Moscovici also outlined what makes minority attempts at social influence successful. In particular, his fourth proposition highlighted *the importance of behavioural styles* – namely how consistent, autonomous, fair and invested minorities appear to be in the change process. He argued that these behavioural styles are important because they affect the attributions that targets of change make about the sources of social influence (see Chapter 5). Finally, proposition five argues that *the course of the influence process is determined by objective norms, preference norms and originality norms.* Sometimes, majority groups seek to verify opinions against reality (*objectivity norms,* which prevent social change); at other times they may seek consensus between group members, allowing the possibility that alternatives exist (*preference norms,* which allow social change). Finally, groups may sometimes have an originality norm which actively encourages novelty (which in turn actively encourages social change). Moscovici also made an important distinction between *compliance* (doing something because you feel you must) and *conversion* (doing something because you change your mind and agree with it). Importantly, Moscovici argued that conversion was the only way minorities could affect social change.

Behavioural styles and the green-blue paradigm

Much of the empirical work that Moscovici undertook looked at the effectiveness of minorities undertaking different behavioural styles. The studies were often lab-based and utilised the *blue-green slide paradigm.* A good example of this paradigm is Moscovici, Lage, and Naffrechoux (1969). In this study, participants were placed in a group of six people. In reality, two of the group members were confederates. The participants' task was to identify whether each of 36 slides they were shown were blue or green in colour. All the slides were actually blue, but the colour varied in intensity. Before the trial, participants were tested to make sure they were not colour-blind (so could actually tell the difference between the slides!). The study had two experimental conditions. In the *consistent condition,* the minority stated that every single slide they saw was green in colour. In the *inconsistent condition*, they only said the slide was green in two thirds of the trials. Moscovici was interested in finding out the extent to which this minority would influence the real participants to also say the slide was green. In the consistent condition, participants said the slides were green in 8.4 per cent of trials. Moreover, 32 per cent participants in this condition said at least one slide was green. In contrast, in the inconsistent condition, only in 1.3 per cent of trials did participants say the slides were green. Moscovici interpreted these findings as being evidence that minorities whose behavioural style was consistent were more likely to be successful in influencing majorities than those who adopted an inconsistent style.

Although Moscovici's model was (and is) tremendously influential, and has received considerable empirical support, it also has some limitations. The focus on behavioural styles suggests that these factors are more important than others (such as, for example, the majority's preparedness to change). It is also the case that many minorities don't have the resources to be nomic in the way Moscovici suggests, and it is very unclear how such agency can be acquired. Finally, the blue-green paradigm's emphasis on experimental control resulted in a fairly contrived situation (like much research into conformity which was produced around this time). However, since Moscovici's original work there have been many studies on minority influence that have supported his general idea, conducted in both laboratory and field contexts. A meta-analysis conducted by Wood et al. (1994) examined 97 studies which explored minority influence. They conclude that, of the behavioural styles, consistency is particularly important. However, they also highlight some subtle nuances in the data. For instance, majorities seem to be persuaded on issues *around* the position the minority takes, rather than being directly persuaded. They are also less likely to be persuaded if asked to agree with the minority publicly (as opposed to privately). Wood et al. also suggest that the minority influence is a combination of informational and social comparison effects (see *group polarisation*, above).

One example of minority influence in action is the experience of women's rights protestors. In 1897, Millicent Fawcett founded a movement which would later be known as the suffragettes. This group's aim was to secure for women the right to vote. In contrast, the prevailing view amongst the (at the time more powerful) male population was that women should not take part in the electoral process (on the assumed basis that they would not understand it!). Many of the assumptions of Moscovici's model can be seen in the suffragette movement. Their appeal generated *conflict* (the movement itself involved peaceful and non-peaceful protests) and they were *consistent* in their message across a long period of time (women were eventually given the vote in 1918). The suffragettes also showed themselves to have high levels of *personal investment* – many went to prison for their actions or went on hunger strikes, and one suffragette, Emily Davison, was knocked over and killed by a horse at a prominent horse-racing event during a protest. The use of Moscovici's model in analysing this movement, and others like it, is part of the reason it is so influential, amongst both academics and also people attempting to affect social change.

SOCIAL FACILITATION AND SOCIAL LOAFING

The topics we have covered above are primarily about how social influence affects how people think and behave. In the next chapter on this theme, we will consider the mechanisms via which people attempt to persuade one another. Before that, however, we will look at another way groups influence members: through facilitating (or inhibiting) task performance.

Think of a time you have worked in a group, and everything has gone very wrong – perhaps group members did not contribute as much as they could, or someone behaved like a bit of a 'free-rider'. Maybe the group struggled to co-ordinate itself well, and wasn't as effective as you hoped it would be? Now, think of other times when things were very different – everyone worked together well, people produced great things and lots of work got done. Hopefully, you can bring some examples of this to mind. These two concepts are regarded by psychologists to be examples of *social loafing* and *social facilitation* respectively.

SOCIAL LOAFING

Although early work by Triplett (1898) suggested that people may work harder in the presence of others, it often seems to be the case

that the opposite occurs. Social loafing (a decrease in individual-
and group-level outputs resulting from the presence of others) has
been observed both in and out of the lab. For instance, Ringlemann
(1913, see Kravitz & Martin, 1986) had adult males undertake a
rope-pulling task (with the goal being to pull as hard as possible) on
their own and then as part of a group. These groups ranged in size
between two and eight people. Ringlemann observed that the larger
the group, the lower the percentage of possible maximum effort that
people put in – with people only achieving about 50 per cent of
their potential when other people were in the group. This study was
repeated by Ingham et al. (1974) using a new comparison condition – 'pseudo-groups' made up of a single participant, pulling for
real, and confederates who only pretended to. Ingham et al. observed
that real groups suffered the most detriment but, importantly, also
that the pseudo-group did less well. This suggests social loafing is
caused by *co-ordination loss* (problems co-ordinating effort within
groups) and also by *motivation loss* (people trying less hard when in a
group). In a laboratory context, the same effects have been observed
in simple tasks such as cheering, clapping and public speaking, but
also in more complex tasks such as air-traffic control games (see Bond
& Titus, 1983) In real-life contexts, loafing has been linked to poor
outcomes amongst work teams and a lack of action in emergencies
(Price, Harrison & Gaving 2006).

HOW CAN WE REDUCE LEVELS OF SOCIAL LOAFING?

Social loafing seems to be caused by a variety of factors. It seems
that *diffusion of responsibility* (the assumption that someone else will
take care of a problem, explored in Chapter 8) plays a large part in
social loafing (Latané, Williams, & Harkins, 1979). Loafing may also
be caused by individuals being unwilling to contribute more than
they feel others are, or wishing to avoid being the victim of others'
attempts to free-ride, (see Karau & Williams, 2001, and the discussion
of social dilemmas in Chapter 4). In group tasks, people may also make
only sufficient effort to meet, but not exceed, group targets (known
as *submaximal goal setting*). However, social loafing can be reduced if
people feel (i) they are personally identifiable, (ii) their individual
outputs are evaluated, (iii) their efforts are required to achieve success

(i.e. they are not 'dispensable') and (iv) they are given a say in how work will be undertaken (Price, Harrison & Gavin, 2006).

SOCIAL FACILITATION

The social loafing literature paints a bleak picture of group productivity. However, as we saw in Chapter 1, having others present can also *boost* performance. Earlier studies into social facilitation observed increases in performance during maths and word-generation tasks (see Strauss, 2002). Later research by Hazel Markus (Markus, 1978) involved participants undertaking tasks which combined both practised and unpractised elements (specifically, getting dressed in familiar and unfamiliar clothes) while alone, while being watched by an attentive person or while in the presence of an inattentive one. Markus observed that having people present facilitated the speed with which people completed the practised task. The presence of others, however, inhibited performance in the unpractised task. This happened even when the other person was not attending to the situation.

Why does the presence of others act in this way? One early approach explains this effect through *activation theory* (see Zajonc, 1965). This perspective assumes that the presence of others increases *arousal*. This arousal facilitates practised responses (called *dominant responses*) but inhibits unpractised ones (*non-dominant responses*). Later approaches argue that other people cause a *distraction* to the extent that they generate social comparison. This *distraction hypothesis* was tested by Sanders, Baron and Moore (1978) in a study in which participants completed a task alone or while in the presence of someone doing the same activity or a different one. They argued (and observed) that only in the same-task condition would social comparisons be possible. Similar effects are observed when people are doing the same task as others who provide upwards comparisons (where you compare yourself to someone superior to yourself on a given dimension) relative to downwards ones (comparisons between yourself and someone less superior) – presumably because upwards comparisons are threatening and thus cause more distraction (Muller, Atzeni & Butera, 2004). Although a plausible explanation, the distraction hypothesis doesn't explain *mere presence* effects completely – for instance, it is unclear how it would explain the findings in Markus's study that inattentive people facilitated and inhibited responses. Interestingly, social facilitation and inhibition effects seem relatively stable across groups: studies have shown effects in both younger and older people, and amongst both men and women (Triplett 1898; Chapman 1973; De Castro 1994). They have also been shown in animal populations, most famously amongst cockroaches (in the presence of other cockroaches; see Zajonc, 1965).

CHAPTER SUMMARY

In this chapter we have seen how other people can change the way we behave. Research into conformity and obedience suggests that the groups we are in, and the figures of authority in our lives, can exert considerable influence on our lives, often making us behave in ways in which we wouldn't otherwise. While much of this research is ethically ambiguous by modern standards, it also highlights the dramatic impact groups can have on our behaviour – in both extra-ordinary and everyday situations. In contrast, research on minority influence highlights that we are not passive respondents to group influence. Rather, we are active agents who can push back against the majority and can, sometimes, change the direction of the group as a whole. In this chapter we have also explored how groups can inspire us to work harder, or encourage us to free-ride on others' efforts. Why not try and look out for evidence of all these processes in your life? You may be surprised, and the act of noticing them may encourage you to act differently.

KEY CHAPTER POINTS

- Early laboratory-based work into conformity highlighted that people followed others when situations were ambiguous. Later, often field-based, work into obedience highlighted that groups and authority figures could make people act against their moral beliefs.
- The ethics of much historical conformity research has been widely criticised.
- Research into minority influence highlights that we are not passive recipients of groups' social influence: consistent, invested and fair minorities can change the majority position.

- Groups can motivate us to work harder, or encourage us to put in less effort.

SUGGESTED FURTHER READING

1. Milgram, S. (2017). *Obedience to authority*. New York: Harper Perennial.
2. Zimbardo, P. (2008). *The Lucifer effect: How good people turn evil.* London: Rider.
3. Zajonc, R. B. (1965). Social facilitation. *Science, 149*(3681), 269–274.
4. Moscovici, S., Mugny G., & Van Avermaet, E. (eds) (1985 [2008]). *Perspectives on minority influence.* Cambridge: Cambridge University Press.

7

PERSUASION

WHAT IS PERSUASION?

One of the most endemic forms of social influence is *persuasion*. Every day, people try to persuade us to change our attitude about one thing or another. It could be to support a new project at work, buy a particular product, adopt a behaviour or believe (or disbelieve) in a particular deity or political position, or even something as mundane as encouraging us to do our share of the washing-up. Persuasion, in contrast to many other sources of social influence, is an active process: somebody is, in a fairly conscious and planned way, aiming to change the opinions of somebody else. Of course, we ourselves try to do the same thing to other people! Researchers involved in marketing, political propaganda, health promotion and many other fields have devoted considerable time to understanding how persuasion works at a psychological level. In this section, we explore some of the key ideas in the area – focusing on both classic and more contemporary approaches.

SIX SOURCES OF INFLUENCE

One of the classic works in the persuasion literature (and, arguably, social psychology in general) was first published in 1984, authored by Robert Cialdini and entitled *Influence: Science and practice* (Cialdini, 2007). Cialdini researched this book 'in the field' for almost half a decade before writing it – working at places where people tried to persuade other people (such as car dealership and in telemarketing firms). His aim was to identify key principles in persuasion. His conclusion was that considering six key principles of persuasive communication (namely *reciprocity*, *commitment/consistency*, *social proof*, *authority*, *liking* and *scarcity*) can make it more effective.

Reciprocity is widely recognised to be an important principle in social influence. Many researchers believe that we have evolved to reciprocate favours or kindly acts to keep groups functioning effectively (for a more in-depth discussion of *evolutionary psychology*, see Trivers, 1971). In terms of persuasion, this means giving something to somebody which makes them feel obliged to do something for you in return. A classic example of reciprocity is the use of free samples: I give you a small sample of something and you feel obliged to engage with me while I present a sales pitch in return. It also feeds into negotiation strategies: if you start high and then drop your requirement, you are more likely to have a higher end result (so-called 'high-balling'). Reciprocity is a powerful device – when we feel that we cannot return a favour it can generate considerable discomfort, much like cognitive dissonance (see Chapter 3).

Being put in a position that involves publicly stating what one is planning to do can engage the principle of *commitment and consistency*. Drawing on cognitive dissonance, this principle argues that if we are compelled to commit, either orally or in writing, to a course of behaviour we are more likely to see it through – even if the reasons that we originally committed to the idea are removed. Cialdini uses an example of American prisoners of war being 'brainwashed' into publicly denouncing their beliefs through coercion, but then subsequently maintaining the new beliefs once freed. Less-extreme examples involve generating an intent ('"Do you want cleaner carpets?", "Of course!"') and then providing an opportunity to act consistently ('"Are you going to buy a Magivac3000?", "I must!"'). Interestingly, this is a tool which can be applied effectively to the self as well as others. Indeed, many self-help books suggest we apply commitment and consistency (in the form of *public affirmation* of intent) to persuade *ourselves* to do something!

Cialdini also recognised the power of social influence on behaviour. As we have seen, conformity is a strong influence: we often do what other people are doing, particularly in ambiguous situations. Providing *social proof* for products involves demonstrating that people similar to a target of influence behave in the same way towards an object as you wish the target to. Cialdini uses this device effectively himself on the cover of his own book – making it very clear that there have been 'over a quarter of a million copies sold'! Doubtless the book you are currently reading will also be marketed with testimonials, review quotes and other forms of social proof! The number of people providing social proof also appears to be important: research on online marketing sites suggests that a large number of reviews of a product resulting in an average 'star' rating generates more sales than only a few reviews which rate the product very highly. The source of the social proof is significant too: the more similar the source is to the target of influence, the more effective it will be.

However, the principle of *authority* also explains how people who are quite different from us can influence our behaviour. Cialdini argued that we take the point of view of people in authority very seriously because they often have legitimate expertise, and our own well-being is also often contingent upon their approval of us. We have also seen the power of authority in the Milgram studies we discussed in Chapter 6. Advertising may rarely involve electric shocks, but the use of important scientific, sporting and celebrity figures to endorse products is widespread. Expertise and source authority also feature heavily in other models of persuasion which we will discuss shortly, including the Yale model (Hovland, Janis & Kelley, 1953) and the heuristic systematic model (Chaiken, 1980).

However, the power of authorities (or any sources of influence) can be magnified by *liking* them. If you are trying to persuade someone, try and be likeable! For instance, if a salesperson can build rapport with us we are more likely to make a purchase (even though, from a rational point of view, whether we like the person selling something should be relatively unimportant). As such, anything which increases likability (such as similarity, physical attractiveness etc.; see our discussion of first impressions in Chapter 4) is an important factor. Marketing using 'Tupperware party' models (in which people sell a product to their friends) also rely heavily on this principle.

Ciadlini's final principle is something which we all know, but never seem to overcome: we are all suckers for *scarcity*. When we are worried that we're going to miss an opportunity (*opportunity scarcity*) or that there are only a limited number of an item available (*resource scarcity*), we are more likely to pursue it strongly. This principle has many parallels with the idea of *loss and gain framing* discussed by Kahneman and Tversky (see Chapter 3). In marketing, 'ending soon' promotions and 'limited edition' product are both examples of scarcity being used to drive higher sales.

In a later edition of his book, Cialdini also highlights the importance of *unity*, a principle which argues that a shared social identity between the source and target of influence (described as a 'sense of unity') is also important. Generating a connection increases influence – even if it is relatively arbitrary and unrelated to the discussion. For instance, a used-car salesman may remind a potential customer that they are both fans of the same baseball team. The more powerful the connection, the greater the influence. Some recent events – such as the rise and decline of UKIP in the UK and the 2016 presidential election success of Donald Trump (and, arguably, Obama Barack before him) – are all in part a result of individuals generating an apparently meaningful connection with a large number of segments of society, despite there being (very objectively) tremendous differences between them.

As this section hopefully shows, Cialdini provides a comprehensive account of how we can become successful in persuading people. This work is important from a psychological perspective because it highlights that persuasion is not a rational process, and the psychological principles outlined elsewhere in this book have been used in applied contexts for decades. It is also perhaps one of the most influential social psychology works (alongside, I would argue, Allport's work on prejudice; see Chapter 5) ever written. But don't trust me (although I have some expertise in the area, and you and I both love the same baseball team, breakfast cereal and singer). If you need proof of this assertion, just look at the cover of Cialdini's book – a quarter of a million other readers can't be wrong, can they …?

CRITICAL SPOTLIGHT: WHY DO ADS GO VIRAL?

An advert going 'viral' is perhaps the ultimate expression of social proof in marketing. Adverts get passed on simply because so many *other* people have passed them on in the past. The marketer who figures out how to consistently generate viral adverts is likely to get very rich, very quickly! However, little is understood about the actual mechanisms of viral advertising. What research there is suggests that adverts can go viral when they help people connect emotionally, and when recipients trust both the originator of the advert and the person who sent it on to them (Dobele et al., 2007; Cho, Huh & Faber, 2014). A decision to forward an ad also seems to be sensitive to concepts such as reciprocal altruism (the returning of favours). In contrast, being overly familiar with a brand and seeing it as irrelevant can depress sharing intentions (Huang & Zhou, 2016). Given the amount of money involved in marketing, you can be sure there are also a lot of hunches and in-house expertise that people keep to themselves. Watch this space for more empirical work in this area!

THE YALE MODEL AND SOCIAL JUDGEMENT THEORY

While Cialdini's classic work provides a great 'how-to' and begins to outline some of the processes underpinning persuasion, other researchers have broken down factors related to persuasion in a more granular fashion, often examining the topic from a social-cognitive perspective. One early approach (the *Yale model*, developed by Hovland, Janis & Kelley, 1953). Argues that we need to consider three core concepts when understanding persuasive communication – the *source*, the *message* and the *target* (audience). The source (the 'who') has a greater impact to the extent that they're seen as reliable, trustworthy, expert and, perhaps most importantly, similar to ourselves. Similarly, likeable and attractive sources are more persuasive than less attractive ones. For instance, Eagly and Chaiken (1975) showed that an attractive source persuaded 41 per cent of people to sign a petition. In contrast, a less–attractive source was only successful 30 per cent of the time. As you may have realised, lots of Cialdini's ideas around the six sources of influence revolve around the message source. But is not just the source which matters; other features of the message are also thought to be important. The different ways people *cognitively process* messages are also vital to consider, as factors such as argument length, consistency, balance and the sheer number of exposures to a message can all affect how efficacious it is. Finally, the *audience* is important. For instance – some (but not all) research suggests that women can be more easily persuaded than men – possibly because they may be more focused on co-operating (see Eagly & Carli, 1981 for a review of studies in this area). It also seems that people in their late teens and early adulthood are more easily influenced than those who are older (though some research also shows that we become increasingly persuadable again as we hit late adulthood; Visser and Krosnick, 1998).

One thing to note about the Yale model is that audiences cannot be thought of as passive targets: they will be motivated to engage with a message to greater or lesser extent (as will see when we discuss the *elaboration likelihood model*), and this changes which sort of messages are most effective. There are also individual differences. For instance, some people have a high need for *cognitive closure* (they want to quickly arrive at surety). Such people appear to be harder to influence – possibly because once they have established an attitude they are less likely to change it, and they are also less likely to scrutinise arguments and thus take them in (Webster & Kruglanski, 1994; Klein & Webster, 2000). In contrast, some people have a high *need for cognition* – they actively seek out and enjoy thinking about things (see Cacioppo et al., 1996). As you may expect, people high in need for cognition are generally swayed only by strong arguments. However, high need for cognition also makes people more prepared to consider changing their minds in the first place (Haugtvedt, Petty & Cacioppo, 1992).

Two related concepts in this area are individual differences in *latitude of acceptance* and *latitude of rejection*, specified by *social judgement theory* (Sherif & Hovland, 1961). This model assumes that individuals will have an initial attitude – an *anchor*. Around this anchor we will have a latitude of acceptance – the distance from our initial opinion we would be prepared to shift. Arguments attempting to persuade us to adopt a position within this range are likely to be successful. In contrast, we also have a latitude of rejection; arguments within this range will likely fail – no matter how strong they are. Between this we have the *latitude of non-commitment* – a grey area where persuasion is possible, but more difficult. Different individuals will have latitudes of different sizes in each of the zones: a wide latitude of acceptance make someone easier to persuade on an issue, while a wide latitude of rejection make things harder for a would-be influencer. From a persuasion point of view, this model suggests that one wants to generate the greatest discrepancy between the anchor and the attitude, while staying out of the latitude of rejection. The individual nature of the zones also suggests that the more one's message is palatable to an individual target, the more effective one will be – but achieving this effectively also requires knowledge of where the zones lie for each person/target demographic.

Both the Yale model and social judgement theory have beauty in their simplicity: they make us think about the various crucial elements for effective persuasion. However, like the six sources of influence, they again still do not really explain *how* we are persuaded. To address this, we will now look at more motivational and social-cognitive models of persuasion, in particular the *elaboration likelihood model* (Petty & Cacioppo, 1986) and the *heuristic systematic model* (Chaiken, 1980).

DUAL-PROCESS THEORIES OF PERSUASION

Both the elaboration likelihood model (ELM; Petty & Cacioppo, 1986) and the heuristic systematic model (HSM; Chaiken 1980) argue that the way we process information has an effect on how we interact with persuasive messages, and how efficacious they will be. They also both argue that persuasion is a *dual-route* process – implying that one route to persuasion is slow and reasoned, while the other is faster and automatic (see Chapter 3).

THE ELABORATION LIKELIHOOD MODEL

The ELM argues that there are two distinct processing modes that come into play when we are being persuaded: the *central processing route* and the *peripheral processing route*. Central processing is characterised by effortful processing of the persuasive communication. When in this mode we engage in *elaborate thinking*, scrutinising *central cues* (for instance, scientific evidence, complex reasoned arguments etc.) while placing less weight on more *peripheral*, irrelevant information. When we are in this mode it is difficult to persuade us. But if the persuasion attempt is successful it's also long-standing and more difficult to reverse (i.e. more stable). The alternative to this is the peripheral route. When thinking in this mode, we rely more on peripheral cues – things such as the source (are they an expert?), how the subject matter makes us feel and other objectively less relevant information. In essence, we begin to rely more on *heuristics* than upon reason. If we are persuaded of something by this route it is likely that the attitude change will be less stable.

Whether we take a central or a peripheral approach to processing information is thought to depend on our levels of *motivation* and *ability*. When the issue being considered is important to us (perhaps when we are making a major purchase or a life-changing decision) we are more inclined to engage in elaborate thinking. In contrast, things we are less motivated to think about (for instance, spontaneous purchases of small-value items, or the choice of what we eat for lunch on a particular day) tend to be processed through the peripheral route. We also have to have the *ability* to engage in elaborate thinking. This can include *aptitude* towards processing information – some people are simply more able to process complicated information than others. However, situational factors also play an important role: high levels of *cognitive load* (for instance, if we are stressed or doing too many things at once) decrease our ability to engage in elaborate thinking. If we are in a state of *ego depletion* (see Chapter 3) we also seem less able to resist persuasion, which could be suggestive of lower levels of elaboration (Wheeler, Brinol & Hermann, 2007). The ELM is complemented by a similar approach: the HSM.

THE HEURISTIC SYSTEMATIC MODEL

The HSM also takes a dual-process approach to persuasion. It argues that we process information through two routes: *systematic* and *heuristic*. The systematic route is very similar to the idea of elaboration.

We consider arguments in an effortful manner and focus on their quality. In contrast, heuristic thinking revolves around processing information relatively unthinkingly, relying on heuristics. Much like the ELM, persuasion based mostly on heuristics is seen as less stable than that arrived at by systemic thinking. It could be argued that the HSM actually places more value on heuristic thinking: rather than seeing it as a less sophisticated form of evaluation, it more strongly recognises that we must deal with a large volume of information and that often heuristics are the only feasible way of doing so. The HSM also allows for an interplay between these two routes. While at different times our focus may be more on one than the other, heuristic information can also have an influence when we are thinking systematically.

Together, these two models have been highly influential in our understanding of persuasion. Both argue that there are relatively distinct modes of thinking. They also highlight the importance of heuristics (a number of which we will review in a moment), the need to be able to engage in high-level processing and differences in the stability of attitude change. Both models have been (and remain) highly influential in the field of social influence and persuasion.

CRITICAL SPOTLIGHT: DUAL ROUTES OR A UNIMODAL APPROACH?

As you may have gathered from this textbook so far, the idea of *dual-process systems* is very popular in social cognition. The idea of *automatic* and *reflective* thinking, *type I* and *type II systems* and *high* and *low elaboration* are just a few examples of how the concept of dual processes has permeated the discipline. However, this approach is not without its critics. For instance, Kruglanski et al. (2004) argue that these two processing routes in terms of persuasion are effectively the same – variations on a theme rather than distinct processes. To some extent, it's impossible to disentangle whether such a unimodal approach or a dual-process approach is the most objectively 'accurate' – so perhaps it's more profitable to think about which approaches advance our understanding of social cognition more readily.

SOME EXAMPLES OF HEURISTICS

Researchers have identified a number of heuristics which seem to affect our decision-making on top of those described above. While a full survey of all of these heuristics is beyond the scope of the current volume, we here review a few which we broadly categorise as revolving around *reciprocity* (which we have touched already on above, but explore more fully here), *consistency* and *tangential information*.

Reciprocity. Reciprocity is a social norm that seems to be an important heuristic. If we are offered something, we often feel an urge to offer something in return. Reciprocity can be negative (you do something bad to me, so I do something bad to you), or positive (I do something good for you and you do something good for me). For instance, in an early study of reciprocity, Regan (1971) offered participants a soft drink prior to asking them to purchase raffle tickets. Relative to a control condition in which people were not offered a soft drink, participants were more likely to comply with the request. Bargaining can also be seen as a reciprocal exchange: if I lower my request for you somewhat, you should do the same. Interestingly, we feel the need to reciprocate even when the favour offered to us is uninvited (see, for instance, Paese & Gilin, 2000). Thus, a common marketing technique is to give something to somebody in the hope that they will feel the need to give something back (i.e. a purchase or a better deal) later on. A variation of reciprocity is the so-called '*door-in-the-face technique*'. Cialdini et al. (1975) ran a series of experiments in which some participants were asked to undertake an 'extreme favour', which was refused, prior to being asked for a more reasonable one. People who had initially had to refuse an extreme favour were more likely to grant the more reasonable request – presumably because they felt they had to reciprocate the lowered offer.

Consistency. The door-in-the-face technique can also be reversed (and then described as a '*foot-in-the-door technique*'). Freedman and Fraser (1966) made a large request of their participants. In a control condition, this was the first request made. In an experimental condition, this large request was preceded by a small request – which participants usually granted. The large request was granted more often by participants who had previously agreed to a small one. Rather than reciprocity, this approach relies on the fact that we like to be *consistent* across time and within our decisions – I complied before so should probably do so again (see discussions on cognitive dissonance in Chapter 3). Another tactic which relies on the need to be consistent is *low-balling*. Low-balling involves getting people to agree to something at a fairly low price and then introducing new costs once the initial agreement has been reached. For example, you may buy a new TV set and, as you sit down to sign the contracts, be told it will cost extra if you want something very essential – like a remote control. As you feel we've already sunk costs into the TV (despite the fact that you have not yet bought it!), and because you want to feel consistent with yourself, you will often make the 'extra' purchase. A classic example of this is shown in a study by Cialdini et al. (1978). They set the start time of an experiment at 7 o'clock in the morning. Half of the participants were told about the start time *before* being asked to take part. Of these folk, only 24 per cent agreed to participate. In contrast, when people were told about the start time *after* they had agreed to take part a whopping 95 per cent actually showed up!

Tangential information. We can also be affected by information which has little to do with the issue at hand. For instance, the '*length versus strength*' heuristic suggests that the longer an argument is (even if it doesn't provide any more information), the more persuasive it seems to be (Chaiken, Liberman & Eagly, 1989). Similarly, if we find it easier to cognitively access information we are more likely to be swayed by it (see Tversky & Kahneman, 1983). Generally, more arguments and longer (but not necessarily more substantial) arguments will be more persuasive than fewer or shorter ones. However, this effect is not uniformly observed. For instance, if there are a lot of arguments presented, and only some of them are strong, message recipients can average them out – resulting in a lower level of persuasion than if only fewer, stronger arguments are made (Weaver, Hock & Garcia, 2016).

Another source of tangential information is the *mood* we are in when someone attempts to persuade us. Research by Bless et al. (1990) shows that people in a bad mood elaborated more on a persuasive message than did those who were happy – and they were only persuaded by strong arguments. Interestingly, when in a bad mood participants were also less distractible than happy ones. Generally, it seems that being in a positive mood makes us rely more heavily on heuristics and process information less carefully – per-haps making us more persuadable (Schwarz and Bless, 1991: Mackie and Worth, 1991). Mood is related to another source of intangible information: *colour*.

Colour affects mood and signifies other concepts – something marketers are keen to utilise. For instance, research by Gerend and Sias (2009) presented participants with information about receiving a vaccination and asked them about their intentions to get vaccinated. The messages were presented as either a gain or a loss frame (see Chapter 3). The researchers also manipulated whether or not the colour red was included in the advert (versus a grey control). The experimenters reasoned that the colour red is often associated with danger and blood. They found that the colour red, when coupled with the loss-framed message, increased vaccination intentions. Marketers also use different colours to convey different meanings – navy blue, for example, is thought to contain meanings around reli-ability and steadfastness (good for banks, maybe bad for youth fashion labels!). In contrast, green is linked with growth, balance and envir-onment. Oranges and yellows are used to convey feelings associated with warmth or motivation.

THE ROLE OF FEAR IN PERSUASION

One emotion which is widely used in persuasion (and could be con-sider a heuristic in many ways) is *fear*. Fear generates both psycho-logical and physiological arousal. It is used routinely in public health promotions (think of 'stop smoking' adverts), but almost everything from antifreeze to zebra conservation has been promoted using fear-based appeals at some point. However, the evidence on the effective-ness of this approach is mixed (see Boster & Mongeau, 1984). One reason for this may be because too much fear drives us into a state of *denial* about the problem being presented. This can be understood in terms of the '*inverted U*' hypothesis (applied to fear-based persuasion by Janis, 1967). This approach suggests that low levels of fear gen-erate a small amount of attitude change. Moderate levels of fear are expected to generate the most attitude change. However, high levels of fear are expected to lead to disengagement and low levels of atti-tude change. Plotted on a graph, these produce an inverted U-curve.

At very low levels of fear, people may have no motivation to engage with the message because are simply not interested. At the very high end of the fear spectrum, anxiety and denial prevent people from processing the model effectively. In line with this, a general caveat about using fear in persuasive communication is that the message must also offer an achievable solution to the problem being posed. For instance, scaring people about climate change has a greater effect on issue engagement when people are given a clear, achievable solution which they can enact themselves (see O'Neill & Nicholson-Cole, 2009). Fear-based messages can also lead to *rebound effects* in persuasion, which we will discuss shortly.

CONTEMPORARY APPROACHES TO PERSUASION: NUDGES

The 'nudge' approach became popular with the publication of a book of the same name by economist Richard Thaler and Law professor Cass Sunstein in 2008 (Thaler & Sunstein, 2008). The authors argue that people's decisions can (and should) be swayed towards 'better' options through the use of a system of *choice architecture*. An option can be considered 'better' when it has positive impacts on people – for instance by encouraging them to make better pension-provision investment decisions or healthier food choices.

Choice architecture relies on the fact that we think both fast and slow (drawing on ideas outlined in Chapter 3, and similar to the dual-process models of persuasion we discussed above). It also assumes that people generally choose to do what is easy over what they know to be correct (or best for them). Given this, the ways people make decisions should be set up to take advantage of the various biases that we have (i.e. heuristics) in every stage of the decision-making process. Choice architecture also highlights that, as we sometimes simply cannot be bothered at all, we often rely on an offered 'default' option (assuming someone else has done the thinking for us). Choice architects can carefully select these default options to nudge people to behave in the desired way. Thaler and Sunstein also suggest that choice architects should ensure they avoid '*choice overload*' –in terms of both the number of products offered and the detail given about each of them. The nudge concept also suggests that architects try and ensure that people think in the longer term by highlighting long-term outcomes prominently (particularly important for issues like saving for retirement). Comparisons between options can themselves be a nudge – by providing a 'less good' option as an alternative to the preferred option to boost engagement. The uptake of a default option can also be increased by putting time pressure on people to make a decision.

In many ways, the nudge approach is a fairly natural extension of dual-process work on persuasion such as the ELM and the HSM: all recognise the importance of cognitive biases and the limited motivation and ability of people to think in a manner which could be considered 'rational'. What makes the nudge approach different is that is it has been systematically applied to finance, health and environmental behaviours, and in the public school system. Its impact, both in terms of popular perception and in changing actual policy implications, has arguably been much greater than that of previous approaches. Both former US president Barack Obama and former prime minister of the UK David Cameron set up dedicated 'behavioural insight units', which drew on the ideas of nudge techniques to steer public policy and implementation. Many businesses and marketers also routinely use the nudge philosophy to fine-tune their marketing and sales offerings. The impact of this work was such that, in 2017, Richard Thaler won the Nobel Prize for Economics for it. The nudge approach is one of the few bodies of Nobel-winning work which could in the broadest sense be considered psychological (other examples include Kahneman for his work on thinking biases, awarded in 2002, and Elinor Ostrom's work on social dilemmas, awarded in 2009).

WHEN PERSUASION FAILS: REBOUND EFFECTS

We end our discussion of persuasion by examining a situation which influencers want to avoid. One risk of persuasion attempts is that they backfire: you may actually generate an attitude change in the opposite direction to that which you intended. When this occurs, a *'reactance'*, *'ironic'* or *'rebound'* effect is said to be present. Rebound effects quite often appear when core aspects of one's self-belief system are challenged, or when the message serves to prime the unwanted behaviours for automatic activation and implementation, but fail to cognitively inhibit them. For instance, Moss et al. (2015) had participants view one of a number of posters which contrasted the positive aspects of drinking on a night out with the negative after-effects (with a call for viewers to 'drink responsibly'). Participants then took part in a 'taste task' in which they rated ostensibly alcoholic drinks on dimensions such as taste and appearance. The results showed the people viewing the posters actually ended up drinking *more* than controls! Examining which part of the poster people looked at using an eye tracker suggests that this effect is in part due to people focusing on the positive aspects of the message ('drink', 'have fun!'). Even when no contradiction is present, messages can backfire: anti-smoking campaigns which are entirely negative have been shown to actually increase positive attitudes towards cigarettes amongst some smokers (see e.g. Henriksen et al., 2006; Wolburg, 2006). In general, it's very hard to predict when backlash effects will occur – but many researchers now recommend piloting messages in controlled contexts before putting them 'out in the field'. However, such piloting can be costly in contexts where resources are scarce and can also slow down the delivery of messages, so they are less commonplace than one might assume.

CHAPTER SUMMARY

In our overview of the psychology of persuasion, we have seen various approaches to understanding it. Some take a 'how-to' approach, detailing psychological techniques which make persuasion more effective. In contrast, others represent more conceptual models which describe how attitude change takes place at a cognitive level. What all these different approaches agree on is the importance of the message, its source, the target and the method of delivery. Most models also recognise (to a greater or lesser extent) that persuasion involves both reflective (explicit) and automatic (implicit) thought processes. Although this book presents persuasion separately from other topics, it is also important to realise that, as a form of *social influence*, it manifests in other areas. Minority influence, impression formation and social norms are but a few areas of social psychology which involve attitude change in some form or other.

KEY CHAPTER POINTS

- Sources of social influence include reciprocity, commitment/consistency, social proof, authority, liking and scarcity.
- Features of the message, its source and the intended target must be taken into account to design a persuasive communication.
- Dual-process models argue that persuasion occurs via rational thought and/or is affected by heuristics.
- The 'nudge' approach argues that choice architects should systematically apply persuasion science to decision-making systems for the public good.

SUGGESTED FURTHER READING

1. Cialdini, R. (2007). *Influence: The psychology of persuasion.* New York: HarperBusiness.
2. Jeffrey, W., Sherman, J. W., Gawronski, B., & Trope, Y. (2014). *Dual process theories of social mind.* New York: Guilford Press.
3. Lord, C. G., Ross, L., & Lepper, M. R. (1979). Biased assimilation and attitude polarization: The effects of prior theories on subsequently considered evidence. *Journal of Personality and Social Psychology, 37,* 2098–2109.
4. Thaler, R. H., & Sunstein, C. R. (2008). *Nudge: Improving decisions about health, wealth, and happiness.* New York: Yale University Press.

THEME SUMMARY: SOCIAL INFLUENCE

In this theme we have seen how social influence operates on us in various ways (for instance via conformity, persuasion and social facilitation) and at various levels – making us comply, or change our mind. We've also seen how we are the sources of social influence as well as recipients of it, and how our own social influence has the potential to radically change society. Throughout this, it becomes clear that we have less control over our behaviour than we think. Sometimes, the situations we find ourselves in makes us behave in ways we would not normally. Othertimes, we simply don't have the energy, motivation or ability to be as thoughtful as we would like before acting. We've also seen how persuasion operates, and how the study of persuasion draws on other areas of psychology and has widespread real-life implications.

Over the next few days, try to keep an eye out for social influences in your own life. When do you comply with others? Are there decisions you have made without much thought? How did you try to persuade someone to do something? When you spot these situations, you can ask yourself how the material we have covered here applies to it. Reflect on not only why you behaved the way you did, but also whether you'd like to behave differently (and, if so, how?) next time around.

8

SOCIAL PSYCHOLOGY IN APPLIED CONTEXT

HOW DOES SOCIAL PSYCHOLOGY HELP IN 'THE REAL WORLD'?

Social psychology is, fundamentally, an applied discipline. Social psychologists are interested in phenomena playing out in the real world, and often seek answers to the most pressing questions and problems society presents. Before you embark on this chapter it may be worth thinking about the ideas and themes that we've already discussed: *social influence research*, for example, is routinely applied in real-life situations (in fact, it's probably been applied to the marketing material accompanying this very book!). Similarly, work on *motivation*, the *social self* and *intergroup processes* has all been applied to the real world in manifold ways. Given this diversity, a full review of all the ways that social psychology is applied is beyond the scope of this volume. As a result, we'll focus on four strands of research within the field which are each clearly linked to real-world problems. At a (relatively) inter-individual level, we look at the biological and psychosocial predictors of *aggression* (and the ways media consumption may feed into these). We then examine the related question of *why people choose to help* (or not) in emergency situations. Then we move on to the role that social psychology plays in broader public policy grounds – looking at the way we understand *jury decision-making*, and the potential role of *social connections in improving physical and mental health*.

AGGRESSION

Aggression is a powerful and often destructive emotion which underpins a lot of problematic behaviours. For instance, many of us experience so-called 'micro-aggressions' in our day-to-day lives, when people behave in small ways designed to upset or antagonise us. At the other end of the scale, aggression can lead to entire populations turning upon one another during times of war. As a result, social psychologists have been particularly interested in understanding the causes of aggression, and the processes which underpin aggressive thoughts and behaviours. However, exactly how to define aggression has been the subject of some debate. For instance, we must consider whether or not it is the *behaviour* or the preceding *intention* we are considering, whether aggression is always a physical activity and whether it needs to be aimed at particular person. Most contemporary psychologists argue that the *intent to harm another living being* constitutes aggression (See Geen, 1990). This broad definition includes both physical aggression and also non-physical aggression (e.g. shouting at someone or using racist language).

BIOLOGICAL APPROACHES

Early psychological accounts of aggression revolved around the idea of *catharsis*. Here aggression is seen to be a forceful, primarily biological drive, which gradually builds up, creating tension. A trigger event then occurs which enables the release of this tension into either a form of aggression or a 'cathartic' harmless outlet (perhaps going for a run). However, empirical research that gives people the opportunity to behave cathartically does not consistently seem to reduce levels of aggression – in fact, it can even increase it (Bushman, Baumeister & Stack, 1999)! So, while the idea of cathartic activities may be popular in therapeutic contexts, their efficacy in reducing aggression remains questionable.

Although these attempts to understand aggression as an innate process may not have been successful, this does not mean that aggression doesn't have some biological basis. For instance, biologists Belyaev and Trutt undertook a long-term selective breeding programme of wild foxes (by allowing only animals which appeared to be 'least wild' to breed). After 30 generations, Belyaev and Trutt observed that the percentage of foxes which could reasonably be considered 'tame' (and non-aggressive) rose from almost none to over 66 per cent (see Trutt, 1999). In contrast, Lagerspetz and Lagerspetz (1971) selectively bred mice on the basis of being highly aggressive or territorial, and after only 26 generations had created a strain of mouse which demonstrated significantly higher levels of aggression. In human populations, research has measured levels of aggression in *monozygotic* twins (identical twins, who share the same genetic make-up) and *dizygotic* twins (non-identical twins, who only share 50 per cent of their genetic make-up). These studies typically show that monozygotics are more similar to one another in aggression levels than are dizygotics, suggesting that a genetic component can explain up to 50 per cent of the variance in aggression (see Tuvblad et al., 2009). Some research suggests that physical aggression may have a stronger genetic component than do more social forms of aggression (Brendgen et al., 2005).

The biological basis of aggression is also reflected in research identifying the role of neurochemicals such as *serotonin* or, amongst men, *testosterone*. For instance, in humans, low levels of serotonin are linked with increased aggression (e.g. Coccaro, 1989). However, these effects do not always occur: injecting 'subordinate' animals with extra serotonin has been shown to increase their willingness to engage in competitive situations or, in other studies, to trigger escape-orientated behaviours (Edwards & Kravitz, 1997). In contrast, high levels of testosterone have been linked to both increases in aggressive behaviour and lower investment in caring for offspring. Testosterone itself seems to be increased by both sexual arousal and interpersonal challenges involving other men, suggesting that being aggressive may be an evolved *reproductive strategy* (see Archer, 2006). It is interesting to note that the effects of these neurochemicals seem to be highly interactive with our physical and social environment. For instance, dominating an aggressive physical encounter can increase levels of serotonin, but the effects of serotonin seem to be different for animals with higher and lower levels of social status (Edwards & Kravitz, 1997; McGuire & Raleigh, 1987).

PSYCHOSOCIAL APPROACHES

Aggression is not solely a biological process. Alternative, psycho-social approaches to aggression traditionally revolved around how we deal with a sense of *frustration* (e.g. Dollard et al., 1939). Dollard and colleagues' *frustration-aggression hypothesis* suggested that frustration is particularly likely to lead to aggression when the goal we are trying to achieve is valuable to us, when all hope of achieving it is lost, when we are thwarted multiple times and when we almost (but don't quite) achieve our aims. Later versions of this theory (i.e. Berkowitz, 1989) included the generation of negative emotions as a form of frustration which is likely to translate into aggression. In this formulation, aversive conditions such as high levels of heat, crowding or physical pain can also be a source of frustration. Scaling up frustration to the group level, the feeling of *relative deprivation* between one's own and others' outcomes is also linked to (but does not fully explain) increased intergroup aggression (Crosby, 1976). This form of aggression can be exhibited in ways which include social protest, riots and crime (Gurney & Tierney, 1982; Miller, Bolce & Halligan, 1977; Kawachi, Kennedy & Wilkinson, 1999). The idea of such '*displaced aggression*' continues to attract both the interest of researchers and also considerable empirical support (see Marcus-Newhall et al., 2000).

Aggression can also be understood as a learned behaviour. Bandura's *social learning theory* argues that we understand how to behave through a process of 'vicarious learning'. Specifically, we observe other people's actions and the results that arise from them. In the case of aggression, if we see somebody enjoying being aggressive, and we also observe that it generates some contingent reward for them, we are more likely to be aggressive ourselves. This was famously demonstrated in a series of studies by Bandura (e.g. Bandura, Ross & Ross, 1961). In these *bobo doll experiments*, children aged between three and six observed an adult interacting with a 'bobo doll' – an inflatable figure which when knocked down would bounce right back again. In the *aggressive model* condition, the adult behaved in an aggressive way physically and verbally towards the doll, kicking and punching it and hitting it with a toy mallet while shouting at it. In a control condition, the adult played peacefully with the toys in the room, ignoring the doll. After observing one of these situations, the children themselves were (individually) placed in another room filled with toys, but only allowed to play with them for two minutes (to build a sense of frustration). The children were then moved into the room where they had seen the adult previously. Children who had seen the aggressive model were far more likely to engage in *imitative violence* (i.e. kicking and punching the bobo doll and verbally abusing it). It also appeared that the more similar the model was to the children, the greater effect the model's behaviour had on their own. For instance, a male aggressive model encouraged boys but not girls to behave more aggressively, while the opposite was true for a female model. Bandura, Ross and Ross (1963) conducted a replication of the study in which the model was either rewarded or punished for aggressive behaviour. They concluded that when the model's aggression appeared to be rewarded, subsequent imitative violence became more likely. This research has been criticised on a number of grounds (for instance, that hitting a doll with a toy mallet is very different from hitting a living person with a real one, the children were explicitly engaging in play and there was no intent to harm). However, the idea that we learn to be aggressive from others has received a variety of other empirical support. These findings, and many similar others, led Bandura (1978, p. 12) to argue that social learning is one of the most powerful factors influencing the 'principled resort to aggression'.

CULTURAL EFFECTS ON AGGRESSION

As well as learning from others, culture also seems to define our understanding of *when* it is appropriate to respond to a situation with aggression. For instance, a series of studies suggest that in the American South (where the concept of personal honour is important), the likelihood of insults or slights surrounding one's masculinity being met with aggression is higher than in the American North (e.g. Cohen et al., 1996). Similarly, patterns have been found in Mediterranean societies which have a 'culture of honour', but driven by threats to one's family honour rather than one's masculinity (Van Osch et al., 2013). It is important to note that such honour systems are not uniformly negative: they may encourage stronger social connections (which we will see are important when we discuss the idea of the 'social cure'). *Honour systems* may also guide positive behaviours – for instance, there is some evidence to suggest that those who endorse unrelated aggression are also more likely to reciprocate favours (Leung & Cohen, 2011).

AGGRESSION AND THE MEDIA

Cultural effects similar to the 'honour system' are likely to have been around since the dawn of society. However, the effect they have on our behaviour may well be dwarfed by the widespread impacts of media such as television, computer games and, more recently, the internet (in particular, video upload sites). These increasingly give both adults and children exposure to huge numbers of violent acts. Many of these (for instance, in computer games or TV dramas) are realistic-looking but, ultimately, fictitious. However, in contrast, the news, social networks and video-sharing sites all host content which depicts real graphic violence. This is likely to increase an individual propensity for aggression in several ways. We have already seen that people model their behaviour on that of others. Similarly, Berkowitz's (2012) *cognitive neo-association model* specifically argues that the more you see violence, the more likely you are to engage in it, as the concept of violence becomes more salient and easily activated cognitively. We may also come to see the world as a more threatening place as a result of being exposed repeatedly to narratives around violence in society. A response to living in a *mean world* may well be to become more mean and aggressive ourselves (Gerbner et al., 1977). Repeated exposure to violence may also serve to desensitise us to its meaning and effects (Bandura, 1978). Drawing this work together, Anderson and Bushman (2001) argue that a link between media violence and aggression is extremely well supported. They go as far as to say that the size of the effect is larger than others which have a significant impact on social policy – for instance, the link between homework and academic achievement, or between passive smoking and lung cancer. However, it is also worth noting that for some forms of media (for instance, computer games) the picture is not so straightforward (see the next Critical Spotlight).

CRITICAL SPOTLIGHT: DO COMPUTER GAMES ALWAYS INCITE AGGRESSION?

We have all heard negative media stories about the relationship between the latest video game and aggressive behaviour. As we have seen, there is also a well-established evidence base showing that violent media is linked to increased aggression in general. Video games may increase aggression to a greater extent the more the individual is immersed in the on-screen action. Experimental evidence has certainly linked exposure to video game violence to increased aggression (e.g. Bartholow, Sestir & Davis, 2005). However, the link may not be straight-forward. Some authors have argued that there is a *publication bias* in the literature, which over-inflates the actual effects of video game violence (Ferguson, 2007). Other authors provide evidence which suggests that playing computer games can be linked to better social connections, lower levels of substance misuse, and better social engagement and mental health (Durkin & Barber, 2002). In an era of online games involving thousands of people (e.g. massive online multiplayer role-play games), the goal of companionship and co-operation can be more important than aggression (see Colwell & Kato, 2003). Thus, it can be argued that video gaming is not automatically negative. In recent years, the emergence of so-called '*prosocial gaming*' has been linked to increased co-operation and prosocial interpersonal behaviours (Gentile et al., 2009). It is also worth remembering that people playing computer games do not do so in isolation. The access to these games (and media in general) by young people is to some extent moderated by their parents, and a desire to play may be shaped by our upbringing more generally. It is also likely that the way people understand violence in video games is shaped by the broader context of their world.

AGGRESSION AND AUTOMATICITY

Aggression has also been understood from the implicit cognition perspective, and this may help explain the effects of media on violence. From this point of view, *primes* in our environments which are cognitively linked to aggression are more likely to generate aggressive thoughts and behaviours. For instance, in Berkowitz and Lepage (1967), the physical presence of a gun in the experimental context made people more likely to react aggressively to the experience of being given electric shocks. In similar work, Bargh, Chen and Burrows (1996) showed that being primed with rudeness made people more likely to interrupt a conversation. Primes beneath conscious awareness also seem to have an effect: priming aggression subliminally leads to more ambivalent and ambiguous behaviours being perceived as aggressive (Todorov & Bargh, 2002). As you can imagine, many researchers have argued that violent computer games are a rich source of such aggressive primes.

As we've seen, aggression has been a source of considerable interest for researchers and psychology for many decades, and a number of theories and practical implications have been posited from different perspectives. When considering these, it is important to understand aggression as a *systemic concept*. Causes of aggression are a combination of physical, socio-cultural and situational factors. Because of this, interventions need to consider the role of each of these factors in order to maximise the likelihood that they will be successful.

WHEN DO WE HELP OTHERS? BYSTANDER HELPING

Have you ever been in a situation where you needed help, but other people around you seemed not to notice or care? Or maybe you have been on the other side of this equation and seen someone who may have needed help but, for whatever reason, you failed to intervene? In this section, we review the evidence around *bystander helping* (or its alternative, *bystander apathy*).

Much research into bystander apathy was prompted by the high-profile murder of Catherine Genovese (known to friends as 'Kitty'). Kitty was murdered in the early hours of March 1968, over a prolonged ordeal lasting over 30 minutes. During the attack she was stabbed once in front of the building where she lived in sight of the other residents, and then later around the back of the building, where she was also raped. During this period, Kitty screamed for help several times. An ambulance picked Kitty up around an hour after the start of the attack, but she died on the way to hospital. Newspaper reports of this terrible event highlighted that there were a large number of witnesses (37, according to some sources) to the crime.

They also focused on the fact that it appeared the attacker left and then returned. Had somebody intervened at this point, Kitty may very well have survived the attack. The idea that the victim's neighbours had watched her being attacked and killed in front of them, without seemingly attempting to do anything about it, generated considerable public consternation. Later accounts of the events suggest that a significant degree of misreporting occurred and, in reality, several people had called the police (who were slow to respond) and/or had intervened directly. Despite this, the murder of Kitty Genovese (and other tragic events which evolved in front of witnesses, such as the torture and murder of two-year-old Jamie Bulger in 1993, after his being seen with his two ten-year-old killers by around 38 people) casts a long shadow over the belief that other people will help us when we need it. These cases have also prompted a large body of research attempting to understand how and when people choose to intervene in emergency situations.

EVOLUTIONARY PERSPECTIVES

One way of understanding helping behaviour is from an *evolutionary perspective*. Helping people can often involve a cost to the self. At the very least, your helping will involve investing time and energy in somebody else, and in many situations you may be actively putting yourself at risk. From an evolutionary point of view this is only *adaptive* to the extent that it helps to spread one's own genes. If you help somebody that you are related to, you are also helping your own genetic code (that they share) to thrive. There is evidence for this idea in both human and non-human studies. Focusing on people, Burnstein, Crandall and Kitayama (1994) observed that we choose to help people more the greater the degree of kinship we have with them. For instance, in life-or-death situation people would help someone who was their sibling (50 per cent shared genes) more than somebody who was a cousin (25 per cent), who in turn will be helped more than someone more distantly related (such as a half-cousin sharing 12.5 per cent of one's genes). This helping seems to be strategic, however: we appear to preferentially help close kin in life-and-death situations. In everyday situations, we seem to also prefer to help sick people over healthy ones. In contrast, in life-or-death situations such as famine we prefer to help healthy people over sick ones. These results are interpreted as showing that we are (knowingly or not) very calculating in our decisions to help. This raises the question of to what extent people are ever 'altruistic', or if all help is a form of helping oneself in some way. One limitation of such evolutionary accounts is that although they describe likelihoods, they do not really pin down the processes which influence whether or not somebody decides to assist somebody else in emergency. These processes are the focus of more psychological models, including Latané and Darley's *five-step model*, and Piliavin, Rodin and Piliavin's *arousal cost–reward approach*.

LATANÉ AND DARLEY'S FIVE-STEP MODEL

One model which arose in the aftermath of the Kitty Genovese murder was Latané and Darley's (1970) five-step model. This model assumes that people choose to help in an emergency. Emergencies can be defined as situations which involve dangers to persons or property, that are unusual and unforeseen to the extent that they can't be planned for and that require instant action, allowing little time for planning. The model argues that when we encounter an emergency we have to go through five steps to give help. Each step presents opportunities for the process to fail, and for no helping to take place.

To begin with, we must *notice* something is happening – we need to actually see the event. Subsequent research by Hyman et al. (2009) has shown that if we are particularly focused on something (for instance, talking on our phone), we may well miss extremely unusual events which seem unmissable (such as clowns on unicycles, in their study!). If we do notice the event, we next need to *interpret* this as an emergency. For instance, in the Jamie Bulger case many people saw (and interacted with) the young child being accompanied by the ten-year-olds who subsequently killed him, but subsequently reported that they assumed his assailants were simply family members looking after him. If we do interpret a situation as an emergency, the next step is to take *responsibility for action*. If we feel that somebody else is likely to step in, we are less likely to help. This effect is captured in the so-called *diffusion of responsibility* phenomenon, where having an increasing number of people witnessing an emergency disproportionately decreases the probability of any one person helping (although the *overall* probability of help occurring does increase at the same time). If we do take responsibility, the next step is to *decide how to help*. If we don't feel competent to help, we are unlikely to be able to take this step (and, conversely, feeling competent increases the chance of doing so). Finally, even if we decide how we can help we may not *implement the action*: if we feel the costs are too high, or something about the situation suggests that not doing so is most appropriate, we may not follow through on our intentions.

One of the strengths of this model is that it identifies a clear number of stages which need to be achieved and also suggests a number of ways we can increase the chances of people helping (for instance, making people aware of what constitutes an unusual situation, educating them about the dangers of diffusion of responsibility or equipping them to act if an emergency arises). However, one limitation of model is that it is fairly 'cold' and unemotional in nature.

A model which complements Latané and Darley's model by focusing more on the 'hot' cognition side of helping is the *arousal cost–reward model* (see Piliavin, Rodin & Piliavin, 1969). This model argues that (i) when we see someone who is in distress this generates a state of negative psychological arousal and (ii) we are motivated to reduce this arousal. We decide how to behave by looking at the costs and benefits of helping (versus not helping). The costs of helping can include the effort helping will involve, being embarrassed if it turns out help was not needed and the risk of physical harm. In contrast, helping can be rewarding to the extent that it attracts praise from others and may generate 'peace of mind' in ourselves. In contrast, the cost of not helping can include blaming oneself for the negative outcome and the risk of being frowned upon by others. Finally, the rewards of not helping include the opportunity to get on with whatever it is you're doing and saving the time and effort involved. How we choose to respond depends on the balance of these *push* and *pull* factors. If there are a lot of these factors encouraging us to help, and few of them inhibiting us, direct action is likely. This reduces the psychological arousal we feel. In contrast, if there is a lot discouraging us from helping directly, combined with very few things encouraging it, we try to reduce arousal by avoiding the situation (e.g. leaving the scene). Of course, sometimes there is a lot pushing us towards helping but also a lot pulling us away from such a course of action. In these situations, the arousal cost–reward model argues that we will engage in some other form of behaviour which serves to reduce the arousal. This can include cognitive reframing (e.g. reinterpreting the event as a non-emergency, thus removing the need to act) or indirect action (e.g. contacting someone you feel is more qualified to deal with the situation – thus reducing the arousal without becoming directly involved). The arousal cost–reward model has been used to explain the findings of Piliavan, Rodin & Piliavin's (1969) famous 'good Samaritan' study.

THE GOOD SAMARITAN STUDY

The 'good Samaritan study' involved observing the helping behaviour of members of the public travelling on a subway car in Queens, New York City, when presented with someone who appeared to become very ill. The field experiment was set up such that observers were strategically placed within one area of the subway car. From here, they could observe the reactions of people in the adjacent area of the car (the 'critical' area). On average, there were around 8.5 people in the critical area during this trial, roughly half of these being African American while the remainder were white Caucasian. During each trial, a confederate in the critical area appeared to become very ill – they staggered around, collapsed onto the floor and stared at the ceiling. The observers measured how long it took somebody to get up and help the person, as well as the gender and ethnic background of the helper. Importantly, the experimenters also manipulated the appearance of the victim. In all cases, the male victim was dressed in jacket and trousers and not wearing a tie. However, in one condition the victim carried a black cane, whereas in the other the victim smelled of alcohol and carried a bottle in a brown paper bag. The researchers observed that the victim with the cane was helped far more often (95 per cent of the time) than the drunk victim was (50 per cent of the time). They also observed that 90 per cent of the helpers were male and 64 per cent were white. These differences may be in part due to the perceived costs and rewards that people considered when deciding how to act. When the victim was drunk, the costs of helping may have been perceived as higher ('he may be sick on me!'), and the risks of not helping lower ('who'd blame me for not stepping in?'). There were probably also more possibilities for *cognitive reframing* ('by the looks of it, he's like this all the time!'). In the case of the victim with the cane, the opposite of all of these things was likely to be the case. Perhaps slightly more controversially, the research team argued that women may be less likely to help because they felt less able and also that (given the stereotypes around chivalry which were more prevalent at the time) they may also perceive a lower cost of *not* acting.

Taken together, these two models (and the variety of research which has subsequently investigated them) suggest that helping behaviour depends on a combination of our realising that an emergency is occurring, deciding whether or not to help and, if we decide to do so, working out how best to do it. They have been widely applied in real-life situations. For instance, training people in first aid makes them more likely to actually assist people, and training them to not feel embarrassed about attracting attention to suspicious objects or people is a cornerstone of public anti-terrorism campaigns.

JURY DECISION-MAKING

The jury system is the bedrock of the majority of Western legislative systems. Every day, thousands of juries across the world make decisions which can drastically change (or, in some cases, even end) people's lives. Juries differ from place to place – for instance in the amount of training individual jurors receive prior to the trial, the way jurors are selected and the number of people they comprise. However, what they have in common is that they are a group of people who come together to have a discussion and then make a decision (i.e. reach a verdict or decide upon a sentence). Given the gravity of their work, it is unsurprising that social psychologists have devoted a lot of attention to understanding how juries work, and the biases which may affect them.

Many of the systematic biases in decision-making that we have already observed in this book will apply to joint decision-making. For example, when deciding on a sentence juries may be prone to polarisation effects, they may be obedient to authority figures, act on stereotypes, be inappropriately persuaded by information, rely on automatic or heuristic processing, or find it hard to overcome majority opinion. However, alongside this body of work is research focusing specifically on *jury decision-making*. Although a complete treatment of this topic is beyond the scope of this book, we will examine issues around the features of defendants and litigants, the importance and complexity of polling issues and jury size, and the role of the jury foreperson.

FEATURES OF DEFENDANTS AND LITIGANTS

As well as being part of the jury itself, jurors themselves are part of a variety of other groups. Social identities associated with race and socioeconomic status have been identified as particularly important factors which can bias jury members. In general, people are more likely to be biased in favour of similar others when deciding guilt. This seems to be particularly true when majorities judge minorities. For instance, white majority juries judge black and Hispanic defendants guilty more often (see Devine et al., 2001; Perez et al., 1993). White, reasonably affluent group members are disproportionately over-represented on juries. In contrast, defendants are more likely to be from ethnic minorities, and to be of lower socioeconomic status. These effects combine, resulting in defendants who are from ethnic minorities and/or poorer than average being systematically more likely to be found guilty than those who are more similar to the majority.

Jurors also bring their preconceptions about individuals into the mix. The physical features of defendants can have an enormous impact on how likely they are to be found guilty. For instance, physically attractive defendants are less likely to be found guilty of crimes (e.g. Efran, 1974), more lenient sentences are given to attractive defendants (e.g. Kulka & Kessler, 1978) and, perhaps most famously, so-called '*baby-faced*' defendants are less likely to be found guilty of violent crimes, but more likely to be found guilty of crimes of negligence (see Berry & Zebrowitz-McArthur, 1988). These effects likely spring from the stereotypes we have about particular sorts of people. We've already seen from the literature on first impressions that we presume individuals who are attractive also possess other positive qualities (the halo effect; see Chapter 4). The 'baby-face' effects described above could be due to the fact that a cherubic appearance does not sit well with the idea of violence, but does not violate expectancies around negligence. This idea of *expectancy confirmation* is supported by findings which seemingly contradict those we just discussed. For instance, attractive women accused of crimes such as conning middle-aged men out of cash are *more likely* to be found guilty than are less attractive women (Piehl, 1977). In summary, our beliefs about how similar a defendant is to us, and our preconceived expectations about the defendant's character and likely behaviour, introduce systematic bias in the way we make decisions about them. Unfortunately, the trouble does not stop there: other research suggests that additional biases can be generated through procedural issues such as polling methods and the use of a foreperson.

POLLING AND FOREPEOPLE

The way that juries decide to solicit group members' opinions can have a serious effect on the final outcomes. For instance, juries quite often poll people to see if they believe the defendant is guilty or not guilty. Consider the work we've already discussed on the Asch paradigm (see Chapter 6). Now imagine that five out of twelve jury members felt that the defendant was guilty, five more felt that the defender was innocent and the final juror was on the fence. If the jury did a 'round robin', each declaring their opinions in turn, the conformity effect could present real problems. For instance, what do you think would happen if five people who wanted a guilty verdict had their turns first, followed by the unsure person? Research suggests that such *local majorities* can influence the decisions of voters that follow them (before deliberation) on guilty/not guilty decisions, and the same processes can also affect damage payouts (Davis et al., 1989).

A foreperson is typically elected to help organise the discussion and report back on the jury's final decision. Forepeople have a disproportionate effect on the jury. Some research suggests that they take up between 25 per cent and 35 per cent of speaking time, that they often decide on procedural issues such as voting format, and that their initial opinions strongly affect final outcomes (see Strodtbeck & Lipinski, 1985; Diamond & Casper 1992). Forepersons are likely to have high socioeconomic status, and to be male and highly educated. They are often also people who choose to sit at the head of the table and to speak first, and, perhaps unsurprisingly, the person who raises the need to have a foreperson in the first place! This combination of the selection bias and disproportionate influence on the final result introduces further systematic bias against defendants from minority groups. The effect of a foreperson may depend in part on the size of the jury.

JURY SIZE

Does jury size influence the likelihood you will be found guilty? If so, are larger or smaller juries more accurate? Psychologists Saks and Marti (1997) undertook a meta-analysis of the research available on this topic and drew a number of important conclusions. The results of their analysis suggest that larger juries bring about an increased chance of multiple individuals being present from minority groups. This is particularly important when we consider that a single dissenting group member is unlikely to overturn a majority attitude, while consistent group members may stand a chance (see Chapter 6). However, it also appears that larger juries seem to result in less participation from any one group member, are more likely to fail to come to a decision (to 'hang') and are no more accurate than smaller ones.

PRACTICAL APPLICATION OF JURY DECISION-MAKING RESEARCH

Many of these findings have led to significant changes in the way juries operate. For instance, jury selection methods which draw on list of automobile driver registrations (which tend to exclude minority group members disproportionately) are in many places being phased out. While juries are usually free to make a decision however they choose, in many jurisdictions they are now also given advice about how to avoid biases such as those we discussed above (in particular, around the importance of blind versus open polling). However, there is still a lot of work to be done: while jury members may (mostly) try their best, they are no more or less fallible than anybody else. Issues such as stereotyping and the other biases associated with social psychology make it unlikely that the problem will really go away until society *as a whole* adjusts its attitudes. While this should not preclude efforts to improve jury decision-making at the level of the jury, it is also important to note that these attempts are likely to be unsuccessful in isolation.

CRITICAL SPOTLIGHT: THE EFFECTS OF WRONGFUL CONVICTION

Although researchers have identified a number of systematic biases in jury decision-making, procedural changes have been slow or non-existent in many judicial systems. As systematic biases are likely to lead to wrongful convictions, this has a number of important implications. The National Registry of Exonerations (a project involving the University of California Irvine Newkirk Centre, the University of Michigan Law School and Michigan State University College of Law) aims to keep track of exonerations of innocent criminal defendants. They also study false convictions in the US, aiming to understand what the causes and consequences were and how future mistakes can be avoided. At the time of writing they've documented 2128 exonerations since 1989 (representing over 18,500 years spent wrongly imprisoned). There are also likely to be a large number of wrongly convicted individuals still in the penal system. Little research to date has examined the psychological effects of being wrongly convicted of a crime. However, it seems that such an experience can do lasting psychological damage. The research that does exist suggests that wrongful conviction and imprisonment can lead to symptoms similar to post-traumatic stress disorder (PTSD) and a heightened intolerance for injustice (Grounds, 2004; Campbell & Denov, 2004). Other researchers have noted that exonerated convicts struggle to generate positive social identity, avoid social stigma and achieve reintegration into their own community (Westervelt & Cook, 2012).

THE 'SOCIAL CURE'

One way in which social psychology has been applied the domain of health is through the '*social cure*' approach. The core idea of the social cure is that both the social identities we hold and the social networks we are connected to form important psychological resources which we can draw upon when we face psychological and/or physical challenges (Jetten, Haslam & Haslam, 2011). More specifically, having connections with multiple groups, maintaining membership during times of transition and successfully building new ties are all linked to better outcomes. In this section, we will examine how research has thought about social cures in domains such as trauma, addiction recovery and dealing with old age. We'll also look at how the social cure has been applied to treatment settings.

TRAUMA AND ADAPTATION

The social identities we hold buffer us against stressful experiences and help us recover quicker from traumatic events. Haslam et al. (2005) undertook two studies exploring this effect. The first examined patients recovering from heart surgery, and the second was undertaken with two populations of bomb disposal officers and bar staff. In both studies, the greater the extent to which people identified with their group, the less stress they experienced on an everyday basis. It also appears that identifying with *multiple* groups is important. For instance, research has shown that multiple group membership encourages people to adapt quickly to physical challenges such as learning to bobsleigh, or to dramatic life transitions such as acquired brain injuries (Jones & Jetten, 2011). This importance of social identity for adapting to difficult situations has been seen in many other domains. Kellezi, Reicher and Cassidy (2009) conducted interviews exploring mental well-being amongst individuals directly affected by the Kosovo conflict (which took place in 1999). They concluded that individuals who were able to understand the war as affirming their social identity subsequently experienced lower levels of depression and anxiety, and greater perceptions of available social support. This seems to hold for people recovering from more 'routine' traumas as well: a study by Bule and Frings (2016) suggested that individuals who are fitted with a stoma experience less negative emotions to the extent that they were able to maintain multiple group memberships. Social connections also help us during more predictable changes, such as getting old.

OLD AGE

Old age is inevitable, and with populations living longer it is important that we make the most out of people's later years.

Research suggests that social connections are incredibly important in maintaining psychological and physical health. *Social isolation* is a real risk for those in later life and men appear to be particularly vulnerable, even in contexts where the possibility for social interactions exist, such as in care-home settings. Research by Gleibs and colleagues (Gleibs et al., 2011) found that male participants who took part in social clubs experienced better psychological outcomes across a three-month period. Specifically, women who took part in clubs maintained their cognitive function and psychological well-being better than those who did not. For men the effect was even more pronounced, with a significant reduction in levels of depression and anxiety – apparently related to an increasing sense of social identification with other residents. Generally, it appears that the more people are involved with their community, the greater the sense of freedom and autonomy they had (Gleibs, Sonnenberg & Haslam, 2014).

It is worth noting at this point that the effects of identity for those in later life are not uniformly positive. If one's self-identity as being elderly is linked to negative stereotypes (such as poor cognitive performance, decreased motor skills etc.) this can negatively impact outcomes. Some life transitions can disproportionately change the extent to which people identify with these more negative versions of their social identities. For instance, being unable to continue to drive has been linked with perceiving oneself as being less independent and more frail. Activating old-age stereotypes has also been linked to stereotype threat, and the stereotypes may actually be a greater cause of performance detriment than exists in reality (Abrams, Eller & Bryant, 2006; Lamont, Swift & Abrams, 2015). Similar effects have been observed in other areas of mental health, including depression – to which our discussion now turns.

SOCIAL IDENTITY AND DEPRESSION

Until recently, depression was seen as primarily an organic brain-based disease, and its treatment often involves the use of strong psychotropic medication combined with one-to-one counselling or group therapy sessions. However, it can also be understood from a more *psychosocial perspective*. In line with the work previously described, it seems that fostering positive social identities can buffer against and reduce the effects of depression. Work by Tegan Cruwys and colleagues (Cruwys et al., 2015) suggests that this may be in part because social identities help people make more positive attributions about their own behaviour and outcomes (see Chapter 4). For instance, instead of thinking 'I failed because I'm stupid – I'll always fail', an individual may think 'I failed because the task was impossible – next time I may well succeed'. Cruwys et al. (2013) also suggest social connections are linked to the alleviation of depression symptoms, reduced relapse risk and a decreased likelihood of people becoming depressed in the future. Again, research in this area suggests social identities are not *always* helpful. For instance, Cruwys and Gunaseelan (2016) surveyed 250 people with depression in 23 countries. They found that the extent to which people identified as being depressed also predicted the extent to which they had low levels of psychological well-being. The fact that identities can both help and hinder is particularly relevant in domains such as *addiction*.

ADDICTION

A recent application of the social cure approach which has received considerable attention is in the arena of *addiction recovery*. Investigating the success of people struggling to recover from addiction, a number of research groups have observed that the extent to which people identify with being in recovery can affect their outcomes (e.g. Buckingham, Frings & Albery, 2013; Dingle et al., 2015). The number of social connections that such individuals have with people who have nothing to do with addiction also seems to predict better recovery (Best et al., 2016). These processes appear to be related to the group's ability to help individuals contextualise their experience, boost self-efficacy and conform to protective (as opposed to risky) behavioural norms (Frings & Albery, 2015). Processes around behaviours such as alcohol consumption seem to occur at both explicit and implicit (automatic) levels (Lindgren et al., 2013; Frings, Melichar & Albery, 2016). For instance, Lindgren and colleagues (Lindgren et al., 2013) show that associations between the concept of self and the concept of drinking identity (measured using a reaction-time task) predicted the amount of alcohol people intended to drink at a later date.

SOCIAL CURE: PROSPECTS FOR TREATMENT

What impact could ideas around a social cure have on treatment for psychological and physical health? The idea of the social cure is important not only theoretically, but also because it suggests that *psychosocial interventions* (i.e. those which target aspects of people's social and environmental context) may be beneficial in improving outcomes. For instance, the 'Groups 4 Health' intervention developed by Catherine Haslam and colleagues (Haslam et al., 2016) uses a series of exercises which help people identify the strengths and opportunities within their social networks and also equips them with skills to make new connections. Although in its infancy, this programme has been shown to help improve the mental health of those who undertake it (Haslam et al., 2016). More generally, the notion of 'social prescribing', where patients are facilitated to undertake locally available services (ranging from arts classes to zoo trips) and activities (such as volunteering, hobby groups and the like), is becoming an increasingly popular addition to (or substitute for) traditional medicine-based approaches to both physical and psychological health problems (see South et al., 2008). One example of this is the setting up of 'Men's Shed' schemes. These involve men coming together to undertake practical activities and hobbies in a social group revolving around – as the name suggests – a shed. These schemes seem to be successful in promoting mental health and reducing social isolation (e.g. Morgan et al., 2007).

CHAPTER SUMMARY

This chapter set out to examine social psychology in applied contexts. It did this by focusing on four particular areas in which the insights of psychologists are clearly applicable to real-world situations. In reality, there are very few experiences in our personal and professional lives which have not been studied by social psychologists in some form or another. Sports performance, consumer behaviour, education, organisational and health contexts are just some of the arenas in which social psychology has a major impact. When considering other ways that social psychology has been (or could be) applied to the real world, it is worth looking back at the previous chapters.

You'll notice that almost every single section this book covers work which has been or could potentially be transferred to a real-life situation. This is a strength of the discipline, but also raises a number of serious questions. For instance, it is worth considering whether social psychology is *morally neutral*. Both the questions researchers ask and the way they present the results feed into social narratives. They can also have potentially large-scale social effects. Often, the ways that authorities attempt to socially engineer situations (for good or for bad) is informed by research, and their agendas may not always be for the common good. This is relevant in the context of applied social psychology as it raises questions around the extent to which research should be used to manipulate people's behaviour on a large scale. We also need to bear in mind that the conclusions we draw from studies are only as good as the studies themselves – a notion highlighted by the 'second crisis' in social psychology (see Chapter 1).

KEY CHAPTER POINTS

- Social psychology is an applied discipline, which impacts many areas.
- Topics such as aggression and helping behaviours can be understood from biological, social-cognitive and cultural perspectives.
- Social psychology can have important policy implications – for instance in areas such as jury decision-making.
- The importance of social connections is increasingly being recognised in the sphere of physical and psychological health.

SUGGESTED FURTHER READING

1. Krahé, B. (2013). *The social psychology of aggression.* Hove, East Sussex: Psychology Press.
2. Stürmer, S., & Snyder, M. (eds) (2009). *The psychology of prosocial behavior: Group processes, intergroup relations, and helping.* Oxford: Wiley-Blackwell.
3. Devine, D. J., Clayton, L. D., Dunford, B. B., Seying, R., & Pryce, J. (2001). Jury decision making: 45 years of empirical research on deliberating groups. *Psychology, Public Policy and Law, 7,* 622–727.
4. Jetten, J., Haslam, C., & Alexander, S. H. (eds) (2012). *The social cure: Identity, health and well-being.* Hove, East Sussex: Psychology Press.

9

FUTURE DIRECTIONS AND COMMON THEMES

WHAT LIES AHEAD FOR SOCIAL PSYCHOLOGY?

Across the last eight chapters and three key themes, we have taken a tour of the major areas which constitute social psychology. We have met some of the major figures in the field and learnt about how it has developed from the musing of Aristotle to the cutting-edge of social neuroscience techniques. We have also seen how tensions about the methods and philosophical underpinnings have changed the face of the discipline. In terms of the areas of study themselves, we have outlined how the self is defined and what motivates us, how we interact on an interpersonal and intergroup basis, the processes of social influence, and some examples of how social psychology is applied in the real world. But we are not (quite!) done. In this final chapter we will conclude our discussion by speculating a little about what social psychologists may be interested in in the future, and by looking at some key themes which emerge consistently across the field.

FUTURE DIRECTIONS IN SOCIAL PSYCHOLOGY

What might social psychologists be studying in the coming decades? Much of social psychology is '*basic*' *research* – which will likely continue to investigate the basic social-cognitive processes which govern our behaviour. However, social psychology is also a responsive discipline, and thus likely to be affected by future *geopolitical events* – some of which we can predict, but many of which we cannot. Interest is also likely to be affected by *emerging social demands* and *new technology*. Predicting the future accurately is tricky – so before proceeding, please promise not quote me on the following in years to come!

DIRECTIONS INFLUENCED BY CONFLICT AND GEOPOLITICS

As we have seen, many of the historically key themes in the discipline (in particular around obedience and conformity) were, in part, generated by the terrible events of World War II. Since then, both industrialised Europe and the US have enjoyed an unprecedented period of relative peace – there have been few inter-state conflicts on 'home ground'. This may be associated with the reduced interest in intergroup relations research over the last 15 years – work on *acculturation* being a notable exception (see Chapter 5). However, both Europe and the US have experienced levels of attacks from domestic and overseas paramilitary/terrorist movements which arguably match the high levels experienced by the UK in the 1980s (associated with the conflict over Northern Ireland). This rise in terrorist activity may well lead to a resurgence in research looking at how *intergroup relations* (in particular around political and religious differences) can be addressed. It is also likely to lead to the increasingly rich and more systematic study of *radicalisation* (how people are nurtured to become 'fanatical' or terrorists). Indeed, governments around the world are already investing more and more in this research area in a number of academic fields such as political science, sociology and psychology. Outside of Europe and the US, there are unfortunately many parts of the world still affected by inter- or intra-state conflict. One effect that these conflicts have had is the movement of large numbers of civilians from one country and culture to another – often in very short periods (the recent movements of populations from Syria being a prime example). Research in the acculturation tradition specifically addressing such *conflict-displaced populations* has become more prevalent as a result. Finally, the uncertainty which the world has recently faced (politically and economically) has led to an increase in *populist politics*. Many emerging parties have policies very right of centre, and often with explicitly nationalist attitudes. Understanding the processes which underpin a move towards nationalism is likely to be a key aim of (often fairly liberal) social psychologists. A final geopolitical issue which may affect the direction of social psychology is a *widening of participation* in setting the research agenda. As we have discussed, social psychology has historically been based in Europe and the US. This situation may well change. Many countries in the Middle East are explicitly aiming to propel their institutions to the top of the world rankings. India is expanding its university sector at a tremendous pace to meet the demands of an aspiring generation of young people, and China's annual research output is increasing at a phenomenal rate. While much of the research these institutions currently undertake is in physical sciences and engineering, more and more are also engaging in social science (particularly in China). These emerging 'research powers' will have their own social priorities, and their own views on what social psychology is (and is not). This area of growth is exciting – and likely to be the source of the next set of major 'paradigm shifts' (where the direction of a field is changed significantly) that the field goes through.

DIRECTIONS INFLUENCED BY SOCIAL DEMANDS AND NEW TECHNOLOGY

Alongside direct geopolitical influences, the future of social psychology may be affected by other emerging social demands. With increasing lifespans and a resulting *ageing population* in many countries, issues which affect those who are older are likely to become increasingly important. Research which helps us understand how people can make the most of their later lives is likely to be a source of interest. In particular, the effects of *social isolation* on the elderly (or, in contrast, *social enrichment* and participation programmes) will likely be the focus of much research.

Finally, social psychology is likely to be influenced by *new technologies and research tools*. Social cognition is still limited by the relative coarseness of the measures it has at its disposal, and new developments in this field may help bridge the gap between this area of the field and others. For instance, better measures of cognitive associations may bring together the disparate areas of automaticity and social identity. Similarly, new developments in social neuroscience may make this field more directly applicable to mainstream social psychology. Of course, new technology may also present the ability to explore new questions: *wearable technologies* such as activity- and sleep-trackers are developing rapidly, and may present the opportunity for more sophisticated behavioural measures. For instance, new systems can now measure blood alcohol levels non-invasively in real time via an ankle bracelet, and mobile eye-trackers are now less bulky than some spectacles! Together, future developments in this area may lead to a consolidation of the various levels of analysis we use – *with multilevel explanations* (taking into account both qualitative and quantitative approaches) becoming more normative.

In summary, the field of social psychology is likely to be an exciting place in the coming decades. Discussions about how the field positions itself as a science (expressed through the debate about *replication* and *scientific integrity*) will combine with an ever-changing political and technological landscape. Although I have risked taking a (sort of informed!) guess at how some of these issues will pan out, it's impossible to say with certainty how things will end up and, ultimately, only time will tell …

COMMON THEMES IN SOCIAL PSYCHOLOGY

As we have seen, social psychology is a diverse and often contradictory discipline – so how can we sum it up? Despite the apparent variety, there are some similarities. Across social psychology's history and over the various debates, research fads and fashions, and changing methods it can be argued that a number of core themes are present. In this section we will briefly explore how the discipline can be seen as an applied and basic science, which benefits from encouraging multiple levels of explanation, but also is in constant flux. We also make an argument that one aspect seems ever-present – it all seems to come back to the idea of *social influence* in the end.

SOCIAL PSYCHOLOGY AS A BASIC AND APPLIED DISCIPLINE

In any given period, pressing concerns inspire social psychologists to find out 'how things work' and, increasingly, move them to develop new ways of intervening. The nature of these concerns can be varied: the study of social norms can be used to sell more toothpaste, but also to heal the social rifts left by sectarian violence, for example. However, what brings all these interventions together is a foundation of rigorously tested theoretical models. These models and evidence from interventions in turn inform the development of the next generation of ideas. As such, *social psychology is both a basic and an applied discipline.*

SOCIAL PSYCHOLOGY AS A MULTILEVEL PHENOMENON

The days when any one methodological approach could reasonably claim to be 'the best' are, thankfully, well in the past. Social psychology encompasses an enormous range of methods, each of which is particularly suited to answering its own particular set of research questions. Although this diversity can present challenges, it also highlights a distinct strength of social psychology: it can generate multiple explanations in response to the same question, each pitched at different levels. For instance, take the experience of 'being in a group'. The study of implicit social cognition consistently highlights the role of processes which we may not be able to consciously inspect, or even be aware of, which affect intergroup processes (see Chapters 3 and 5). Similarly, neuroscientific approaches explore how our brain responds to social stimuli – including meeting ingroup and outgroup members. At the other end of the scale, *critical social psychology* approaches – in particular *qualitative* perspectives – highlight how our self-reported experience is key to achieving a full understanding of our social lives. Increasingly, these differing approaches are seen as complementary rather than antagonistic. As such, social psychology is a field which assumes *multiple levels of causation* and *multiple levels of explanation.* The challenge, of course, is achieving a useful integration of the various ideas.

SOCIAL PSYCHOLOGY AS A DYNAMIC PROCESS

Social psychology as a discipline is in a state of constant flux. Trends in research methods (in particular, *qualitative* versus *quantitative*) have waxed and waned over the years, as has the interest and effort invested in specific topic areas. At times, the very philosophical basis of the discipline has been (and still is) questioned. New methods of investigation are developed, and old ones challenged. The current debate about replications and the statistical methods we use represent the latest iteration of these ongoing changes. The long-term impact of this particular debate remains to be seen – but it is certain that practices within the discipline will change fundamentally as a result of it. Equally, it is likely that new debates will arise (and be resolved) in due course. The backdrop against which social psychology 'happens' also changes: variation across cultures and changes within a given culture over time often limit the generalisability of findings. As a result, psychological processes that at times have been seen as almost 'proven' themselves become in need of revaluation. As more of the world becomes involved in the study of social psychology, this process is likely to accelerate. As such, *social psychology is constantly evolving*, in both its focus and its methodologies.

SOCIAL PSYCHOLOGY AS SOCIAL INFLUENCE

From the earliest work by Triplett to current research showing how neurons in our brain are activated by the behaviour of others, one thing that is clear from social psychology is that no-one is truly isolated from others – and that *social influence* is a fundamental process in our social psychology. Allport's observation that we can be affected by the actual, implied or imagined presence of others is as well supported today as it was when first developed. Whether we are thinking about social norms, being subjected to online advertising or being inspired to try harder to benefit the group, the interplay between our self and others is a constant feature in our psychological lives. Partly as a result of this interconnectedness, we can also see our social selves as being dynamic. 'Who we think we are' is shaped not only by how we think others see us, but also by the roles we play in a given social situation. Sources of social influence can temporarily (or more permanently) change how we behave – sometimes in ways we'd prefer to avoid. These effects are interactive: as well as our own self being affected by the social world, we are also a source of influence which affects others. Across virtually all of the evidence presented in this book you can see an underlying implication that people are *dynamic selves within dynamic systems* and that interaction between these systems, or *social influence*, is a fundamental part of the human condition.

KEY CHAPTER POINTS

- Social psychology is likely to change significantly as time goes on.
- Changes are likely to be driven by geopolitical, social and technological developments.
- Social psychology is a basic and applied discipline which assumes multiple levels of causation and explanation.
- Social psychology can be understood as having social influence as a common, perhaps defining, theme.

AFTERWORD

So, we have reached the end of our journey! I have had a marvellous time writing this book, and I hope you have enjoyed learning about the history, context, insights and future that social psychology offers. I also hope that along the way you have been inspired to think about the ways in which social psychology explains some of your own behaviour, and that of others. Finally, I would be really pleased if this book has inspired you to look further into the discipline. As you have seen, each of the chapters presents a number of recommended readings. Some of these are textbooks which explore a given area in more depth; others are papers which summarise a given field, or that I feel have been particularly influential. However, don't let the list restrict you! More and more, the research produced by social psychologists is available as '*open access*': this means that the academic journals it is published in make it available, free of charge, for anyone to view. Various search engines (including Google Scholar) let anybody access this growing repository − so find a topic you are interested in, search and learn! I hope the end of this book represents the start of your longer journey of exploring social psychology. Enjoy!

Daniel Frings, 30 April 2018

REFERENCES

Abrams, D., Eller, A., & Bryant, J. (2006). An age apart: The effects of intergenerational contact and stereotype threat on performance and intergroup bias. *Psychology and Aging, 21,* 691–702. https://doi.org/10.1037/0882-7974.21.4.691

Abrams, D., Rutland, A., Cameron, L., & Marques, J. (2003). The development of subjective group dynamics: When in-group bias gets specific. *British Journal of Developmental Psychology, 21,* 155–176. https://doi.org/10.1348/026151003765264020

Ackerman, J. M., Nocera, C. C., & Bargh, J. A. (2010). Incidental haptic sensations influence: Social judgments and decisions. *Science, 328,* 1712–1715. https://doi.org/10.1126/science.1189993

Adams, J. S. (1965). Inequity in social exchange. *Advances in Experimental Social Psychology, 2,* 267–299. https://doi.org/10.1016/S0065-2601(08)60108-2

Adorno, T. W., Frenkel-Brunswik, E., Levinson, D. J., & Sanford, R. N. (1950). *The authoritarian personality.* Oxford: Harpers.

Alberici, A. I., & Milesi, P. (2013). The influence of the internet on the psychosocial predictors of collective action. *Journal of Community & Applied Social Psychology, 23,* 373–388. https://doi.org/10.1002/casp.2131

Allport, F. H. (1924). *Social psychology.* Boston: Houghton Mifflin Company.

Allport, G. W. (1954a). The historical background of social psychology. In G. Lindzey (ed.), *Handbook of social psychology* (pp. 3–56). Reading, MA: Addison-Wesley.

Allport, G. (1954b). *The nature of prejudice.* Reading, MA: Addison-Wesley.

Altemeyer, B. (1981). *Right-wing authoritarianism*. Manitoba: University of Manitoba Press.

Anderson, C. A., & Bushman, B. J. (2001). Effects of violent video games on aggressive behavior, aggressive cognition, aggressive affect, physiological arousal, and prosocial behavior: A meta-analytic review of the scientific literature. *Psychological Science, 12*, 353–359. https://doi.org/10.1111/1467-9280.00366

Anderson, N. H. (1965). Averaging versus adding as a stimulus-combination rule in impression formation. *Journal of Experimental Psychology, 70*, 394–400. https://doi.org/10.1037/h0022280

Archer, J. (2006). Testosterone and human aggression: An evaluation of the challenge hypothesis. *Neuroscience & Biobehavioral Reviews, 30*, 319–345. https://doi.org/10.1016/J.NEUBIOREV.2004.12.007

Argyle, M., & Dean, J. (1965). Eye-contact, distance and affiliation. *Sociometry, 28*, 289–304. https://doi.org/10.2307/2786027

Aristotle, trans. Jowett, B. (2000). *Politics*. Mineola, NY: Dover Publications.

Arkin, R., Cooper, H., & Kolditz, T. (1980). A statistical review of the literature concerning the self-serving attribution bias in interpersonal influence situations. *Journal of Personality, 48*, 435–448. https://doi.org/10.1111/j.1467-6494.1980.tb02378.x

Aronson, E., & Carlsmith, J. M. (1963). Effect of the severity of threat on the devaluation of forbidden behavior. *The Journal of Abnormal and Social Psychology, 66*, 584–588. https://doi.org/10.1037/h0039901

Aronson, E., & Mills, J. (1959). The effect of severity of initiation on liking for a group. *The Journal of Abnormal and Social Psychology, 59*, 177–181. https://doi.org/10.1037/h0047195

Arrow, H., McGrath, J., & Berdahl, J. (2000). *Small groups as complex systems: Formation, coordination, development, and adaptation.* Thousand Oaks, CA: Sage Publications.

Asch, S. E. (1946). Forming impressions of personality. *The Journal of Abnormal and Social Psychology, 41*, 258–290. https://doi.org/10.1037/h0055756

Asch, S. E., Solomon, E., & Guetzkow, H. (1951). Effects of group pressure upon the modification and distortion of judgments. In H. Guetzkow (ed.), *Groups, leadership, and men* (pp. 117–190). Pittsburgh: Carnegie Press.

Ashforth, B. E., Sluss, D. M., & Saks, A. M. (2007). Socialization tactics, proactive behavior, and newcomer learning: Integrating socialization models. *Journal of Vocational Behavior, 70*, 447–462. https://doi.org/10.1016/J.JVB.2007.02.001

Balliet, D. (2010). Communication and cooperation in social dilemmas: A meta-analytic review. *Journal of Conflict Resolution, 54*, 39–57. https://doi.org/10.1177/0022002709352443

Balliet, D., & Joireman, J. (2010). Ego depletion reduces proselfs' concern with the well-being of others. *Group Processes & Intergroup Relations, 13*, 227–239. https://doi.org/10.1177/1368430209353634

Bandura, A. (1978). Social learning theory of aggression. *Journal of Communication*, *28*, 12–29. https://doi.org/10.1111/j.1460-2466.1978.tb01621.x

Bandura, A., Ross, D., & Ross, S. A. (1961). Transmission of aggression through the imitation of aggressive models. *Journal of Abnormal and Social Psychology*, *63*, 575–582. http://dx.doi.org/10.1037/h0045925

Bandura, A., Ross, D., & Ross, S. A. (1963). Vicarious reinforcement and imitative learning. The *Journal of Abnormal and Social Psychology*, *67*, 601–607. https://doi.org/10.1037/h0045550

Bargh, J. A., & Chartrand, T. L. (1999). The unbearable automaticity of being. *American Psychologist*, *54*, 462–479. https://doi.org/10.1037/0003-066X.54.7.462

Bargh, J. A., & Williams, E. L. (2006). The automaticity of social life. *Current Directions in Psychological Science*, *15*, 1–4. https://doi.org/10.1111/j.0963-7214.2006.00395.x

Bargh, J. A., Chen, M., & Burrows, L. (1996). Automaticity of social behavior: Direct effects of trait construct and stereotype activation on action. *Journal of Personality and Social Psychology*, *71*, 230–244. http://dx.doi.org/10.1037/0022-3514.71.2.230

Bar-Tal, D. (2000). From intractable conflict through conflict resolution to reconciliation: Psychological analysis. *Political Psychology*, *21*, 351–365. https://doi.org/10.1111/0162-895X.00192 C

Bar-Tal, D., Halperin, E., & De Rivera, J. (2007). Collective emotions in conflict situations: Societal implications. *Journal of Social Issues*, *63*, 441–460. https://doi.org/10.1111/j.1540-4560.2007.00518.x

Bartholow, B. D., Sestir, M. A., & Davis, E. B. (2005). Correlates and consequences of exposure to video game violence: Hostile personality, empathy, and aggressive behavior. *Personality and Social Psychology Bulletin*, *31*, 1573–1586. https://doi.org/10.1177/0146167205277205

Bartlett, F. C., & Burt, C. (1933). Remembering: A study in experimental and social psychology. *British Journal of Educational Psychology*, *3*, 187–192. https://doi.org/10.1111/j.2044-8279.1933.tb02913.x

Baumeister, R. F., & Bratslavsky, E. (1999). Passion, intimacy, and time: Passionate love as a function of change in intimacy. *Personality and Social Psychology Review*, *3*, 49–67. https://doi.org/10.1207/s15327957pspr0301_3

Baumeister, R. F., & Leary, M. R. (1995). The need to belong: Desire for interpersonal attachments as a fundamental human motivation. *Psychological Bulletin*, *117*, 497–529.

Baumeister, R. F., & Vohs, K. D. (2007). Self-regulation, ego depletion, and motivation. *Social and Personality Psychology Compass*, *1*, 115–128. https://doi.org/10.1111/j.1751-9004.2007.00001.x

Baumeister, R. F., Bratslavsky, E., Muraven, M., & Tice, D. M. (1998). Ego depletion: is the active self a limited resource? *Journal of Personality and Social Psychology*, *74*, 1252–1265. https://doi.org/10.1037/0022-3514.74.5.1252

Baumeister, R. F., Smart, L., & Boden, J. M. (1996). Relation of threatened egotism to violence and aggression: The dark side of high self-esteem. *Psychological Review, 103*, 5–33. https://doi.org/10.1037/0033-295X.103.1.5

Baumeister, R. F., Sparks, E. A., Stillman, T. F., & Vohs, K. D. (2008). Free will in consumer behavior: Self-control, ego depletion, and choice. *Journal of Consumer Psychology, 18*, 4–13. https://doi.org/10.1016/j.jcps.2007.10.002

Baumeister, R. F., Tice, D. M., & Hutton, D. G. (1989). Self-presentational motivations and personality differences in self-esteem. *Journal of Personality, 57*, 547–579. https://doi.org/10.1111/j.1467-6494.1989.tb02384.x

Beck, A., Rush, A., Shaw, B., & Emery, G. (1979). *Cognitive therapy of depression.* New York: Guilford Press.

Becker, J. C., Wagner, U., & Christ, O. (2011). Consequences of the 2008 financial crisis for intergroup relations. *Group Processes & Intergroup Relations, 14*, 871–885. https://doi.org/10.1177/1368430211407643

Bekkering, H., & Neggers, S. F. W. (2002). Visual search is modulated by action intentions. *Psychological Science, 13*, 370–374. https://doi.org/10.1111/j.0956-7976.2002.00466.x

Bem, S. L. (1981). Gender schema theory: A cognitive account of sex typing. *Psychological Review, 88*, 354–364. https://doi.org/10.1037/0033-295X.88.4.354

Berkowitz, L. (1989). Frustration-aggression hypothesis: Examination and reformulation. *Psychological Bulletin, 106*, 59–73. https://doi.org/10.1037/0033-2909.106.1.59

Berkowitz, L. (2012). A different view of anger: The cognitive-neoassociation conception of the relation of anger to aggression. *Aggressive Behavior, 38*, 322–333. https://doi.org/10.1002/ab.21432

Berkowitz, L., & Lepage, A. (1967). Weapons as aggression-eliciting stimuli. *Journal of Personality and Social Psychology, 7*, 202–207. https://doi.org/10.1037/h0025008

Berlin, B., & Kay, P. (1991). *Basic color terms: Their universality and evolution.* Berkley: University of California Press.

Berry, D. S., & Zebrowitz-McArthur, L. (1988). What's in a face? *Personality and Social Psychology Bulletin, 14*, 23–33. https://doi.org/10.1177/0146167288141003

Berry, J. (1967). Independence and conformity in subsistence-level societies. *Journal of Personality and Social Psychology, 7*, 415–418. http://dx.doi.org/10.1037/h0025231

Berry, J. (1997). Immigration, acculturation, and adaptation. *Applied Psychology, 46*, 5–34. https://doi.org/10.1111/j.1464-0597.1997.tb01087.x

Berry, J., Phinney, J., Sam, D., & Vedder, P. (2006). Immigrant youth: Acculturation, identity, and adaptation. *Applied Psychology, 55*, 303–332.

Berscheid, E., Dion, K., Walster, E., & Walster, G. W. (1971). Physical attractiveness and dating choice: A test of the matching hypothesis. *Journal of Experimental Social Psychology, 7*, 173–189. https://doi.org/10.1016/0022-1031(71)90065-5

Best, D., Beckwith, M., Haslam, C., Alexander Haslam, S., Jetten, J., Mawson, E., & Lubman, D. I. (2016). Overcoming alcohol and other drug addiction as a process of social identity transition: The social identity model of recovery (SIMOR). *Addiction Research & Theory, 24*, 111–123. https://doi.org/10.3109/16066359.2015.1075980

Bettencourt, B. A., & Sheldon, K. (2001). Social roles as mechanism for psychological need satisfaction within social groups. *Journal of Personality and Social Psychology, 81*, 1131–1143. https://doi.org/10.1037/0022-3514.81.6.1131

Blascovich, J., Ginsburg, G. P., & Veach, T. L. (1975). A pluralistic explanation of choice shifts on the risk dimension. *Journal of Personality and Social Psychology, 31*, 422–429. https://doi.org/10.1037/h0076479

Blascovich, J., Mendes, W. B., Hunter, S. B., Lickel, B., & Kowai-Bell, N. (2001). Perceiver threat in social interactions with stigmatized others. *Journal of Personality and Social Psychology, 80*, 253–267.

Blass, T. (1991). Understanding behavior in the Milgram obedience experiment: The role of personality, situations, and their interactions. *Journal of Personality and Social Psychology, 60*, 398–413. https://doi.org/10.1037/0022-3514.60.3.398

Bless, H., Bohner, G., Schwarz, N., & Strack, F. (1990). Mood and persuasion. *Personality and Social Psychology Bulletin, 16*, 331–345. https://doi.org/10.1177/0146167290162013

Bliuc, A., Best, D., Beckwith, M., & Iqbal, M. (2017). Online support communities in addiction recovery: capturing social interaction and identity change through analyses of online communication. In S. Buckingham and D. Beat (eds), *Addiction, behavioural change and social identity: The pathway to resilience and recovery* (pp. 137–155). Oxon: Routledge.

Blumer, H. (1986). *Symbolic interactionism: perspective and method.* University of California Press.

Boen, F., Vanbeselaere, N., & Feys, J. (2002). Behavioral consequences of fluctuating group success: An internet study of soccer-team fans. *Journal of Social Psychology, 142*, 769–781. https://doi.org/10.1080/00224540209603935

Bond, C. F., & Titus, L. J. (1983). Social facilitation: A meta-analysis of 241 studies. *Psychological Bulletin, 94*, 265–292. https://doi.org/10.1037/0033-2909.94.2.265

Bond, R., & Smith, P. B. (1996). Culture and conformity: A meta-analysis of studies using Asch's (1952b, 1956) line judgment task. *Psychological Bulletin, 119*, 111–137. https://doi.org/10.1037//0033-2909.119.1.111

Borkenau, P., & Liebler, A. (1992). Trait inferences: Sources of validity at zero acquaintance. *Journal of Personality and Social Psychology, 62*, 645–657. https://doi.org/10.1037/0022-3514.62.4.645

Boster, F. J., & Mongeau, P. (1984). Fear-arousing persuasive messages. *Annals of the International Communication Association, 8*, 330–375. https://doi.org/10.1080/23808985.1984.11678581

Bradshaw, J. L., & Nettleton, N. C. (1982). Language lateralization to the dominant hemisphere: Tool use, gesture and language in hominid evolution. *Current Psychological Reviews, 2*, 171–192. https://doi.org/10.1007/BF02684498

Brendgen, M., Dionne, G., Girard, A., Boivin, M., Vitaro, F., & Perusse, D. (2005). Examining genetic and environmental effects on social aggression: A study of 6-year-old twins. *Child Development, 76*, 930–946. https://doi.org/10.1111/j.1467-8624.2005.00887.x

Bressler, E. R., Martin, R. A., Balshine, S., & Quinter, V. E. (2006). Production and appreciation of humor as sexually selected traits. *Evolution and Human Behavior, 27*, 121–130. https://doi.org/10.1016/j.evolhumbehav.2005.09.001

Brewer, M. B. (1999). The psychology of prejudice: Ingroup love and outgroup hate? *Journal of Social Issues, 55*, 429–444. https://doi.org/10.1111/0022-4537.00126

Broadbent, D. E. (1957). A mechanical model for human attention and immediate memory. *Psychological Review, 64*, 205–215. https://doi.org/10.1037/h0047313

Bromet, E., Andrade, L. H., Hwang, I., Sampson, N. A., Alonso, J., de Girolama, G., … & Kessler, R. C. (2011). Cross-national epidemiology of DSM-IV major depressive episode. *BMC Medicine, 9*, 90. https://doi.org/10.1186/1741-7015-9-90

Buckingham, S. A., Frings, D., & Albery, I. P. (2013). Group membership and social identity in addiction recovery. *Psychology of Addictive Behaviors, 27*, 1132–1140. https://doi.org/10.1037/a0032480

Bule, B., & Frings, D. (2016). The role of group membership continuity and multiple memberships on mental well-being amongst post-operative stoma patients. *Psycho-Oncology, 25*, 726–728. https://doi.org/10.1002/pon.4006

Burnstein, E., & Vinokur, A. (1975). What a person thinks upon learning he has chosen differently from others: Nice evidence for the persuasive-arguments explanation of choice shifts. *Journal of Experimental Social Psychology, 11*, 412–426. https://doi.org/10.1016/0022-1031(75)90045-1

Burnstein, E., Crandall, C., & Kitayama, S. (1994). Some neo-Darwinian decision rules for altruism: Weighing cues for inclusive fitness as a function of the biological importance of the decision. *Journal of Personality and Social Psychology, 67*, 773–789. https://doi.org/10.1037/0022-3514.67.5.773

Bushman, B. J., Baumeister, R. F., & Stack, A. D. (1999). Catharsis, aggression, and persuasive influence: Self-fulfilling or self-defeating prophecies? *Journal of Personality and Social Psychology, 76*, 367–376. https://doi.org/10.1037/0022-3514.76.3.367

Buss, D. M. (1989). Sex differences in human mate preferences: Evolutionary hypotheses tested in 37 cultures. *Behavioral and Brain Sciences, 12*, 1–14. https://doi.org/10.1017/S0140525X00023992

Buss, D. M., & Schmitt, D. P. (1993). Sexual strategies theory: An evolutionary perspective on human mating. *Psychological Review, 100*, 204–232. https://doi.org/10.1037/0033-295X.100.2.204

Cacioppo, J., & Berntson, G. (1992). Social psychological contributions to the decade of the brain: Doctrine of multilevel analysis. *American Psychologist, 47*, 1019–1028.

Cacioppo, J. T., Petty, R. E., Feinstein, J. A., & Jarvis, W. B. G. (1996). Dispositional differences in cognitive motivation: The life and times of individuals varying in need for cognition. *Psychological Bulletin, 119*, 197–253. https://doi.org/10.1037/0033-2909.119.2.197

Campbell, D. (1958). Common fate, similarity, and other indices of the status of aggregates of persons as social entities. *Systems Research and Behavioral Science, 3*, 14–25. https://doi.org/10.1002/bs.3830030103

Campbell, K., & Denov, M. (2004). The burden of innocence: Coping with a wrongful imprisonment. *Canadian Journal of Criminology and Criminal Justice, 46*, 139–164. https://doi.org/10.3138/cjccj.46.2.139

Carney, D. R., Colvin, C. R., & Hall, J. A. (2007). A thin slice perspective on the accuracy of first impressions. *Journal of Research in Personality, 41*, 1054–1072. https://doi.org/10.1016/J.JRP.2007.01.004

Carpenter, A. (2008). Kant on the embodied cognition. *Falsafeh, 36*(1), 59–68.

Carter, E. C., & McCullough, M. E. (2014). Publication bias and the limited strength model of self-control: Has the evidence for ego depletion been overestimated? *Frontiers in Psychology, 5*, 823. https://doi.org/10.3389/fpsyg.2014.00823

Carver, C. S., & Scheier, M. F. (1981). *Attention and self-regulation: A control-theory approach to human behavior*. New York: Springer.

Cash, T. F., & Derlega, V. J. (1978). The matching hypothesis: Physical attractiveness among same-sexed friends. *Personality and Social Psychology Bulletin, 4*, 240–243. https://doi.org/10.1177/014616727800400213

Chaiken, S. (1980). Heuristic versus systematic information processing and the use of source versus message cues in persuasion. *Journal of Personality and Social Psychology, 39*, 752–766. https://doi.org/10.1037/0022-3514.39.5.752

Chaiken, S., Liberman, A., & Eagly, A. H. (1989). Heuristic and systematic information processing within and beyond the persuasion context. In J. S. Uleman & J. A. Bargh (eds), *Unintended thought* (pp. 212–253). London: Guilford Press.

Chapman, A. J. (1973). Social facilitation of laughter in children. *Journal of Experimental Social Psychology, 9*, 528–541. https://doi.org/10.1016/0022-1031(73)90035-8

Cheng, P. W., & Novick, L. R. (1990). A probabilistic contrast model of causal induction. *Journal of Personality and Social Psychology, 58*, 545–567. https://doi.org/10.1037/0022-3514.58.4.545

Cho, S., Huh, J., & Faber, R. J. (2014). The influence of sender trust and adver-
tiser trust on multistage effects of viral advertising. *Journal of Advertising, 43*,
100–114. https://doi.org/10.1080/00913367.2013.811707

Choi, I., & Nisbett, R. (2000). Cultural psychology of surprise: Holistic theories
and recognition of contradiction. *Journal of Personality and Social Psychology, 79*,
890–905.

Chowdhury, A. N. (1996). The definition and classification of Koro. *Culture,
Medicine and Psychiatry, 20*, 41–65. https://doi.org/10.1007/BF00118750

Cialdini, R. B. (2007). *Influence: The psychology of persuasion*. New York:
HarperBusiness.

Cialdini, R. B., Borden, R., & Thorne, A. (1976). Basking in reflected glory:
Three (football) field studies. *Journal of Personality, 34*, 366–375.

Cialdini, R. B., Cacioppo, J. T., Bassett, R., & Miller, J. A. (1978). Low-ball
procedure for producing compliance: Commitment then cost. *Journal
of Personality and Social Psychology, 36*, 463–476. https://doi.org/10.1037/
0022-3514.36.5.463

Cialdini, R. B., Reno, R. R., & Kallgren, C. A. (1990). A focus theory of normative conduct: Recycling the concept of norms to reduce littering in public
places. *Journal of Personality and Social Psychology, 58*, 1015–1026. https://doi.
org/10.1037/0022-3514.58.6.1015

Cialdini, R. B., Vincent, J. E., Lewis, S. K., Catalan, J., Wheeler, D., & Darby,
B. L. (1975). Reciprocal concessions procedure for inducing compliance: The
door-in-the-face technique. *Journal of Personality and Social Psychology, 31*, 206–
215. https://doi.org/10.1037/h0076284

Coccaro, E. F. (1989). Central serotonin and impulsive aggression. *The British
Journal of Psychiatry, 155*, 52–62.

Cohen, D., Nisbett, R. E., Bowdle, B. F., & Schwarz, N. (1996). Insult, aggression,
and the southern culture of honor: An 'experimental ethnography'. *Journal
of Personality and Social Psychology, 70*, 945–960. https://doi.org/10.1037/
0022-3514.70.5.945

Cohen, E. G. (1982). Expectation states and interracial interaction in school
settings. *Annual Review of Sociology, 8*, 209–235. https://doi.org/10.1146/
annurev.so.08.080182.001233

Colwell, J., & Kato, M. (2003). Investigation of the relationship between
social isolation, self-esteem, aggression and computer game play in Japanese
adolescents. *Asian Journal of Social Psychology, 6*, 149–158. https://doi.org/
10.1111/1467-839X.t01-1-00017

Cooley, C. H. (1902). *Human nature and the social order*. New York: Scribner.

Cosmides, L., & Tooby, J. (2005). Neurocognitive adaptations designed for social
exchange. In D. Buss (ed.), *The handbook of evolutionary psychology* (pp. 584–
627). Hoboken, NJ: Wiley.

Crisp, R. J., & Turner, R. N. (2009). Can imagined interactions produce positive perceptions? Reducing prejudice through simulated social contact. *American Psychologist, 64*, 231–240. https://doi.org/10.1037/a0014718

Crocker, J., & Major, B. (1989). Social stigma and self-esteem: The self-protective properties of stigma. *Psychological Review, 96*, 608–630. https://doi.org/10.1037/0033-295X.96.4.608

Crosby, F. (1976). A model of egoistical relative deprivation. *Psychological Review, 83*, 85–113. https://doi.org/10.1037/0033-295X.83.2.85

Crossley, K. L., Cornelissen, P. L., & Tovée, M. J. (2012). What is an attractive body? Using an interactive 3d program to create the ideal body for you and your partner. *PLoS ONE, 7*, e50601. https://doi.org/10.1371/journal.pone.0050601

Cruwys, T., & Gunaseelan, S. (2016). 'Depression is who I am': Mental illness identity, stigma and wellbeing. *Journal of Affective Disorders, 189*, 36–42. https://doi.org/10.1016/J.JAD.2015.09.012

Cruwys, T., Dingle, G. A., Haslam, C., Haslam, S. A., Jetten, J., & Morton, T. A. (2013). Social group memberships protect against future depression, alleviate depression symptoms and prevent depression relapse. *Social Science & Medicine, 98*, 179–186. https://doi.org/10.1016/J.SOCSCIMED.2013.09.013

Cruwys, T., South, E. I., Greenaway, K. H., & Haslam, S. A. (2015). Social identity reduces depression by fostering positive attributions. *Social Psychological and Personality Science, 6*, 65–74. https://doi.org/10.1177/1948550614543309

Darley, J. M., & Berscheid, E. (1967). Increased liking as a result of the anticipation of personal contact. *Human Relations, 20*, 29–40. https://doi.org/10.1177/001872676702000103

Davis, J. H., Kameda, T., Parks, C., Stasson, M., & Zimmerman, S. (1989). Some social mechanics of group decision making: The distribution of opinion, polling sequence, and implications for consensus. *Journal of Personality and Social Psychology, 57*, 1000–1012. https://doi.org/10.1037/0022-3514.57.6.1000

Davis, K. (2012). Tensions of identity in a networked era: Young people's perspectives on the risks and rewards of online self-expression. *New Media & Society, 14*, 634–651. https://doi/abs/10.1177/1461444811422430

De Castro, J. M. (1994). Family and friends produce greater social facilitation of food intake than other companions. *Physiology & Behavior, 56*, 445–455. https://doi.org/10.1016/0031-9384(94)90286-0

Derné, S. (1999). Handling ambivalence toward 'Western' ways: Transnational cultural flows and men's identity in India. *Studies in Symbolic Interaction, 22*, 17–45.

Devine, D. J., Clayton, L. D., Dunford, B. B., Seying, R., & Pryce, J. (2001). Jury decision making: 45 years of empirical research on deliberating groups. *Psychology, Public Policy, and Law, 7*, 622–727. https://doi.org/10.1037/1076-8971.7.3.622

Diamond, S. S., & Casper, J. D. (1992). Blindfolding the jury to verdict consequences: Damages, experts, and the civil jury. *Law & Society Review, 26*, 513–564. https://doi.org/10.2307/3053737

Diener, E., Fraser, S. C., Beaman, A. L., & Kelem, R. T. (1976). Effects of deindividuation variables on stealing among Halloween trick-or-treaters. *Journal of Personality and Social Psychology, 33*, 178–183. https://doi.org/10.1037/0022-3514.33.2.178

Dijksterhuis, A., & Bargh, J. A. (2001). The perception–behavior expressway: Automatic effects of social perception on social behavior. *Advances in Experimental Social Psychology, 33*, 1–40. https://doi.org/10.1016/S0065-2601(01)80003-4

DiMatteo, M. R., Friedman, H. S., & Taranta, A. (1979). Sensitivity to bodily nonverbal communication as a factor in practitioner–patient rapport. *Journal of Nonverbal Behavior, 4*, 18–26. https://doi.org/10.1007/BF00986909

Dingle, G. A., Stark, C., Cruwys, T., & Best, D. (2015). Breaking good: Breaking ties with social groups may be good for recovery from substance misuse. *British Journal of Social Psychology, 54*, 236–254. https://doi.org/10.1111/bjso.12081

Dion, K., Berscheid, E., & Walster, E. (1972). What is beautiful is good. *Journal of Personality and Social Psychology, 24*, 285–290. http://dx.doi.org/10.1037/h0033731

Dittes, J. E., & Kelley, H. H. (1956). Effects of different conditions of acceptance upon conformity to group norms. *Journal of Abnormal and Social Psychology, 53*, 100–107. https://doi.org/10.1037/h0047855

Dobele, A., Lindgreen, A., Beverland, M., Vanhamme, J., & van Wijk, R. (2007). Why pass on viral messages? Because they connect emotionally. *Business Horizons, 50*, 291–304. https://doi.org/10.1016/J.BUSHOR.2007.01.004

Dollard, J., Miller, N. E., Doob, L. W., Mowrer, O. H., & Sears, R. R. (1939). *Frustration and aggression.* New Haven, CT: Yale University Press. https://doi.org/10.1037/10022-000

Dovidio, J. F., & Ellyson, S. L. (1985). Pattern of visual dominance behavior in humans. In J. F. Dovidio & S. L. Ellyson (eds), *Power, dominance, and nonverbal behavior* (pp. 129–149). New York: Springer New York. https://doi.org/10.1007/978-1-4612-5106-4_7

Doyen, S., Klein, O., Pichon, C.-L., Cleeremans, A., & Higgins, E. (2012). Behavioral priming: it's all in the mind, but whose mind? *PLoS ONE, 7*, e29081. https://doi.org/10.1371/journal.pone.0029081

Drury, J., & Reicher, S. (2009). Collective psychological empowerment as a model of social change: Researching crowds and power. *Journal of Social Issues, 65*, 707–725. https://doi.org/10.1111/j.1540-4560.2009.01622.x

Dunbar, R., & Dunbar, R. (1998). *Grooming, gossip, and the evolution of language.* London: Harvard University Press.

Duncan, B. L. (1976). Differential social perception and attribution of intergroup violence: testing the lower limits of stereotyping of blacks. *Journal of Personality and Social Psychology, 34*, 590–598. Retrieved from www.ncbi.nlm.nih.gov/pubmed/993976

Duriez, B., & Van Hiel, A. (2002). The march of modern fascism. A comparison of social dominance orientation and authoritarianism. *Personality and Individual Differences, 32*, 1199–1213. https://doi.org/10.1016/S0191-8869(01)00086-1

Durkin, K., & Barber, B. (2002). Not so doomed: Computer game play and positive adolescent development. *Journal of Applied Developmental Psychology, 23*, 373–392. https://doi.org/10.1016/S0193-3973(02)00124-7

Dutton, D. G., & Aron, A. P. (1974). Some evidence for heightened sexual attraction under conditions of high anxiety. *Journal of Personality and Social Psychology, 30*, 510–517. https://doi.org/10.1037/h0037031

Eagly, A. H., & Carli, L. L. (1981). Sex of researchers and sex-typed communications as determinants of sex differences in influenceability: A meta-analysis of social influence studies. *Psychological Bulletin, 90*, 1–20. https://doi.org/10.1037/0033-2909.90.1.1

Eagly, A. H., & Chaiken, S. (1975). An attribution analysis of the effect of communicator characteristics on opinion change: The case of communicator attractiveness. *Journal of Personality and Social Psychology, 32*, 136–144. https://doi.org/10.1037/h0076850

Eastwick, P. W., Finkel, E. J., Mochon, D., & Ariely, D. (2007). Selective versus unselective romantic desire: Not all reciprocity is created equal. *Psychological Science, 18*, 317–319. https://doi.org/10.1111/j.1467-9280.2007.01897.x

Ebbesen, E. B., & Bowers, R. J. (1974). Proportion of risky to conservative arguments in a group discussion and choice shift. *Journal of Personality and Social Psychology, 29*, 316–327. https://doi.org/10.1037/h0036005

Edwards, D. H., & Kravitz, E. A. (1997). Serotonin, social status and aggression. *Current Opinion in Neurobiology, 7*, 812–819. https://doi.org/10.1016/S0959-4388(97)80140-7

Edwards, R., Manstead, A. S. R., & Macdonald, C. J. (1984). The relationship between children's sociometric status and ability to recognize facial expressions of emotion. *European Journal of Social Psychology, 14*, 235–238. https://doi.org/10.1002/ejsp.2420140212

Efran, M. G. (1974). The effect of physical appearance on the judgment of guilt, interpersonal attraction, and severity of recommended punishment in a simulated jury task. *Journal of Research in Personality, 8*, 45–54. https://doi.org/10.1016/0092-6566(74)90044-0

Ekman, P., & Friesen, W. (1975). *Unmasking the face: A guide to recognizing emotions from facial cues.* Englewood Cliffs, NJ: Prentice Hall.

Ekman, P., & Friesen, W. V. (1982). Felt, false, and miserable smiles. *Journal of Nonverbal Behavior, 6*(4), 238–252.

Ellemers, N., De Gilder, D., & Haslam, S. (2004). Motivating individuals and groups at work: A social identity perspective on leadership and group performance. *Academy of Management Review, 29*, 459–478. http://dx.doi.org/10.2307/20159054

Eltantawy, N., & Wiest, J. B. (2011). The Arab Spring: Social media in the Egyptian revolution. Reconsidering resource mobilization theory. *International Journal of Communication, 5*, 1207–1224.

Enli, G., & Thumim, N. (2012). Socializing and self-representation online: exploring Facebook. *Observatorio, 6*, 87–105. http://dx.doi.org/10.15847/obsOBS612012489

Exline, R. V., Ellyson, S. L., & Long, B. (1975). Visual behavior as an aspect of power role relationships. In P. Pliner, L. Krames & T. Alloway (eds), *Nonverbal communication of aggression* (pp. 21–52). Boston: Springer US. https://doi.org/10.1007/978-1-4684-2835-3_2

Eysenck, H., & Eysenck, S. (1974). *Manual for the Eysenck personality questionnaire: (EPQ-R adult)*. San Diego: Educational & Industrial Testing Services. https://doi.org/10.3200/JRLP.139.6.545-552

Eysenck, H., & Eysenck, S. (1977). *Psychoticism as a dimension of personality*. London: Hodder & Stoughton.

Ferguson, C. J. (2007). Evidence for publication bias in video game violence effects literature: A meta-analytic review. *Aggression and Violent Behavior, 12*, 470–482. https://doi.org/10.1016/J.AVB.2007.01.001

Festinger, L. (1954). A theory of social comparison processes. *Human Relations, 7*, 117–140. https://doi.org/10.1177/001872675400700202

Festinger, L., & Carlsmith, J. M. (1959). Cognitive consequences of forced compliance. *Journal of Abnormal and Social Psychology, 58*, 203–210. https://doi.org/10.1037/h0041593

Festinger, L., Schachter, S., & Back, K. (1950). *Social pressures in informal groups: A study of human factors in housing*. Oxford: Harper.

Fisher, R. J. (1990). *The social psychology of intergroup and international conflict resolution*. New York: Springer-Verlag.

Fiske, S. T. (2010). *Social beings: A core motives approach to social psychology*. Hoboken, NJ: John Wiley.

Fiske, S. T., & Taylor, S. E. (1982). *Social cognition*. New York: McGraw-Hill.

Fiske, S. T., Cuddy, A. J. C., Glick, P., & Xu, J. (2002). A model of (often mixed) stereotype content: competence and warmth respectively follow from perceived status and competition. *Journal of Personality and Social Psychology, 82*, 878–902.

Fletcher, G., & Ward, C. (1988). Attribution theory and processes: A cross-cultural perspective. In M. Bond (ed), *The cross-cultural challenge to social psychology* (pp. 230–244). Thousand Oaks, CA: Sage Publications.

Freedman, J. L., & Fraser, S. C. (1966). Compliance without pressure: The foot-in-the-door technique. *Journal of Personality and Social Psychology, 4*, 195–202. https://doi.org/10.1037/h0023552

Freud, S. (1920). *Beyond the pleasure principle.* New York: W. W. Norton.

Friese, M., Messner, C., & Schaffner. Y. (2012). Mindfulness meditation counteracts self-control depletion. *Consciousness and Cognition, 21*, 1016–1022. https://doi.org/10.1016/J.CONCOG.2012.01.008

Frings, D., & Abrams, D. (2010). The effect of difference oriented communication on the subjective validity of an in-group norm: Doc can treat the group. *Group Dynamics: Theory, Research, and Practice, 14*, 281–291. http://dx.doi.org/10.1037/a0019162

Frings, D., & Albery, I. P. (2015). The social identity model of cessation maintenance: Formulation and initial evidence. *Addictive Behaviors, 44*, 35–42. https://doi.org/10.1016/j.addbeh.2014.10.023

Frings, D., & Albery, I. P. (2016). Developing the social identity model of cessation maintenance: Theory, evidence and implications. In S. Buckingham and D. Best (eds), *Addiction, behavioral change and social identity: The path to resilience and recovery* (pp. 116–136). London. Routledge.

Frings, D., Collins, M., Long, G., Pinto, I. R., & Albery, I. P. (2016). A test of the social identity model of cessation maintenance: The content and role of social control. *Addictive Behaviors Reports, 3*, 77–85. https://doi.org/10.1016/j.abrep.2016.02.003

Frings, D., Hurst, J., Cleveland, C., Blascovich, J., & Abrams, D. (2012). Challenge, threat, and subjective group dynamics: Reactions to normative and deviant group members. *Group Dynamics, 16*, 105–121. https://doi.org/10.1037/a0027504

Frings, D., Melichar, L., & Albery, I. P. (2016). Implicit and explicit drinker identities interactively predict in-the-moment alcohol placebo consumption. *Addictive Behaviors Reports, 3*, 86–91. https://doi.org/10.1016/J.ABREP.2016.04.002

Furnham, A., & Quilley, R. (1989). The Protestant work ethic and the prisoner's dilemma game. *British Journal of Social Psychology, 28*, 79–87. https://doi.org/10.1111/j.2044-8309.1989.tb00848.x

Gaertner, S. L., Mann, J., Murrell, A., & Dovidio, J. F. (1989). Reducing intergroup bias: The benefits of recategorization. *Journal of Personality and Social Psychology, 57*, 239–249. https://doi.org/10.1037/0022-3514.57.2.239

Gailliot, M. T., Baumeister, R. F., DeWall, C. N., Maner, J. K., Plant, E. A., Tice, D. M., … & Schmeichel, B. J. (2007). Self-control relies on glucose as a limited energy source: willpower is more than a metaphor. *Journal of Personality and Social Psychology, 92*, 325–336. https://doi.org/10.1037/0022-3514.92.2.325

Gallace, A., & Spence, C. (2010). The science of interpersonal touch: An overview. *Neuroscience & Biobehavioral Reviews, 34*, 246–259. https://doi.org/10.1016/j.neubiorev.2008.10.004

Garfinkel, H. (1967). *Ethnomethodological studies*. Englewood Cliffs, NJ: Prentice Hall.

Gawronski, B., & Bodenhausen, G. V. (2011). The associative-propositional evaluation model. Theory, evidence, and open questions. *Advances in Experimental Social Psychology, 44*, 60–108. https://doi.org/10.1016/B978-0-12-385522-0.00002-0

Geen, R. G. (1990). *Human Aggression*. Buckingham: Open University Press.

Gentile, D. A., Anderson, C. A., Yukawa, S., Ihori, N., Saleem, M., Lim Kam Ming, L. K., … & Sakamoto, A. (2009). The effects of prosocial video games on prosocial behaviors: International evidence from correlational, longitudinal, and experimental studies. *Personality and Social Psychology Bulletin, 35*, 752–763. https://doi.org/10.1177/0146167209333045

Gerard, H. B., & Mathewson, G. C. (1966). The effects of severity of initiation on liking for a group: A replication. *Journal of Experimental Social Psychology, 2*, 278–287. https://doi.org/10.1016/0022-1031(66)90084-9

Gerbner, G., Gross, L., Eleey, M. F., Jackson-Beeck, M., Jeffries-Fox, S., & Signorielli, N. (1977). TV violence profile No. 8: The highlights. *Journal of Communication, 27*, 171–180. https://doi.org/10.1111/j.1460-2466.1977.tb01845.x

Gerend, M. A., & Sias, T. (2009). Message framing and color priming: How subtle threat cues affect persuasion. *Journal of Experimental Social Psychology, 45*, 999–1002. https://doi.org/10.1016/J.JESP.2009.04.002

Gergen, K. J. (1973). Social psychology as history. *Journal of Personality and Social Psychology, 26*, 309–320. https://doi.org/10.1037/h0034436

Gilbert, D. (1989). Thinking lightly about others: Automatic components of the social inference process. In J. Uleman & J. Bargh (eds), *Unintended thought* (pp. 189–211). New York: Guilford Press.

Gilbert, D., & Malone, P. (1995). The correspondence bias. *Psychological Bulletin, 117*(1) 21–38. http://dx.doi.org/10.1037/0033-2909.117.1.21

Gildersleeve, K., Haselton, M. G., & Fales, M. R. (2014). Do women's mate preferences change across the ovulatory cycle? A meta-analytic review. *Psychological Bulletin, 140*, 1205–1259. https://doi.org/10.1037/a0035438

Gillen, C. T. A., Bergstrøm, H., & Forth, A. E. (2016). Individual differences and rating errors in first impressions of psychopathy. *Evolutionary Psychology, 14*. https://doi.org/10.1177/1474704916674947

Gleibs, I. H., Haslam, C., Jones, J. M., Alexander Haslam, S., McNeill, J., & Connolly, H. (2011). No country for old men? The role of a 'gentlemen's club' in promoting social engagement and psychological well-being in residential care. *Aging & Mental Health, 15*, 456–466. https://doi.org/10.1080/13607863.2010.536137

Gleibs, I. H., Sonnenberg, S. J., & Haslam, C. (2014). 'We get to decide': The role of collective engagement in counteracting feelings of confinement and lack of autonomy in residential care. *Activities, Adaptation & Aging, 38*, 259–280. https://doi.org/10.1080/01924788.2014.966542

Glick, P., & Fiske, S. T. (1996). The Ambivalent Sexism Inventory: Differentiating hostile and benevolent sexism. *Journal of Personality and Social Psychology, 70*, 491–512. https://doi.org/10.1037/0022-3514.70.3.491

Grammer, K., & Thornhill, R. (1994). Human (Homo sapiens) facial attractiveness and sexual selection: The role of symmetry and averageness. *Journal of Comparative Psychology, 108*, 233–242. https://doi.org/10.1037/0735-7036.108.3.233

Grasmick, H., Bursik, Jr, R., & Kinsey, K. A. (1991). Shame and embarrassment as deterrents to noncompliance with the law: The case of an antilittering campaign. *Environment and Behavior, 23*, 233–251. https://doi.org/10.1177/0013916591232006

Greenwald, A. G., McGhee, D. E., & Schwartz, J. L. K. (1998). Measuring individual differences in implicit cognition: The Implicit Association Test. *Journal of Personality and Social Psychology, 74*, 1464–1480. https://doi.org/10.1037/0022-3514.74.6.1464

Greenwald, A. G., Poehlman, T. A., Uhlmann, E. L., & Banaji, M. R. (2009). Understanding and using the Implicit Association Test: III. Meta-analysis of predictive validity. *Journal of Personality and Social Psychology, 97*, 17–41. https://doi.org/10.1037/a0015575

Grossman, P., Niemann, L., Schmidt, S., & Walach, H. (2004). Mindfulness-based stress reduction and health benefits. A meta-analysis. *Journal of Psychosomatic Research, 57*, 35–43. https://doi.org/10.1016/S0022-3999(03)00573-7

Grounds, A. (2004). Psychological consequences of wrongful conviction and imprisonment. *Canadian Journal of Criminology and Criminal Justice, 46*, 165–182. https://doi.org/10.3138/cjccj.46.2.165

Gueguen, N., Jacob, C., & Martin, A. (2009). Mimicry in social interaction: Its effect on human judgment and behavior. *European Journal of Social Sciences, 8*, 253–259.

Gupta, U., & Singh, P. (1982). An exploratory study of love and liking and type of marriages. *Journal of Applied Psychology, 19*, 92–97.

Gurney, J. N., & Tierney, K. J. (1982). Relative deprivation and social movements: A critical look at twenty years of theory and research. *Sociological Quarterly, 23*, 33–47. https://doi.org/10.1111/j.1533-8525.1982.tb02218.x

Hager, J. C., & Ekman, P. (1979). Long-distance of transmission of facial affect signals. *Ethology and Sociobiology, 1*, 77–82. https://doi.org/10.1016/0162-3095(79)90007-4

Hagger, M. S., Chatzisarantis, H., Alberts, C. O., Anggono, C., Batailler, A. R., Birt, R. ... & Zwienenberg, M. (2016). A multilab preregistered replication of the ego-depletion effect. *Perspectives on Psychological Science, 11*, 546–573. http://dx.doi.org/10.1177/1745691616652873

Hagger, M. S., Wood, C., Stiff, C., & Chatzisarantis, N. L. D. (2010). Ego depletion and the strength model of self-control: A meta-analysis. *Psychological
Bulletin, 136*, 495–525. https://doi.org/10.1037/a0019486

Hall, E. (1966.). *The hidden dimension*. New York: Doubleday & Co.

Hall, J. A. (1978). Gender effects in decoding nonverbal cues. *Psychological
Bulletin, 85*, 845–857. https://doi.org/10.1037/0033-2909.85.4.845

Hamilton, D. L., & Rose, T. L. (1980). Illusory correlation and the maintenance
of stereotypic beliefs. *Journal of Personality and Social Psychology, 39*, 832–845.
https://doi.org/10.1037/0022-3514.39.5.832

Haney, C., Banks, W. C., & Zimbardo, P. G. (1973). A study of prisoners and
guards in a simulated prison. *Naval Research Reviews, 9*, 1–17.

Hardin, G. (1968). The tragedy of the commons. *Science, 162*, 1243–1248.

Harper, D. J., Wagstaff, G. F., Newton, J. T., & Harrison, K. R. (1990). Lay casual
perceptions of third world poverty and the just world theory. *Social Behavior
and Personality, 18*, 235–238. https://doi.org/10.2224/sbp.1990.18.2.235

Harré, R., & Secord, P. F. (1972). *The explanation of social behaviour*. Lanham,
MD: Rowman & Littlefield.

Haslam, S. A., & Reicher, S. (2007). Identity entrepreneurship and the
consequences of identity failure: The dynamics of leadership in the BBC
prison study. *Social Psychology Quarterly, 70*, 125–147. https://doi.org/10.1177/
019027250707000204

Haslam, S. A., & Reicher, S. D. (2017). 50 years of 'obedience to authority': From
blind conformity to engaged followership. *Annual Review of Law and Social
Science, 13*, 59–78. https://doi.org/10.1146/annurev-lawsocsci-110316-113710

Haslam, C., Cruwys, T., Haslam, S. A., Dingle, G., & Xue-Ling, M. (2016).
Groups 4 Health: Evidence that a social-identity intervention that builds
and strengthens social group membership improves mental health. *Journal of
Affective Disorders, 194*, 188–195. https://doi.org/10.1016/J.JAD.2016.01.010

Haslam, S. A., O'Brien, A., Jetten, J., Vormedal, K., & Penna, S. (2005). Taking the
strain: Social identity, social support, and the experience of stress. *British Journal
of Social Psychology, 44*, 355–370. https://doi.org/10.1348/014466605X37468

Haslam, S. A., Reicher, S. D., & Birney, M. E. (2014). Nothing but mere
authority: Evidence that in an experimental analogue of the Milgram paradigm participants are motivated not by orders but by appeals to science. *Journal
of Social Issues, 70*, 473–488. https://doi.org/10.1111/josi.12072

Hatfield, E., & Rapson, R. L. (1993). *Love, sex, and intimacy: Their psychology,
biology, and history*. New York: Harper Collins.

Haugtvedt, C. P., Petty, R. E., & Cacioppo, J. T. (1992). Need for cognition
and advertising: Understanding the role of personality variables in consumer
behavior. *Journal of Consumer Psychology, 1*, 239–260. https://doi.org/10.1016/
S1057-7408(08)80038-1

Heider, F. (1958). *The psychology of interpersonal relations* (1st ed.). New York: Erlbaum.

Heider, F., & Simmel, M. (1944). An experimental study of apparent behavior. *American Journal of Psychology, 57,* 243–259.

Hendrick, C., Hendrick, S. S., & Dicke, A. (1998). The Love Attitudes Scale: Short form. *Journal of Social and Personal Relationships, 15,* 147–159. https://doi.org/10.1177/0265407598152001

Henrich, J., Heine, S., & Norenzayan, A. (2010). Most people are not WEIRD. *Nature, 466*(7302), 29.

Henriksen, L., Dauphinee, A. L., Wang, Y., & Fortmann, S. P. (2006). Industry sponsored anti-smoking ads and adolescent reactance: Test of a boomerang effect. *Tobacco Control, 15,* 13–18. https://doi.org/10.1136/tc.2003.006361

Hewstone, M. (1989). Changing stereotypes with disconfirming information. In D. Bar-Tal, C. F. Grumann, A. W. Kriglanski, & W. Stroebe (eds), *Stereotyping and prejudice.* (pp. 207–223). New York: Springer-Verlag. https://doi.org/10.1007/978-1-4612-3582-8_10

Hewstone, M., Hopkins, N., & Routh, D. A. (1992). Cognitive models of stereotype change: (1) Generalization and subtyping in young people's views of the police. *European Journal of Social Psychology, 22,* 219–234. https://doi.org/10.1002/ejsp.2420220303

Hewstone, M., Islam, M. R., & Judd, C. M. (1993). Models of crossed categorization and intergroup relations. *Journal of Personality and Social Psychology, 64,* 779–793. https://doi.org/10.1037/0022-3514.64.5.779

Higgins, E. T. (1989). Self-discrepancy theory: What patterns of self-beliefs cause people to suffer? *Advances in Experimental Social Psychology, 22,* 93–136. https://doi.org/10.1016/S0065-2601(08)60306-8

Hoffman, C., & Hurst, N. (1990). Gender stereotypes: Perception or rationalization? *Journal of Personality and Social Psychology, 58,* 197–208. https://doi.org/10.1037/0022-3514.58.2.197

Hofstede, G. (2001). *Culture's consequences: Comparing values, behaviors, institutions and organizations across nations.* Thousand Oaks, CA: Sage Publications. http://dx.doi.org/10.1016/S0005-7967(02)00184-5

Hogg, M. (2001). A social identity theory of leadership. *Personality and Social Psychology Review, 5,* 184–200. https://doi.org/10.1207/S15327957PSPR0503_1

Hogg, M. A., Hohman, Z. P., & Rivera, J. E. (2008). Why do people join groups? Three motivational accounts from social psychology. *Social and Personality Psychology Compass, 2,* 1269–1280. https://doi.org/10.1111/j.1751-9004.2008.00099.x

Hornsey, M. J., & Hogg, M. A. (2000). Assimilation and diversity: An integrative model of subgroup relations. *Personality and Social Psychology Review, 4,* 143–156. https://doi.org/10.1207/S15327957PSPR0402_03

Hornsey, M. J., Grice, T., Jetten, J., Paulsen, N., & Callan, V. (2007). Group-directed criticisms and recommendations for change: Why newcomers arouse more resistance than old-timers. *Personality and Social Psychology Bulletin, 33,* 1036–1048. https://doi.org/10.1177/0146167207301029

Hovland, C. I., Janis, I. L., & Kelley, H. H. (1953). *Communication and persuasion.* New Haven, CT: Yale University Press.

Huang, J.-S., & Zhou, L. (2016). Negative effects of brand familiarity and brand relevance on effectiveness of viral advertisements. *Social Behavior and Personality: An International Journal, 44,* 1151–1162. https://doi.org/10.2224/sbp.2016.44.7.1151

Hyman, I. E., Boss, S. M., Wise, B. M., McKenzie, K. E., & Caggiano, J. M. (2009). Did you see the unicycling clown? Inattentional blindness while walking and talking on a cell phone. *Applied Cognitive Psychology, 24,* 597–607. https://doi.org/10.1002/acp.1638

Ingham, A. G., Levinger, G., Graves, J., & Peckham, V. (1974). The Ringelmann effect: Studies of group size and group performance. *Journal of Experimental Social Psychology, 10,* 371–384. https://doi.org/10.1016/0022-1031(74)90033-X

Isenberg, D. J. (1986). Group polarization: A critical review and meta-analysis. *Journal of Personality and Social Psychology, 50,* 1141–1151. https://doi.org/10.1037/0022-3514.50.6.1141

Janis, I. L. (1967). Effects of fear arousal on attitude change: Recent developments in theory and experimental research. *Advances in Experimental Social Psychology, 3,* 166–224. https://doi.org/10.1016/S0065-2601(08)60344-5

Janoff-Bulman, R., Timko, C., & Carli, L. (1985). Cognitive biases in blaming the victim. *Journal of Experimental Social Psychology, 21,* 161–177. https://doi.org/10.1016/0022-1031(85)90013-7

Jetten, J., Haslam, C., & Haslam, S. A. (2011). *The social cure: Identity, health and well-being.* London: Psychology Press.

Johnson, D. W., & Johnson, E. P. (1987). *Joining together: Group theory and group skills.* Englewood, NJ: Prentice Hall.

Jones, E., & Davis, K. (1965). From acts to dispositions the attribution process in person perception. *Advances in Experimental Social Psychology, 2,* 219–266. https://doi.org/10.1016/S0065-2601(08)60107-0

Jones, E. E., & Harris, V. A. (1967). The attribution of attitudes. *Journal of Experimental Social Psychology, 3,* 1–24. https://doi.org/10.1016/0022-1031(67)90034-0

Jones, E., & Nisbett, R. (1971). *The actor and the observer: Divergent perceptions of the causes of behavior.* New York: General Learning Press.

Jones, J. M., & Jetten, J. (2011). Recovering from strain and enduring pain. *Social Psychological and Personality Science, 2,* 239–244. https://doi.org/10.1177/1948550610386806

Karau, S., & Williams, K. D. (2001). Understanding individual motivation in groups: The collective effort model. In M. E. Turner (ed.), *Groups at work* (pp. 113–143). New York: Routledge.

Katz, I., & Hass, R. G. (1988). Racial ambivalence and American value conflict: Correlational and priming studies of dual cognitive structures. *Journal of Personality and Social Psychology, 55*, 893–905. https://doi.org/10.1037/0022-3514.55.6.893

Kawachi, I., Kennedy, B. P., & Wilkinson, R. G. (1999). Crime: Social disorganization and relative deprivation. *Social Science & Medicine, 48*, 719–731. https://doi.org/10.1016/S0277-9536(98)00400-6

Kelley, H. (1967). Attribution theory in social psychology. *Nebraska Symposium on Motivation, 15*, 192–238.

Kelley, H. H., & Stahelski, A. J. (1970). Social interaction basis of cooperators' and competitors' beliefs about others. *Journal of Personality and Social Psychology, 16*, 66–91. https://doi.org/10.1037/h0029849

Kelley, H. H., & Thibaut, J. W. (1978). *Interpersonal relations: A theory of interdependence.* New York: Wiley.

Kellezi, B., Reicher, S., & Cassidy, C. (2009). Surviving the Kosovo conflict: A study of social identity, appraisal of extreme events, and mental wellbeing. *Applied Psychology, 58*, 59–83. https://doi.org/10.1111/j.1464-0597.2008.00382.x

Kende, A., van Zomeren, M., Ujhelyi, A., & Lantos, N. A. (2016). The social affirmation use of social media as a motivator of collective action. *Journal of Applied Social Psychology, 46*, 453–469. https://doi.org/10.1111/jasp.12375

Kernis, M. H., Grannemann, B. D., & Barclay, L. C. (1989). Stability and level of self-esteem as predictors of anger arousal and hostility. *Journal of Personality and Social Psychology, 56*, 1013–1022. https://doi.org/10.1037/0022-3514.56.6.1013

Klein, C. T. F., & Webster, D. M. (2000). Individual differences in argument scrutiny as motivated by need for cognitive closure. *Basic and Applied Social Psychology, 22*, 119–129. https://doi.org/10.1207/S15324834BASP2202_5

Koerner, E. F. K. (1992). The Sapir-Whorf hypothesis: A preliminary history and a bibliographical essay. *Journal of Linguistic Anthropology, 2*, 173–198. https://doi.org/10.1525/jlin.1992.2.2.173

Kraut, R., Patterson, M., Lundmark, V., & Kiesler, S. (1998). Internet paradox: A social technology that reduces social involvement and psychological wellbeing? *American Psychologist, 53*, 1017–1031. http://dx.doi.org/10.1037/0003-066X.53.9.1017

Kravitz, D. A., & Martin, B. (1986). Ringelmann rediscovered: The original article. *Journal of Personality and Social Psychology, 50*, 936–941. https://doi.org/10.1037/0022-3514.50.5.936

Kruglanski, A. W., Fishbach, A., Erb, H. P., Pierro, A., & Mannetti, L. (2004). The parametric unimodel as a theory of persuasion. In G. Haddock & G. Maio (eds), *Contemporary perspectives on the psychology of attitudes* (pp. 399–423). Abingdon, Oxon: Psychology Press.

Kulka, R. A., & Kessler, J. B. (1978). Is justice really blind? The influence of litigant physical attractiveness on juridical judgment. *Journal of Applied Social Psychology, 8*, 366–381. https://doi.org/10.1111/j.1559-1816.1978.tb00790.x

Lagerspetz, K. M. J., & Lagerspetz, K. Y. H. (1971). Changes in the aggressiveness of mice resulting from selective breeding, learning and social isolation. *Scandinavian Journal of Psychology, 12*, 241–248. https://doi.org/10.1111/j.1467-9450.1971.tb00627.x

Lamont, R. A., Swift, H. J., & Abrams, D. (2015). A review and meta-analysis of age-based stereotype threat: Negative stereotypes, not facts, do the damage. *Psychology and Aging, 30*, 180–193. https://doi.org/10.1037/a0038586

Latané, B., & Darley, J. (1970). *The unresponsive bystander: Why doesn't he help?* New York: Appleton-Century-Crofts.

Latané, B., Williams, K., & Harkins, S. (1979). Many hands make light the work: The causes and consequences of social loafing. *Journal of Personality and Social Psychology, 37*, 822–832. https://doi.org/10.1037/0022-3514.37.6.822

Le Bon, G. (1896). *The crowd: A study of the popular mind.* New York: Macmillan & Co.

Lea, M., & Spears, R. (1991). Computer-mediated communication, de-individuation and group decision-making. *International Journal of Man-Machine Studies, 34*, 283–301.

Leary, M. R., & Downs, D. L. (1995). Interpersonal functions of the self-esteem motive. In *Efficacy, agency, and self-esteem* (pp. 123–144). Boston: Springer US. https://doi.org/10.1007/978-1-4899-1280-0_7

Lerner, M. J. (1980). *The belief in a just world.* Boston: Springer US.

Leung, A. K.-Y., & Cohen, D. (2011). Within- and between-culture variation: Individual differences and the cultural logics of honor, face, and dignity cultures. *Journal of Personality and Social Psychology, 100*, 507–526. https://doi.org/10.1037/a0022151

Levine, J. M., & Moreland, R. L. (1994). Group socialization: Theory and research. *European Review of Social Psychology, 5*, 305–336. https://doi.org/10.1080/14792779543000093

Levinger, G., & Schneider, D. J. (1969). Test of the 'risk is a value' hypothesis. *Journal of Personality and Social Psychology, 11*, 165–169. https://doi.org/10.1037/h0026966

Lewin, K. (1936). *Principles of topological psychology.* New York: McGraw-Hill.

Lindgren, K. P., Neighbors, C., Teachman, B. A., Wiers, R. W., Westgate, E., & Greenwald, A. G. (2013). I drink therefore I am: Validating alcohol-related implicit association tests. *Psychology of Addictive Behaviors, 27*, 1–13. https://doi.org/10.1037/a0027640

Lipkusa, I. M., Dalbert, C., & Siegler, I. C. (1996). The importance of distinguishing the belief in a just world for self versus for others: Implications for psychological well-being. Personality and Social *Psychology Bulletin, 22*, 666–677. https://doi.org/10.1177/0146167296227002

Mackie, D. M., & Worth, L. T. (1991). Feeling good but not thinking straight: The impact of positive mood on persuasion. In J. P. Forgas (ed.), *Emotion and social judgments* (pp. 201–241). Oxford: Pergamon Press. https://doi.org/10.1080/00049538808259077

Major, B., & Adams, J. B. (1983). Role of gender, interpersonal orientation, and self-presentation in distributive-justice behavior. *Journal of Personality and Social Psychology, 45*, 598–608. https://doi.org/10.1037/0022-3514.45.3.598

Malle, B. F. (2006). The actor–observer asymmetry in attribution: A (surprising) meta-analysis. *Psychological Bulletin, 132*, 895–919.

Mann, T. C., & Ferguson, M. J. (2017). Reversing implicit first impressions through reinterpretation after a two-day delay. *Journal of Experimental Social Psychology, 68*, 122–127. https://doi.org/10.1016/j.jesp.2016.06.004

Maoz, I. (2000). Multiple conflicts and competing agendas: A framework for conceptualizing structured encounters between groups in conflict the case of a coexistence project of Jews and Palestinians in Israel. *Peace and Conflict: Journal of Peace Psychology, 6*, 135–156. https://doi.org/10.1207/S15327949PAC0602_3

Marcus-Newhall, A., Pedersen, W. C., Carlson, M., & Miller, N. (2000). Displaced aggression is alive and well: A meta-analytic review. *Journal of Personality and Social Psychology, 78*, 670–689. https://doi.org/10.1037/0022-3514.78.4.670

Marino, C., Vieno, A., Pastore, M., Albery, I. P., Frings, D., & Spada, M. M. (2016). Modeling the contribution of personality, social identity and social norms to problematic Facebook use in adolescents. *Addictive Behaviors, 63*, 51–56. https://doi.org/10.1016/j.addbeh.2016.07.001

Markus, H. (1978). The effect of mere presence on social facilitation: An unobtrusive test. *Journal of Experimental Social Psychology, 14*, 389–397. https://doi.org/10.1016/0022-1031(78)90034-3

Marques, J. M., & Yzerbyt, V. Y. (1988). The black sheep effect: Judgmental extremity towards ingroup members in inter-and intra-group situations. *European Journal of Social Psychology, 18*, 287–292. https://doi.org/10.1002/ejsp.2420180308

Marques, J., Abrams, D., & Serôdio, R. G. (2001). Being better by being right: Subjective group dynamics and derogation of in-group deviants when generic norms are undermined. *Journal of Personality and Social Psychology, 81*, 436–447. https://doi.org/10.1037/0022-3514.81.3.436

Masicampo, E. J., & Baumeister, R. F. (2007). Relating mindfulness and self-regulatory processes. *Psychological Inquiry, 18*, 255–258. https://doi.org/10.1080/10478400701598363

Mast, M. S. (2002). Female dominance hierarchies: Are they any different from males'? *Personality and Social Psychology Bulletin, 28,* 29–39. https://doi.org/10.1177/0146167202281003

Mattelaer, J. J., & Jilek, W. (2007). Sexual medicine history: Koro – the psychological disappearance of the penis. *The Journal of Sexual Medicine, 4,* 1509–1515. https://doi.org/10.1111/j.1743-6109.2007.00586.x

Mauss, M. (1985). A category of the human mind: The notion of person, the notion of self. In M. Carrithers, S. Collins & S. Lukes (eds), *The category of the person* (pp. 1–23). Cambridge: Cambridge University Press.

McClure, J., Meyer, L., Garisch, J., & Fischer, R. (2011). Students' attributions for their best and worst marks: Do they relate to achievement? *Contemporary Educational Psychology, 36,* 71–81. https://doi.org/10.1016/j.cedpsych.2010.11.001

McConnell, A. R., & Leibold, J. M. (2001). Relations among the Implicit Association Test, discriminatory behavior, and explicit measures of racial attitudes. *Journal of Experimental Social Psychology, 37,* 435–442. https://doi.org/10.1006/JESP.2000.1470

McCrae, R. R., & Costa, P. T. (1987). Validation of the five-factor model of personality across instruments and observers. *Journal of Personality and Social Psychology, 52,* 81–90. https://doi.org/10.1037/0022-3514.52.1.81

McGuire, M. T., & Raleigh, M. J. (1987). Serotonin, social behaviour, and aggression in vervet monkeys. In R. D. Masters & M. T. McGuire (eds), *The neurotransmitter revolution: Serotonin, social behavior, and the law* (pp. 207–222). Dordrecht: Springer. https://doi.org/10.1007/978-94-009-3359-0_13

Mead, G. (1934). *Mind, self and society.* Chicago: University of Chicago Press.

Meier, B. P., Schnall, S., Schwarz, N., & Bargh, J. A. (2012). Embodiment in social psychology. *Topics in Cognitive Science, 1,* 1–12. https://doi.org/10.1111/j.1756-8765.2012.01212.x

Meltzoff, A. N., & Moore, M. K. (1989). Imitation in newborn infants: Exploring the range of gestures imitated and the underlying mechanisms. *Developmental Psychology, 25,* 954–962. https://doi.org/10.1037/0012-1649.25.6.954

Milgram, S. (1963). Behavioral study of obedience. *Journal of Abnormal and Social Psychology, 67,* 371–378. https://doi.org/10.1037/h0040525

Milgram, S. (1973). *The perils of obedience. Harpers, 247,* 62–75.

Miller, A. H., Bolce, L. H., & Halligan, M. (1977). The J-curve theory and the black urban riots: An empirical test of progressive relative deprivation theory. *American Political Science Review, 71,* 964–982. https://doi.org/10.1017/S0003055400265180

Miller, G. (1956). The magical number seven, plus or minus two: some limits on our capacity for processing information. *Psychological Review, 63,* 81–97.

Miller, G., Tybur, J. M., & Jordan, B. D. (2007). Ovulatory cycle effects on tip earnings by lap dancers: Economic evidence for human estrus? *Evolution and Human Behavior, 28*, 375–381. https://doi.org/10.1016/j.evolhumbehav. 2007.06.002

Miller, J. (1984). Culture and the development of everyday social explanation. *Journal of Personality and Social Psychology, 46*, 961–978. http://dx.doi.org/ 10.1037/0022-3514.46.5.961

Miller, N. S., & Brewer, M. B. (1984). Beyond the contact hypotheses: Theoretical perspectives on desegregation. In N. S. Miller & M. B. Brewer (eds), *Groups in contact: The psychology of desegregation* (pp. 281–302). Orlando, FL: Academic Press.

Molden, D. C., Hui, C. M., Scholer, A. A., Meier, B. P., Noreen, E. E., D'Agostino, P. R., & Martin, V. (2012). Motivational versus metabolic effects of carbohydrates on self-control. *Psychological Science, 23*, 1137–1144. https:// doi.org/10.1177/0956797612439069

Morgan, M., Hayes, R., Williamson, M., & Ford, C. (2007). Men's sheds: a community approach to promoting mental health and well-being. *International Journal of Mental Health Promotion, 9*, 48–52. https://doi.org/10.1080/14623730.2007.9721842

Morton, T. A., Postmes, T., & Jetten, J. (2007). Playing the game: When group success is more important than downgrading deviants. *European Journal of Social Psychology, 37*, 599–616. https://doi.org/10.1002/ejsp.385

Moscovici, S. (1976). *Social influence and social change.* London: Academic Press.

Moscovici, S., Lage, E., & Naffrechoux, M. (1969). Influence of a consistent minority on the responses of a majority in a color perception task. *Sociometry, 32*, 365. https://doi.org/10.2307/2786541

Moss, A. C., Albery, I. P., Dyer, K. R., Frings, D., Humphreys, K., Inkelaar, T., … & Speller, A. (2015). The effects of responsible drinking messages on attentional allocation and drinking behaviour. *Addictive Behaviors, 44*, 94–101. https://doi.org/10.1016/j.addbeh.2014.11.035

Muller, D., Atzeni, T., & Butera, F. (2004). Coaction and upward social comparison reduce the illusory conjunction effect: Support for distraction–conflict theory. *Journal of Experimental Social Psychology, 40*, 659–665. https:// doi.org/10.1016/J.JESP.2003.12.003

Munroe, K., Estabrooks, P., Dennis, P., & Carron, A. (1999). A phenomenological analysis of group norms in sport teams. *The Sport Psychologist, 13*, 171–182. https://doi.org/10.1123/tsp.13.2.171

Murstein, B. I. (1972). Physical attractiveness and marital choice. *Journal of Personality and Social Psychology, 22*, 8–12. https://doi.org/10.1037/h0032394

Myers, D. G. (1975). Discussion-induced attitude polarization. *Human Relations, 28*, 699–714. https://doi.org/10.1177/001872677502800802

Myers, D. G., Brown Wojcicki, S., & Aardema, B. S. (1977). Attitude comparison: Is there ever a bandwagon effect? *Journal of Applied Social Psychology, 7*, 341–347. https://doi.org/10.1111/j.1559-1816.1977.tb00758.x

Myers, R., Chou, C.-P., Sussman, S., Baezconde-Garbanati, L., Pachon, H., & Valente, T. W. (2009). Acculturation and substance use: Social influence as a mediator among Hispanic alternative high school youth. *Journal of Health and Social Behavior, 50,* 164–179. https://doi.org/10.1177/002214650905000204

Neisser, U. (1967). *Cognitive psychology.* New York: Appleton-Century-Crofts.

Nelson, T. E., Biernat, M. R., & Manis, M. (1990). Everyday base rates (sex stereotypes): Potent and resilient. *Journal of Personality and Social Psychology, 59,* 664–675. https://doi.org/10.1037/0022-3514.59.4.664

Newcomb, T. M. (1956). The prediction of interpersonal attraction. *American Psychologist, 11,* 575–586. https://doi.org/10.1037/h0046141

Nguyen, H.-H. D., & Ryan, A. M. (2008). Does stereotype threat affect test performance of minorities and women? A meta-analysis of experimental evidence. *Journal of Applied Psychology, 93,* 1314–1334. https://doi.org/10.1037/a0012702

O'Neill, S., & Nicholson-Cole, S. (2009). 'Fear won't do it': Promoting positive engagement with climate change through visual and iconic representations. *Science Communication, 30,* 355–379. https://doi.org/10.1177/1075547008329201

Open Science Collaboration (2015). Estimating the reproducibility of psychological science. *Science,* 349(6251), aac4716.

Ostrom, E. (1991). *Governing the commons: The evolution of institutions for collective action.* Cambridge: Cambridge University Press. http://dx.doi.org/10.2307/3146384

Oswald, F. L., Mitchell, G., Blanton, H., Jaccard, J., & Tetlock, P. E. (2013). Predicting ethnic and racial discrimination: A meta-analysis of IAT criterion studies. *Journal of Personality and Social Psychology, 105,* 171–192. https://doi.org/10.1037/a0032734

Paese, P. W., & Gilin, D. A. (2000). When an adversary is caught telling the truth: Reciprocal cooperation versus self-interest in distributive bargaining. *Personality and Social Psychology Bulletin, 26,* 79–90. https://doi.org/10.1177/0146167200261008

Peng, K., & Nisbett, R. (1999). Culture, dialectics, and reasoning about contradiction. *American Psychologist, 54,* 741–754.

Perez, D. A., Hosch, H. M., Ponder, B., & Trejo, G. C. (1993). Ethnicity of defendants and jurors as influences on jury decisions. *Journal of Applied Social Psychology, 23,* 1249–1262. https://doi.org/10.1111/j.1559-1816.1993.tb01031.x

Pettigrew, T. F. (1979). The Ultimate attribution error: Extending Allport's cognitive analysis of prejudice. *Personality and Social Psychology Bulletin, 5,* 461–476. https://doi.org/10.1177/014616727900500407

Petty R. E., & Cacioppo, J. (1986). The elaboration likelihood model of persuasion. *Advances in Experimental Social Psychology, 19,* 123–205. https://doi.org/10.1016/S0065-2601(08)60214-2

Piehl, J. (1977). Integration of information in the 'courts': Influence of physical attractiveness on amount of punishment for a traffic offender. *Psychological Reports, 41,* 551–556. https://doi.org/10.2466/pro.1977.41.2.551

Piliavin, I. M., Rodin, J., & Piliavin, J. A. (1969). Good Samaritanism: An underground phenomenon? *Journal of Personality and Social Psychology, 13,* 289–299. https://doi.org/10.1037/h0028433

Pinto, I. R., Marques, J. M., Levine, J. M., & Abrams, D. (2010). Membership status and subjective group dynamics: Who triggers the black sheep effect? *Journal of Personality and Social Psychology, 99,* 107–119. https://doi.org/10.1037/a0018187

Polimeni, J., & Reiss, J. P. (2006). The first joke: Exploring the evolutionary origins of humor. *Evolutionary Psychology, 4,* 347–366. https://doi.org/10.1177/147470490600400129

Postmes, T., & Spears, R. (1998). Deindividuation and antinormative behavior: A meta-analysis. *Psychological Bulletin, 123,* 238–259. http://dx.doi.org/10.1037/0033-2909.123.3.238

Potter, J., & Wetherell, M. (1987). *Discourse and social psychology: Beyond attitudes and behaviour.* London: Sage Publications.

Price, K. H., Harrison, D. A., & Gavin, J. H. (2006). Withholding inputs in team contexts: Member composition, interaction processes, evaluation structure, and social loafing. *Journal of Applied Psychology, 91,* 1375–1384. https://doi.org/10.1037/0021-9010.91.6.1375

Rabbie, J. M., & Horwitz, M. (1988). Categories versus groups as explanatory concepts in intergroup relations. *European Journal of Social Psychology, 18,* 117–123. https://doi.org/10.1002/ejsp.2420180204

Regan, D. T. (1971). Effects of a favor and liking on compliance. *Journal of Experimental Social Psychology, 7,* 627–639. https://doi.org/10.1016/0022-1031(71)90025-4

Reicher, S. (1996). 'The battle of Westminster': Developing the social identity model of crowd behaviour in order to explain the initiation and development of collective conflict. *European Journal of Social Psychology, 26,* 115–134. http://dx.doi.org/10.1002/(SICI)1099-0992(199601)26:1<115::AID-EJSP740>3.0.CO;2-Z

Reicher, S., & Haslam, S. A. (2006). On the agency of individuals and groups: Lessons from the BBC Prison Study. In T. Postmes & J. Jetten (eds), *Individuality and the group: Advances in social identity* (pp. 237–257). London: Sage Publications. http://dx.doi.org/10.4135/9781446211946.n13

Reicher, S., Spears, R., & Postmes, T. (1995). A social identity model of deindividuation phenomena. *European Review of Social Psychology, 6,* 161–198. https://doi.org/10.1080/14792779443000049

Richeson, J. A., & Shelton, J. N. (2003). When prejudice does not pay: Effects of interracial contact on executive function. *Psychological Science, 14,* 287–290. https://doi.org/10.1111/1467-9280.03437

Ristic, J., & Kingstone, A. (2005). Taking control of reflexive social attention. *Cognition, 94*, B55–B65. https://doi.org/10.1016/j.cognition.2004.04.005

Ristic, J., Mottron, L., Friesen, C. K., Iarocci, G., Burack, J. A., & Kingstone, A. (2005). Eyes are special but not for everyone: The case of autism. *Cognitive Brain Research, 24*, 715–718. https://doi.org/10.1016/j.cogbrainres.2005.02.007

Robson, K. S. (1967). The role of eye–eye contact in maternal–infant attachment. *Journal of Child Psychology and Psychiatry, 8*, 13–25. https://doi.org/10.1111/j.1469-7610.1967.tb02176.x

Rosenthal, R., & Jacobson, L. (1966). Teachers' expectancies: Determinants of pupils' IQ gains. *Psychological Reports, 19*, 115–118. https://doi.org/10.2466/pro.1966.19.1.115

Ross, L., Greene, D., & House, P. (1977). The 'false consensus effect': An egocentric bias in social perception and attribution processes. *Journal of Experimental Social Psychology, 13*, 219–301.

Rubin, M., & Hewstone, M. (1998). Social identity theory's self-esteem hypothesis: A review and some suggestions for clarification. *Personality and Social Psychology Review, 2*, 40–62. https://doi.org/10.1207/s15327957pspr0201_3

Rudmin, F. W. (2003). Critical history of the acculturation psychology of assimilation, separation, integration, and marginalization. *Review of General Psychology, 7*, 3–37. https://doi.org/10.1037/1089-2680.7.1.3

Rule, N. O. (2017). Perceptions of sexual orientation from minimal cues. *Archives of Sexual Behavior, 46*, 129–139. https://doi.org/10.1007/s10508-016-0779-2

Rusbult, C. E., & Van Lange, P. A. M. (2003). Interdependence, interaction, and relationships. *Annual Review of Psychology, 54*, 351–375. https://doi.org/10.1146/annurev.psych.54.101601.145059

Ryan, W. (1971). *Blaming the victim*. New York: Vintage.

Saks, M. J., & Marti, M. W. (1997). A meta-analysis of the effects of jury size. *Law and Human Behavior, 21*, 451–467. https://doi.org/10.1023/A:1024819605652

Sanders, G. S., Baron, R. S., & Moore, D. L. (1978). Distraction and social comparison as mediators of social facilitation effects. *Journal of Experimental Social Psychology, 14*, 291–303. https://doi.org/10.1016/0022-1031(78)90017-3

Schmader, T., Johns, M., & Forbes, C. (2008). An integrated process model of stereotype threat effects on performance. *Psychological Review, 115*, 336–356. https://doi.org/10.1037/0033-295X.115.2.336

Schofield, T. J., Parke, R. D., Kim, Y., & Coltrane, S. (2008). Bridging the acculturation gap: Parent–child relationship quality as a moderator in Mexican American families. *Developmental Psychology, 44*, 1190–1194. https://doi.org/10.1037/a0012529

Schwarz, N., & Bless, H. (1991). Happy and mindless, but sad and smart? The impact of affective states on analytical reasoning. In J. P. Forgas (ed.), *Emotion and social judgments* (pp. 55–73). Oxford: Pergamon Press. https://doi.org/10.1080/00049538808259077

Scott, C. L., Harris, R. J., & Rothe, A. R. (2001). Embodied cognition through improvisation improves memory for a dramatic monologue. *Discourse Processes, 31*, 293–305. https://doi.org/10.1207/S15326950dp31-3_4

Sedikides, C., & Gregg, A. (2007). Portraits of the self. In M. Hogg & J. Cooper (eds), *Sage handbook of social psychology* (pp. 110–138). London: Sage Publications.

Sherif, M. (1936). *The psychology of social norms*. Oxford: Harper.

Sherif, M. (1937). An experimental approach to the study of attitudes. *Sociometry, 1*, 90. https://doi.org/10.2307/2785261

Sherif, M., & Hovland, C. I. (1961). *Social judgment: Assimilation and contrast effects in communication and attitude change*. Oxford: Yale University Press.

Sherif, M., & Sherif, C. (1969). *Social Psychology*, New York: Harper Row.

Sherif, M., Harvey, O., White, B.J, Hood, W. R., & Sherif, C. W. (1961). *Intergroup conflict and cooperation: The Robber's Cave experiment*. Norman, OK: University of Oklahoma Book Exchange.

Sherman, D. K., Kinias, Z., Major, B., Kim, H. S., & Prenovost, M. (2007). The group as a resource: Reducing biased attributions for group success and failure via group affirmation. *Personality and Social Psychology Bulletin, 33*, 1100–1112. https://doi.org/10.1177/0146167207303027

Shrauger, J. S., & Schoeneman, T. J. (1979). Symbolic interactionist view of self-concept: Through the looking glass darkly. *Psychological Bulletin, 86*, 549–573. https://doi.org/10.1037/0033-2909.86.3.549

Sidanius, J., & Pratto, F. (2001). *Social dominance: An intergroup theory of social hierarchy and oppression*. Cambridge: Cambridge University Press. http://dx.doi.org/10.1017/CBO9781139175043

Singh, D., & Young, R. K. (1995). Body weight, waist-to-hip ratio, breasts, and hips: Role in judgments of female attractiveness and desirability for relationships. *Ethology and Sociobiology, 16*, 483–507. https://doi.org/10.1016/0162-3095(95)00074-7

Singh, D., Dixson, B. J., Jessop, T. S., Morgan, B., & Dixson, A. F. (2010). Cross-cultural consensus for waist–hip ratio and women's attractiveness. *Evolution and Human Behavior, 31*, 176–181. https://doi.org/10.1016/J.EVOLHUMBEHAV.2009.09.001

Singh, R., & Simons, J. J. P. (2010). Attitudes and attraction: Optimism and weight as explanations for the similarity–dissimilarity asymmetry. *Social and Personality Psychology Compass, 4*, 1206–1219. https://doi.org/10.1111/j.1751-9004.2010.00328.x

Smith, C. A., & Konik, J. (2011). Feminism and evolutionary psychology: Allies, adversaries, or both? An introduction to a special issue. *Sex Roles, 64*, 595–602. https://doi.org/10.1007/s11199-011-9985-5

Snyder, M., & Swann, W. B. (1978). Hypothesis-testing processes in social interaction. *Journal of Personality and Social Psychology, 36*, 1202–1212. https://doi.org/10.1037/0022-3514.36.11.1202

Son Hing, L. S., Li, W., & Zanna, M. P. (2002). Inducing hypocrisy to reduce prejudicial responses among aversive racists. *Journal of Experimental Social Psychology, 38*, 71–78. https://doi.org/10.1006/JESP.2001.1484

South, J., Higgins, T. J., Woodall, J., & White, S. M. (2008). Can social prescribing provide the missing link? *Primary Health Care Research & Development, 9*, 310–318. https://doi.org/10.1017/S146342360800087X

Steele, C. M., & Aronson, J. (1995). Stereotype threat and the intellectual test performance of African Americans. *Journal of Personality and Social Psychology, 69*, 797–811. https://doi.org/10.1037/0022-3514.69.5.797

Stier, D. S., & Hall, J. A. (1984). Gender differences in touch: An empirical and theoretical review. *Journal of Personality and Social Psychology, 47*, 440–459. https://doi.org/10.1037/0022-3514.47.2.440

Stone, J., Aronson, E., Crain, A. L., Winslow, M. P., & Fried, C. B. (1994). Inducing hypocrisy as a means of encouraging young adults to use condoms. *Personality and Social Psychology Bulletin, 20*, 116–128. https://doi.org/ 10.1177/0146167294201012

Stoner, J. (1968). Risky and cautious shifts in group decisions: The influence of widely held values. *Journal of Experimental Social Psychology, 4*, 442–459. https://doi.org/10.1016/0022-1031(68)90069-3

Storms, M. D. (1973). Videotape and the attribution process: Reversing actors' and observers' points of view. *Journal of Personality and Social Psychology, 27*, 165–175. https://doi.org/10.1037/h0034782

Strack, F., Martin, L. L., & Stepper, S. (1988). Inhibiting and facilitating conditions of the human smile: A nonobtrusive test of the facial feedback hypothesis. *Journal of Personality and Social Psychology, 54*, 768–777.

Strauss, B. (2002). Social facilitation in motor tasks: A review of research and theory. *Psychology of Sport and Exercise, 3*, 237–256. https://doi.org/10.1016/S1469-0292(01)00019-X

Strodtbeck, F. L., & Lipinski, R. M. (1985). Becoming first among equals: Moral considerations in jury foreman selection. *Journal of Personality and Social Psychology, 49*, 927–936. https://doi.org/10.1037/0022-3514.49.4.927

Sunstein, C., & Thaler, R. (2008). *Nudge: Improving decisions about health, wealth and happiness.* London: Penguin.

Sutton, R. M., & McClure, J. (2001). Covariational influences on goal-based explanation: An integrative model. *Journal of Personality and Social Psychology, 80*, 222–236. https://doi.org/10.1037/0022-3514.80.2.222

Tajfel, H. (1970). Experiments in intergroup discrimination. *Scientific American, 5*, 96–103.

Tajfel, H., & Turner, J. (1979). An integrative theory of intergroup conflict. In W. G. Austin & S. Worchel (eds), *The social psychology of intergroup relations* (pp. 33–47). Monterey, CA: Brooks/Cole.

Tajfel, H., Billig, M. G., Bundy, R. P., & Flament, C. (1971). Social categorization and intergroup behaviour. *European Journal of Social Psychology, 1*, 149–178. https://doi.org/10.1002/ejsp.2420010202

Testa, M., Crocker, J., & Major, B. (1988). The self-protective function of prejudice: Effects of negative feedback and evaluator prejudice on mood and self-esteem. Paper presented at the Annual Meeting of the Midwestern Psychological Association.

Tetlock, P. E. (1983). Accountability and the perseverance of first impressions. *Social Psychology Quarterly, 46*, 285–292. https://doi.org/10.2307/3033716

Thaler, R. H., & Sunstein, C. R. (2008). *Nudge: improving decisions about health, wealth, and happiness.* New York: Yale University Press. https://doi.org/10.1111/j.1468-0270.2009.1884_6.x

Thornhill, R., & Palmer, C. T. (2000). *A natural history of rape.* Cambridge, MA: MIT Press.

Todorov, A., & Bargh, J. A. (2002). Automatic sources of aggression. *Aggression and Violent Behavior, 7*, 53–68. https://doi.org/10.1016/S1359-1789(00)00036-7

Tomeo, O. B., Ungerleider, L. G., & Liu, N. (2017). Preference for averageness in faces does not generalize to non-human primates. *Frontiers in Behavioral Neuroscience, 11*, 129. https://doi.org/10.3389/fnbeh.2017.00129

Tosun, L. (2012). Motives for Facebook use and expressing true self on the internet. *Computers in Human Behavior, 28*, 1510–1517.

Triandis, H. (1989). The self and social behavior in differing cultural contexts. *Psychological Review, 96*, 506–520.

Triplett, N. (1898). The dynamogenic factors in pacemaking and competition. *The American Journal of Psychology, 9*, 507–533. https://doi.org/10.2307/1412188

Triplett, N. (1900). The psychology of conjuring deceptions. *The American Journal of Psychology, 11*, 439–510. https://doi.org/10.2307/1412365

Trivers, R. L. (1971). The evolution of reciprocal altruism. *Quarterly Review of Biology, 46*, 35–57. https://doi.org/10.1086/406755

Trutt, L. N. (1999). Early canid domestication: The farm fox experiment. *American Scientist, 87*, 160–168.

Tuckman, B. W. (1965). Developmental sequence in small groups. *Psychological Bulletin, 63*, 384–399. https://doi.org/10.1037/h0022100

Tuckman, B. W., & Jensen, M. A. C. (1977). Stages of small-group development revisited. *Group & Organization Studies, 2*, 419–427. https://doi.org/10.1177/105960117700200404

Turner, J. (1982). Towards a cognitive redefinition of the social group. In H. Tajfel (ed.), *Social identity and intergroup relations* (pp. 15–40). Cambridge: Cambridge University Press.

Turner, J. C., Hogg, M. A., Oakes, P. J., Reicher, S. D., & Wetherell, M. S. (1987). *Rediscovering the social group: A self-categorization theory.* Oxford. Basil Blackwell.

Tuvblad, C., Raine, A., Zheng, M., & Baker, L. A. (2009). Genetic and environmental stability differs in reactive and proactive aggression. *Aggressive Behavior, 35*, 437–452. https://doi.org/10.1002/ab.20319

Tversky, A., & Kahneman, D. (1983). Extensional versus intuitive reasoning: The conjunction fallacy in probability judgment. *Psychological Review, 90*, 293–315. https://doi.org/10.1037/0033-295X.90.4.293

Tyerman, A., & Spencer, C. (1983). A critical test of the Sherifs' Robber's Cave experiments. *Small Group Behavior, 14*, 515–531. https://doi.org/10.1177/104649648301400407

Vacharkulksemsuk, T., & Fredrickson, B. L. (2012). Strangers in sync: Achieving embodied rapport through shared movements. *Journal of Experimental Social Psychology, 48*, 399–402. https://doi.org/10.1016/j.jesp.2011.07.015

Van Bavel, J., & Cunningham, W. (2012). A social identity approach to person memory: Group membership, collective identification, and social role shape attention and memory. *Personality and Social Psychology, 38*, 1566–1578.

Van Lange, P. A., Otten, W., De Bruin, E. M., & Joireman, J. A. (1997). Development of prosocial, individualistic, and competitive orientations: theory and preliminary evidence. *Journal of Personality and Social Psychology, 73*, 733–746. http://dx.doi.org/10.1037/0022-3514.73.4.733

Van Osch, Y., Breugelmans, S. M., Zeelenberg, M., & Bölük, P. (2013). A different kind of honor culture: Family honor and aggression in Turks. *Group Processes & Intergroup Relations, 16*, 334–344. https://doi.org/10.1177/1368430212467475

Visser, P. S., & Krosnick, J. A. (1998). Development of attitude strength over the life cycle: Surge and decline. *Journal of Personality and Social Psychology, 75*, 1389–1410. https://doi.org/10.1037/0022-3514.75.6.1389

Von Neumann, J., & Morgenstern, O. (1944). *Theory of games and economic behavior.* Princeton, NJ: Princeton University Press.

Weaver, K., Hock, S. J., & Garcia, S. M. (2016). 'Top 10' reasons: When adding persuasive arguments reduces persuasion. *Marketing Letters, 27*, 27–38. https://doi.org/10.1007/s11002-014-9286-1

Weber, J. M., & Murnighan, J. K. (2008). Suckers or saviors? Consistent contributors in social dilemmas. *Journal of Personality and Social Psychology, 95*, 1340–1353. https://doi.org/10.1037/a0012454

Webster, D. M., & Kruglanski, A. W. (1994). Individual differences in need for cognitive closure. *Journal of Personality and Social Psychology, 67*, 1049–1062. https://doi.org/10.1037/0022-3514.67.6.1049

Wegner, D. M. (1989). *White bears and other unwanted thoughts: Suppression, obsession, and the psychology of mental control.* New York: Penguin Press.

Weinstein, N. D., & Klein, W. M. (1996). Unrealistic optimism: Present and future. *Journal of Social and Clinical Psychology, 15*, 1–8. https://doi.org/10.1521/jscp.1996.15.1.1

Weisfeld, G. E., & Beresford, J. M. (1982). Erectness of posture as an indicator of dominance or success in humans. *Motivation and Emotion, 6*, 113–131. https://doi.org/10.1007/BF00992459

Wellman, B., Boase, J., & Chen, W. (2002). The networked nature of community. Online and offline. *IT and Society, 1*, 151–165. https://doi.org/10.1111/j.1468-2958.2008.01338.x

Westervelt, S. D., & Cook, K. J. (2012). *Life after death row: Exonerees' search for community and identity.* New Brunswick, NJ: Rutgers University Press.

Wheeler, S. C., Brinol, P., & Hermann, A. (2007). Resistance to persuasion as self-regulation: Ego depletion and its effects on attitude change processes. *Journal of Experimental Social Psychology, 43*, 150–156. https://doi.org/10.1016/J.JESP.2006.01.001

Wiemann, J. M., & Knapp, M. L. (1975). Turn-taking in conversations. *Journal of Communication, 25*, 75–92. https://doi.org/10.1111/j.1460-2466.1975.tb00582.x

Williams, L. E., & Bargh, J. A. (2008). Experiencing physical warmth promotes interpersonal warmth. *Science, 322*, 606–607. https://doi.org/10.1126/science.1162548

Willis, J., & Todorov, A. (2006). First impressions. *Psychological Science, 17*, 592–598. https://doi.org/10.1111/j.1467-9280.2006.01750.x

Winkielman, P., Halberstadt, J., Fazendeiro, T., & Catty, S. (2006). Prototypes are attractive because they are easy on the mind. *Psychological Science, 17*, 799–806. https://doi.org/10.1111/j.1467-9280.2006.01785.x

Wolburg, J. M. (2006). College students' responses to antismoking messages: Denial, defiance, and other boomerang effects. *Journal of Consumer Affairs, 40*, 294–323. https://doi.org/10.1111/j.1745-6606.2006.00059.x

Wood, W., Lundgren, S., Ouellette, J. A., Busceme, S., & Blackstone, T. (1994). Minority influence: A meta-analytic review of social influence processes. *Psychological Bulletin, 115*, 323–345. https://doi.org/10.1037/0033-2909.115.3.323

Word, C. O., Zanna, M. P., & Cooper, J. (1974). The nonverbal mediation of self-fulfilling prophecies in interracial interaction. *Journal of Experimental Social Psychology, 10*, 109–120. https://doi.org/10.1016/0022-1031(74)90059-6

Wright, S. C., Aron, A., McLaughlin-Volpe, T., & Ropp, S. A. (1997). The extended contact effect: Knowledge of cross-group friendships and prejudice. *Journal of Personality and Social Psychology, 73*, 73–90. https://doi.org/10.1037/0022-3514.73.1.73

Xu, H., Bègue, L., & Bushman, B. J. (2012). Too fatigued to care: Ego depletion, guilt, and prosocial behavior. *Journal of Experimental Social Psychology, 48*, 1183–1186. https://doi.org/10.1016/j.jesp.2012.03.007

Zajonc, R. B. (1965). Social facilitation. *Science, 149*, 269–274. https://doi.org/10.2307/1715944

Zajonc, R. B. (1968). Attitudinal effects of mere exposure. *Journal of Personality and Social Psychology, 9*, 1–27. https://doi.org/10.1037/h0025848

Zimbardo, P. G. (2006). On rethinking the psychology of tyranny: The BBC prison study. *British Journal of Social Psychology, 45*, 47–53. https://doi.org/10.1348/014466605X81720

Zuckerman, M., Blanck, P. D., DePaulo, B. M., & Rosenthal, R. (1980). Developmental changes in decoding discrepant and nondiscrepant nonverbal cues. *Developmental Psychology, 16*, 220–228. https://doi.org/10.1037/0012-1649.16.3.220

INDEX